# GREGOR FISHER

## WITH MELANIE REID

*The Boy from Nowhere*

HarperCollins*Publishers*

To my mother

HarperCollins*Publishers*
1 London Bridge Street
London SE1 9GF
www.harpercollins.co.uk

First published by HarperCollins*Publishers* 2015

1 3 5 7 9 10 8 6 4 2

Plate section: all photos provided by Gregor Fisher except page 6 (bottom)
and page 7 images © RCAHMS, licensor www.rcahms.gov.uk
Cover quote reproduced with kind permission of
*The Telegraph* © Michael Deacon, *The Telegraph*
*The Scotsman* extract © *The Scotsman*
Nancy Banks-Smith/*Guardian* extract © Nancy Banks-Smith

A catalogue record of this book is
available from the British Library

ISBN 978-0-00-815043-3

Printed and bound in Great Britain by
Clays Ltd, St Ives plc

# Contents

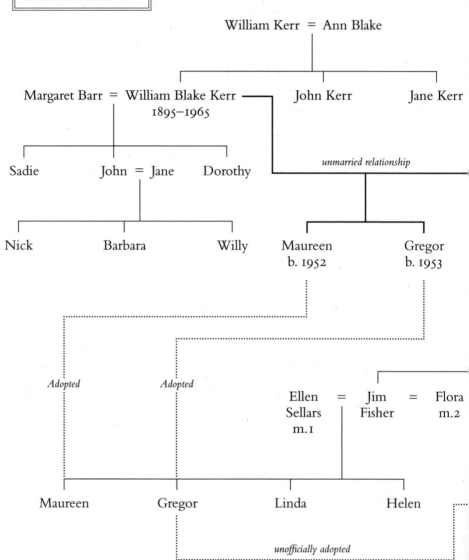

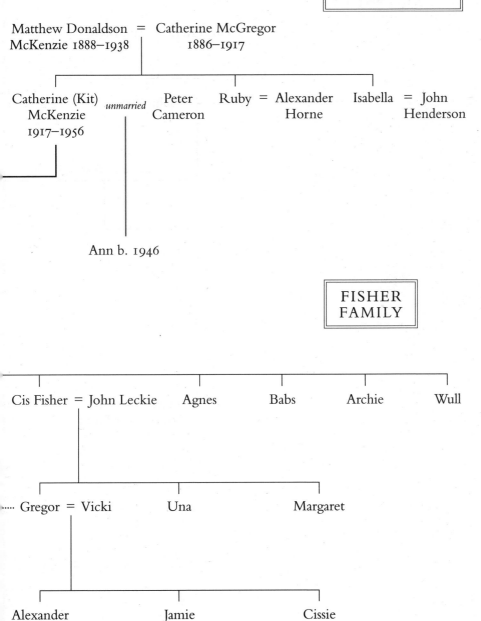

McKENZIE
FAMILY

Matthew Donaldson = Catherine McGregor
McKenzie 1888–1938          1886–1917

Catherine (Kit)    *unmarried*    Peter    Ruby = Alexander    Isabella = John
McKenzie                          Cameron        Horne                  Henderson
1917–1956

Ann b. 1946

FISHER
FAMILY

Cis Fisher = John Leckie    Agnes    Babs    Archie    Wull

····· Gregor = Vicki    Una    Margaret

Alexander    Jamie    Cissie

# Prologue

A story has to start somewhere, so let it begin with two men, strangers to each other, but with lives that will run in parallel. Matthew Donaldson McKenzie and William Blake Kerr were born in Scotland in 1888 and 1895 respectively. Both survived the slaughter of the Somme, married the same year, had children the same age, found jobs and sought to make their way in the world. Eventually their paths would cross, with far-reaching consequences.

Matthew, the elder of the two, returned from the trenches to witness his sick wife give birth, and two days later he was to see her die. He was left with three motherless children, serious trench fever and a damaged leg.

In 1921 he re-married, to a young dressmaker, and took a job at a whisky distillery in a small village in central Scotland.

He moved his family into a tied house – one of the houses under the hills. Remember this place, for we shall return here many times.

William, the younger soldier, returned from war scarred by the sight of filth and disease. Educated and ambitious, he got a job as a customs and excise officer, married and started a family. In 1928 came the move upon which this story hangs. William took a job overseeing three whisky distilleries within a mile of each other. One of them was where Matthew worked.

So the lives of the two men converged at the foot of the stern Ochil Hills. The factory engineer and the feared exciseman were neighbours, briefly, in the houses under the hills, and then work colleagues for the next decade. We have no proof, for time hides such tracks, that they were friends, but it is inconceivable they were not acquainted. William saw Matthew's small daughters playing outside, on the stone steps or on the drying green. They were much the same age as his own little ones.

Victorians by birth, William and Matthew were God-fearing men of status, pillars of the community. One was a government law officer, the other a church organist and teacher at Sunday school. Freemasons, they abided by the social rules of a different age. One would die soon, but tragedy was to stalk them both. And one day scandalous events would unite them in a long-buried tale of betrayal, love and survival.

Let's ask, just this once. Is everything random, or do we believe in fate?

# CHAPTER 1

# The Curly-Haired Boy in the Corner

'I have always depended on the kindness
of strangers'
Blanche DuBois in Tennessee Williams's
*A Streetcar Named Desire*

Thump.
   *Pause.*
   Thump.
   *Pause.*
   Thump.
   Three thumps – never more, never less. No cheery 'Halloo!,' no cry of 'That's me, Cis,' just three dictatorial thuds on the bedroom floor with his foot. John Leckie wanted his breakfast. After a lifetime working the night shift, this was the signal to his wife in the kitchen below to say that he had woken up. It was 5pm, and Cis would prepare tea, toast and marmalade and take it upstairs. Mr Leckie ate upstairs and then came down: a tall,

stern, well-built man, ready to go to work. The child, sitting silently, for it was best to keep quiet, would look up and see the great long legs of his boiler suit appearing down the stairs.

John Leckie was, it's fair to say, as much a creature of routine as he was a man of few words. There was no conversation. He put a long, dark trench coat over his overalls, clapped his grease-stained engineer's bonnet on his head and picked up the lunch-box Cis had prepared earlier. His lunch, his 'piece', was a thing of precise wonderment. It stayed exactly the same for nigh on 50 years: an ancient little Oxo tin containing sugar and loose tea, mixed before it went in, and cheese sandwiches in waxed bread paper, made with the well-fired top of the loaf. John Leckie was as set in his ways as he was undemonstrative. Leckie would nod to his wife and leave for the night shift in the great engineering works in the city. Nor were things much different when he returned home in the morning, weary and grimy. He came in, said little or nothing, took off his overalls, ate the meal Cis had prepared for him and climbed the stairs to bed. Soon it would be time to bang on the floor again for breakfast. Such was the unflinching, unchanging traffic of his life.

At weekends, John Leckie, in an old shirt and trousers and tank top with holes in it, would sit, not in an armchair but on a wooden slat-backed kitchen chair by the fire, his legs spread wide on the hearth, both hugging and hogging the heat. It was always cold in the 1950s. He would spend hours sitting there, hour after hour, in his own silent, still world, staring at the fire. No radio. No books. No conversation. He ignored anyone else who might be in the room. On the mantelpiece were his smoking paraphernalia, neatly arranged – a box of Capstan untipped full strength and the occasional half-smoked cigarette, extinguished early and saved. He would take the tobacco out and re-roll it. There were no matches – he made tapers from tightly rolled sheets of newspaper. When he stood up to smoke, which was frequently, he lit the taper from the fire and put it to the cigarette. The taper was carefully stubbed out and propped at one side of the fire to be re-used. He'd smoke his cigarette standing over the fire, and then sit down again. Occasionally he coughed. And if he needed to fart, he simply lifted one cheek of his backside and farted. No apologies. No glance around. 'This is my house,' announced the fart. 'I'm the main man here.' It was a thing of wonder to the little boy who observed. And Mr Leckie would continue to sit there, legs astride the fire, coal bucket sitting beside him. Eventually the fire would start to burn lower.

'Cis,' he would call in the direction of the kitchen.

Not a question, an order.

'Uh-huh?'

'Coal.'

And she would leave off what she was doing and come through to load coal upon his fire to keep him warm, while he sat there, unmoving. If he did speak, when she had done as he asked, it would only be to criticise the quality of the fuel she had put upon the fire.

'There's too much dross in that.'

The small boy remembered the day he arrived at John and Cis Leckie's house, at the tail end of 1957. It all seemed so simple, back then. He was only three years old and Cis was his mother. Of this he had no doubt. He remembered the day he arrived there because it was snowy and they drove him up to where she lived, at the very top of the hill. He needed a pee and they had

3

to stop the car on the slope. He remembered the pattern his pee made in the snow. He was a sturdy, smiley little chap with heart-melting blond curls and bright blue eyes. That first night, when her husband was at work, Cis carried the child outside to the loo because in 1950s Scotland most people still had outside toilets. The house sat high up to the south above Glasgow and it was a cold, frosty night – he could see the city lights twinkling and he thought he'd died and gone to heaven.

Safe, really safe, in Cis's arms, looking at the lights.

He's outside, pacing the decking, smoking a Gauloise. It's Stirlingshire, Scotland, May 2014, and he's on a flying visit from his home in France. Restless, wary, but eager, he really wants to talk. This has been a long time in the brewing, more than 60 years.

'It's really quite complicated, my story,' says Gregor Fisher, actor, comic legend, man o'pairts. He pauses. 'I just remember thinking that it was like trying to sort out a pile of spaghetti, or finding the ends of a tangled ball of wool. I didn't know how to get to the bottom of this, or if I ever would, actually.'

It was a great place to grow up, that house at the edge of the village of Neilston in Renfrewshire, where there was country-side, animals, freedom, friends, mischief – affection and laugh-ter. The family had an acre of land, once a market garden, up there on the hill, and the new child was the prince of all he surveyed. Some would say kindly that it was an eccentric house, others, more judgemental, that it was like Steptoe's yard. Hens pecked around the back door, the odd goose waddled across the yard, a friendly old dog mooched. Primitive but of its era, the kitchen housed a deep Belfast sink that had a big, wooden step on the floor in front of it, so that Cis, who was not much more than five feet tall, could reach into the water. There was also a very old black range, with a built-in oven and hob. Later, in a nod to the 1960s, it would be taken out and replaced by a Baby Belling: a two-ringed cooker. In the living room was John Leckie's open fire, with chipped tiles around it and a back boiler to heat the water. The fire was his territory; Cis stoked it, but he controlled it. It heated the house and provided any hot water there was. You got scrubbed in the big sink in the kitchen but you had to book a bath and they didn't happen very often.

And if a bath was deserved, Cis used the poker to flick the lever at the back of the fire so the heat would be diverted to the boiler. At night she would load the fire with dross, or slack – the powder left at the bottom of the coal bunker – to keep it going, and it was her job to revive it first thing in the morning before anyone else was up. There was no other heating, but nobody ever thought there was anything odd about that, it was just the way it was. You came down in the morning, you got dressed in front of the fire. Sometimes Cis would stand, back to the flames, and lift up her skirt behind her to get a heat. A fleeting luxury.

'Ah, that's nice!'

Back then Scotland was a thoroughly tough country. It's hard for us, from the comfort of the twenty-first century, to grasp just how tough it was. The gap between rich and poor was vast. As the Historiographer Royal, T. C. Smout, put it, simply and bluntly, the expectations of the working class were a hard life, a poor house and few material rewards. And, we can add, an early death. Basically, this meant 85 per cent of the population. By the 1950s, things were starting to improve, but everything was relative. John Leckie's family, it must be said, were much better placed and more prosperous than many. They owned their sturdy, detached stone-built house; they could grow food and keep poultry to supplement their diet. Nevertheless, life, for them all, was a serious business. In working Scotland, pre-antibiotics, pre-welfare reform, you didn't ask for anything. You sought to survive.

Gregor Fisher, the little boy with the winning blue eyes, landed lucky. Here, his was to be a stable childhood, in a society marked by thrift, hard work, regular church-going and what today's children would regard as sensory deprivation, if not neglect: no television, few toys or holidays, even fewer luxuries, old-fashioned rules of discipline. Waste was unheard of, everything old. Wooden furniture. A 1930s brown sofa with a lever that, when pulled, lowered one end, turning it into a daybed. His new mother's wooden carpet sweeper, circa 1925, with metal wheels, did its best on the old rugs laid on top of the linoleum floor. 'Wax cloth', his mother called the lino. There was a single light bulb hanging from a wire in the middle of the living-room ceiling; if you left it on when you went out of the room there was hell to pay. Always there was a dog that his mother was looking after for some old lady or other who was unwell; or somebody had died and left a dog and Cis, out of the goodness of her huge heart, would take the creature on.

She had a soft spot for animals and she loved her hens. There were lashings of fresh eggs; Gregor remembers yokes like Belisha beacons. At certain wintry times of the year the hens were invited in the latch door at the side of the house and took up residence in the kitchen. A hen that was sitting on eggs, or a nest of chicks, would be kept either side of the range in a cage, and when the chickens got bigger and it was still cold outside, they would perch on the top of the kitchen door. Cis would put sheets of newspaper underneath the door to catch their droppings, but woe betide anyone who forgot and came down in the morning with bare feet.

When Gregor arrived, John Kerr Leckie was 56, and Cis about 50. They had a grown-up family – Margaret, 29, who was a schoolteacher, and Una, 23, who was a school secretary. At that time, the daughters were unmarried and still living at home, but out working every day. The little boy slept at first in bed with his mother when John Leckie was away at work; he remembers the bliss of sleeping in the big, warm bed, safe in her arms, and then, in the morning, when she got up, he used to roll into the cosy nest where her body had been. That was the best moment of all. There in the cocoon he knew for sure that everything was right in the world. Before long, though, before he was old enough for school, his new sisters decreed he should have a room of his own. There was a deep walk-in cupboard upstairs, under the coomb of the roof, with an internal window into their bedroom. It was wide enough to fit a single bed in, so the girls papered it with cowboy wallpaper and after a couple of nights of protest – 'I want to sleep with Mummy!' – he realised having his own room was actually quite nice.

There was no heating in the bedrooms; horsehair mattresses on the beds too. No insulation in the roof or the walls. When it got really cold, coats were piled on top of layers of blankets. Gregor had so many blankets he was riveted to the bed with the weight, and piled on top of them was a moth-eaten fur coat of his mother's to keep him even cosier.

We forget how events of the twentieth century shaped lives, altered personalities. Conditioned by decades of consumerism and relative affluence, we are fast losing the ability to grasp how little ordinary people in those days possessed. Cis and her husband had lived through the Great War, the Depression and the Second World War. Prudence and austerity had defined their lives, were set in their bones.

In an era when people aged fast, where no glossy magazines existed to proclaim that 50 was the new 30, Cis and John Leckie looked and dressed like Gregor's grandparents. It meant nothing to him. In the early days he did not understand that Cis was physically too old to be his birth mother. Why should he? He was too busy surviving on instinct, this child who was as pretty as pie. Butter wouldn't melt in his mouth, he was quite simply the curly-haired boy in the corner; his life revolved around him. He knew his name was Gregor Fisher and Cis Fisher was his mother, except she was married to John Leckie, so she was called Cis Leckie. She was still his mother, nevertheless. He called her Mum, that's just how it was. There were some unexplained things when he was growing up, but he didn't ask any questions, he just accepted that was the way it was. As far as life was concerned, he and his mother *were*. He knew she was different from his pals' mothers, but he didn't care. What mattered was that she adored him. He had what he craved; he was content. Looking back, he realises just how lucky he was to find her – *'Like so many things in my life, it was meant to be.'*

They brought out the joy in each other. He and Cis would constantly set one another off laughing. They laughed when she put him to bed at night, giggling about all kinds of nonsense; they would sing songs and do silly things together. She gave him unconditional love and attention. Maybe she just had a bottomless love for waifs and strays. Whatever the reason, her love saved Gregor Fisher, forged him and still sustains him. He openly acknowledges that he couldn't live without what he got from her, nor would he have achieved what he has. And today, when he talks about her, it is the closest he comes to tears.

Cis can be described as an ordinary, extraordinary woman, or perhaps an extraordinary, ordinary woman. She was just one of hundreds and thousands of wee West of Scotland ladies who were the cement and the oil and the glue and the lifeblood of their families. Every day she wore a wrap-around pinny and coiled her long hair in a bun under a hairnet. Her red hair was going grey. She had a jam jar with red hair dye in it, and Gregor remembers watching her dip her comb in it and spread it into her hair, then shape it into a bun. Her diminutive size belied her determination and strength of personality.

Cis was a full-time housewife. The only time she sat down, Gregor remembers, was with him on her knee to listen to *Listen with Mother* on the wireless or when she read *The People's Friend*. She carried the coal and went for the food, cooked, washed, cleaned, fetched her husband's cigarettes. She got up early and set the fire before any of her family came downstairs. No one ever went hungry in Cis's house, and food is a great way of doling out love. She had a routine of big family suppers late at night: scones, cheese on toast and cups of tea. The family could tell the day of the week by the main meal: one day they had stew, then there was mince, on a Friday there was fish.

Every Friday afternoon Cis and Gregor, in the days before he went to school, would catch the bus to Shawlands in Glasgow to get Scotch mutton pies from Short's in Skirving Street for Saturday and fresh butter in a pat from Henry Healy's, the City grocer.

Cis's sister, Aunt Agnes, conveniently lived in Shawlands too, in what the little boy considered rather an exotic, tenement flat. Best of all, she had a piano, which Gregor was mad for, and for him it was the highlight of a Friday afternoon, going thump, thump, thump on the keys, because somehow music was in his blood but he didn't know it then.

So there was never any choice about what was for supper, nor were those the days of sweet potato with cumin and rocket and a poached egg on top. Plain food, plain lives, few expectations … there was no experimentation whatsoever. It was mince, stew, big pots of really good soup and baking. Gregor enjoyed his food. His mother made rhubarb tarts and apple tarts, she did a top-class fry-up and she also made the best shortbread he could ever hope to taste. Plainly, she and her sisters were a family of bakers, for Aunt Agnes had been at one time industrious enough to start up her own bakery shop.

But this was an extremely male-dominated society. Women like Cis, fathered by and wedded to the stern Presbyterian working men Scotland excelled in, were fantastically strong copers, but they kept their emotions in check. Life taught them not to expect too much. They kept house at a time before bathrooms or washing machines or detergents; they raised children on meals magicked from very small incomes; they toiled from early to late as slaves to men like John Leckie – and he was a saint compared with most men, for he did not drink. Women like Cis were not schooled in any kind of delicate niceties and displays of emotion; kissing and hugging were unheard of. Hers was a loving household but one devoid of displays of physical affection. Until her old age, even a pat on the head was a very unusual thing.

> Decades later, when Gregor went into show business, everyone was hugging and air-kissing each other all the time – the whole luvvie thing. Recalling this, he flaps his hands in comic revulsion. 'Christ, I couldn't cope, I couldn't bear it! It was like, "What are you doing? Get away from me! There's a barrier here, can't you see it? Come on, what's going on? I'm a Scotsman. Please don't do that, you're making me feel very uncomfortable."'

At the time, locked in the intensity of his one-to-one relationship with his new mother, Gregor had little or no concept of the needs of other members of the Leckie family. All children, but especially needy ones, are entirely self-centred. Instinctively, they manipulate the person who gives them most succour and affection. From his perspective, he clung to Cis for emotional and physical survival. Looking back, he realises he caused tensions but he now understands why.

> I don't think I was a very nice little boy. To be honest, I think I was a right little pain in the arse. Looked nice, you know, lots of nice blond curls and all the rest of it; nice to look at, but not nice to spend any time with – the little shit in the Ladybird shorts. I

don't think the rest of the family liked me very much because I was so desperate to gather in every bit of affection that Cis could give me.

Though loved and secure, he was at the same time an outsider who watched and remembered. When John Leckie was around it was best for Gregor to play in the corner. In the silence he absorbed and listened. The other male role model in his life at that time was Uncle Wull, a man every bit as eccentric as John Leckie, both of them rich fodder for the child who would one day put their idiosyncrasies to good use. Wull was a bit simple. Gregor liked him. Cis's half-brother, he was much older and illegitimate – her mother had had a child out of wedlock that nobody knew about. Cis and her siblings didn't know of his existence until much later, when Granny died, and he was then taken under Aunt Agnes's wing. During the week he lived with her in town and went to work at the Parks Department in Glasgow; on weekends he always came to stay at Neilston to be fed and looked after by Cis.

Wull would be classified as special needs now. Back then he was just a bit different and everyone accepted it. He was kind to young Gregor too. Wull mostly communicated by grunting. He'd take out a 10-shilling note and make lots of guttural noises, showing the note to the boy before he folded it up, reached over and squeezed it into his hand. Gregor knew not to say anything – it was between the two of them, an unspoken West of Scotland thing, 'Don't tell your mother.' According to family legend, Wull only spoke once or twice. Every year, when the relatives arrived on their annual visit to Aunt Agnes from the Borders, Wull would open the door and distinctly grunt: 'Are ye back *again*?'

He was once handed a box of Milk Tray and Aunt Agnes said to him, 'Remember and give your cousin one.' And the cousin got one, just one chocolate. No one else got any. That was Wull; he was very literal.

People would find him jobs. Cissie used to send him across the road to Miss McMaster's, an old, retired matron, and he would cut her hedge for her. He cut it with a manual hedge trimmer, a vicious-looking machete-like blade on a pole, which he would flail around wildly, grunting. He was good at that job.

Uncle Wull was small, square-jawed. He didn't impress John Leckie, who sat in his usual spot by the fire and ignored him, dismissed him with his silence. Wull didn't seem to notice. Both men had idiosyncratic toilet habits, which fascinated the small boy. Way before his time John Leckie was the master of recycling. After he had been to the outside loo, he would come back in, carrying the pieces of newspaper used to wipe himself, and throw them on the living-room fire because he didn't want to block the plumbing. And he wouldn't waste money using Izal toilet paper. That was the way he lived.

Sometime in the 1960s the family abandoned the outside loo and had a bathroom and a toilet installed inside the house, which caused a lot of excitement. That was when the bath arrived, insisted on by the girls. All the new facilities were on the ground floor, but upstairs there was still nothing. Gregor watched, wide-eyed with glee, as Uncle Wull would come gingerly downstairs in the morning, carrying a large Ostermilk tin in front of his body.

*'Full to the brim of pish.'*

That was just the way it was, no questions asked. The child stored away the cameos and memories with relish. Besides, at that point in his life Gregor had decided he was going to be a church minister, opening his heart to the frailties of all mankind when he grew up. Apart from John Leckie, who never left the fire, the entire family was very churchy. Gregor's big sister Margaret certainly was, in a vaguely intellectual way, to the extent that she would attend lectures by the famous Scottish theologian Professor William Barclay. There would always be a copy of *Life & Work*, the Church of Scotland magazine, lying about the house. The Leckies' home was next door to the manse, where the minister Robert Whiteford and his family lived. Reverend Whiteford, a striking man with a big shock of hair, cut an imposing figure to a small boy. Two of his four children, John and Bobby, were the same age as Gregor, who often played with them in the large manse garden. They had bikes and he didn't, although he was desperate for one, and he once got into terrible trouble with Mrs Whiteford for stealing one.

'It was Bobby's bike. I took it for a joy ride and then parked it at my house, intending to keep it. It was lunacy – because we were near neighbours, but I thought I would never be discovered.'

Religion was an optionless situation. Gregor attended Sunday school and he went to church; he loved Robert Whiteford who, although he didn't understand half of what he was talking about, gave a very good blessing too.

Gregor Fisher lifts his hand and his diaphragm and slows his voice to its strongest and ripest. '"The blessing of God Almighty, Father, Son and Holy Ghost be with you this day and for evermore." And I went "Ooh" and shuddered. I thought it was all rather fabulous. I think I'd have made a good Catholic, actually – do y'know what I mean? It was the theatricality of it that got me. I just thought it was "Oh, this is marvellous! Gimme some of that!"'

On the wall in the Sunday school there was a big picture of a kindly Jesus in white robes. Gregor loved the robes and the queue of all the children of the world in their national costumes snaking off into the distance, waiting for their chance to sit on Christ's knee. In the picture he was holding a little black child and Gregor decided that this was what he wanted to do when he grew up: be a missionary. That was the job for him, thank you very much. He started praying to be allowed to be one. Gregor was for a while very busy with his prayers.

I was usually asking things like, please make me as good-looking as Bobby Thorpe or somebody else who was the leader of the gang, because that's what I wanted to be. I seemed to take to prayer. Did a lot of it. I think there was plenty of guilt involved when I was a child, I always felt guilty about something. Hellish guilty about the fact that I wasn't very good at school or even Sunday school ... you had to learn by rote the Beatitudes, or the Ten Commandments, and you would get a little badge. The Reverend Whiteford would test you on this – it was almost Victorian.

So those were abiding memories, walking up the hill to church holding Cis's hand. With her faith, and her Sunday hat and her huge heart. She was the patron saint of lost people, blessed were those she found. Cis looked after the simple Wull; certainly she rescued Gregor, and she also rescued old dogs and nurtured chickens by the fire. She would never see anyone, or anything, in trouble.

Some family secrets remain buried forever, with the complicity of everyone involved. Others, however, are shared at a certain point. It was inevitable that there would come a time when Gregor would question why his mother was so old and where, if she hadn't given birth to him, had he come from, that day in the snow? Given the bond between them, this was always going to carry a lot of emotional freight. When it did happen, it was devastating, leaving both in distress. This was the only time Gregor ever rejected his mother; shut her out from him, closed the door on her love.

It was during one of those scones-and-jam family suppers when the mood had lifted because Mr Leckie had gone to work. There must have been a christening in the family because it was the subject of discussion. Churches, godparents, babies … Cis, Margaret and Una chatting.

Out of the blue, Gregor, unthinking, opened his mouth.

'Where was I christened?'

An awkward, loaded silence fell over the room; an ear pop of tension. Sensing something, and never slow at coming forward, Gregor repeated his question. Immediately the subject was changed. One of his sisters offered him another scone, his mother chipped in with a change of subject. *'Uh-oh,'* he thought.

Preoccupied with himself, like all 14-year-olds, he picked up on the evasion, the awkwardness in the room. There was a mystery, some secret being withheld from him. Something that pertained to him, which everyone else was party to.

Nothing more was said and he went to bed as usual. Then came a knock on his door – an unusual occurrence because it was the sort of household where no one locked or knocked on doors. His mother came into the room.

'You're adopted,' she said.

She stood there awkwardly, looking at him, unsure what to do next. It was the classic, blunt-edged West of Scotland way of doing things. In the 1960s no one was schooled in communication and child psychology; no one read manuals on how to discuss sensitive issues with children. Unlike today, there weren't numerous books and websites on how to deal with an adopted child. There were few social workers, hoops to jump through or guidelines to follow. What followed was a moment of most extraordinary drama. Cis was not given to physical demonstrativeness, but she reached out with her hand and patted her beloved son on the head.

Not once. Twice.

A single pat was unheard of. Two was a sign of almost uncontrollably high emotion. Cis was obviously as moved as she was uncomfortable.

'We look after you now, you know. We wanted you, we love you,' she muttered.

And she turned and left the room.

*We're on our first expedition together, Gregor Fisher and me. A most unlikely Johnson and Boswell, more Dastardly and Muttley. It must surely be a comedown for him – usually he's in a Mercedes. This time he's in my silver VW Polo; a man both cheery and wary, a passenger I barely know. I wonder what he's thinking. I know more about his ancestors than him, the living flesh and blood. Some months ago he had approached me out of the blue, through a mutual friend, because he wanted, finally, to pin down the story of his life.*

*We're heading up the hill into the village of Neilston, me driving, him navigating.*

*Gregor is telling me about what happened when Cis died, in 1983.*

*'She left me some money.'*

*He is silent for a bit.*

*'I'll never forget it – it said in her will, "I leave so much to my daughters and I leave so much to Gregor Fisher, who lived with me."'*

*His voice catches. I suddenly realise he's crying.*

*'Why did they have to say that? "To Gregor Fisher, who lived with me".'*

*Tears are running down his cheeks. She was his mum but he wasn't her son. Even beyond the grave he wasn't allowed to be her son. The authorities wouldn't even give him that comfort: a rejection from the woman who never rejected him.*

*'It's just legal language,' I say, desperate to console him. 'Bloody lawyers, they have to say these things just so. A technicality.'*

*He's wiping his face with a hankie.*

*'I know that, I just can't forget it,' he says. 'Gets me every time.'*

# CHAPTER 2

# Fisher, You're Playing Pooh-Bar

'All the world's a stage and most of us are
desperately unrehearsed'
Sean O'Casey

Gregor lay in the dark, his mind churning with the unwelcome news. Cis was his mother but if this revelation about his adoption was true – and he knew deep down it was, because he'd grasped, somewhere along the line, that neither of them were really his parents – then vague memories dimly made sense. What he didn't know, however, was far greater than what he *thought* he didn't know. The secret was to get a whole lot more complicated yet.

When he woke the next morning he decided to play the sympathy card for all it was worth. If this revelation was true, then he was going to make Cis hurt as much as he was hurting. He would punish her for not being his mother.

'I was very nasty. I was a bastard. Much to my shame now, I behaved terribly. I did horrible things like ... oh, she would give me cereal in the morning and I remember holding up the cereal bowl disdainfully and saying, "What's this?" She said, "Well, that's the cereal you like" and I ... I was a bastard.'

He stopped speaking to her for what seemed a long, long time. Withdrawing his love was the only weapon he had. For those two, maybe three weeks of being sent to Coventry, Cis accepted his sulk and treated him as if nothing were different. She didn't get cross, or try to encourage him to talk, or command him to sit down and discuss things with her. She simply took the hurt on the chin and carried on, loving, generous and undemonstrative as ever.

And then Gregor woke up to the realisation, in glorious technicolor, that he was behaving appallingly. Inside that mix of child and young man, beset by hormones, some logic asserted itself. Taking a deep breath, he went downstairs and, as best a 14-year-old boy can, he apologised to her. He told her that as far as he was concerned she was his mother, and he had to put things right and make it better.

'I realised what an absolute shit I had been. I can't remember what I said. No hugs or kisses, just "I'm sorry, Mum." I think there was another pat of my head involved, which meant a state of high emotion, you know. But it was a case of her saying, "Ach well, it'll be fine" and that's it, passed, finished, you know? That's it, gone.'

He laughs.

'It was a loving household, my household, but it wasn't the thing, it's just not what you did. It was never discussed again.'

Everything carried on as normal. We are all good at burying secrets. Gregor wanted his life to have started when he was three, when he met Cissie. Before that, he had only the vaguest of brief, confusing memories, unexplained stuff – the instinctive sense of trouble a child picks up when grown-ups around are acting strangely. There were assumptions he had grown up with, but had chosen not to address. The revelation that he was adopted helped a few things make sense.

His name, for one: Fisher, Cis's maiden name. And with that the conscious acceptance, finally, that she was not his real mother, even though deep down he'd always known she wasn't. He also knew – and he had always known this – that John Leckie was not his father. But Cis had two other brothers, apart from Uncle Wull, called Jim and Archie. Gregor began to accept, from fragments of memory, that Jim Fisher might be his real father. Something had happened to his first mother and he had been sent to live with his father's sister. So, Cis was really his aunt. That explained everything. Well … nearly. But it explained enough for a big, young lad who preferred eating cake to rocking any boats.

The 14-year-old Gregor, head deep in the sand, did not want to ask questions. He knew what family tension felt like, and he didn't relish it. And he sensed, around the adoption issue, there lay trouble, so why go looking for it? He wasn't sure about details, but people said he looked like Jim Fisher. When he walked, he turned in one foot exactly the same way Jim did. He shrugged, end of story. Much more importantly, what was for tea?

Nearly 50 years later, Gregor still struggles to articulate how he felt. 'It was that I wasn't part of anybody; I felt I didn't belong, I didn't fit in. I wasn't part of this lot, or that lot, or any bloody lot. It wasn't discussed again because I think like a lot of adopted people the reason I was so keen not to ask was because it seemed like a reflection on my mother. If I'd started digging about and trying to find out stuff, that was like saying I wasn't happy in my present situation with her. But I was – I adored her.'

Jim Fisher was a shadowy figure in Gregor's early memory but one incident stuck in his mind. He was at a family christening at Aunt Agnes's flat, a happy, come-one-come-all kind of place. Games were always played on these Fisher family get-togethers, children and adults having fun. They would string a sheet across a door and then someone would flash a leg from behind it, and the rest of the family would have to guess whose leg it was.

Gregor, not yet five, excited by the family nonsense, bouncing off walls, was looking for Cis. He went running into a room where Jim Fisher was, with a woman. Later, the child learnt that she was Jim's new wife, Flora. He has a fragment of memory as sharp and scary as a shard of glass.

'"Where's Mum?" I said.

'Flora leant forward, took my arm and looked into my eyes.

'"I'm your mum," she said.

'I remember feeling freaked out because I thought, "Shit, she's going to take me away from Cis, my mother."

'"No, no, no, no, you're not his mother, I'm his mother," said Cis (it was her way of saying, try if you dare).

'I remember a bad atmosphere after that. None of them were child psychologists, were they? It wasn't the time, those weren't the days. I remember my little red-haired mother getting angry. Looking back, there was obviously some kind of power struggle between her and Jim's new wife, though that makes it sound more dramatic than it was.'

Years later, Cis's daughter Una told Gregor that Jim and Flora had arrived in Neilston at one point and said they had come to take him back. There was a big silence. 'Mummy wasn't happy. She said, "Well, I think we'll just keep him because you've got enough on your plate, haven't you?"' Una recalled. Jim was not very pleased but Gregor stayed with Cis. She didn't want to let him go. After that, Gregor didn't see much of his father.

Not that he was bothered. He had better things to do, like going out to play with his friends. It was the kind of childhood where, at weekends, he left the house on a Saturday morning at half past seven and didn't get back until night-time. Nobody turned a hair then; it's what kids did, nobody fretted about where he was. From an early age, Gregor and his gang, full of nonsense and mischief, would be raking about the village, building dens, climbing trees or catching up on the goings-on in Sherwood Forest.

The old lady across the road, a retired matron, had a television set. Gregor was allowed to go over and watch *Ivanhoe* or, his favourite, the actor Richard Greene, in the black and white series of *The Adventures of Robin Hood*. The signature tune is imprinted in the minds of anyone born in the 1950s: 'Robin Hood, Robin Hood, riding through the glen, Robin Hood, Robin Hood, with his band of men, feared by the bad, loved by the good, Robin Hood, Robin Hood, Robin Hood'. Greene, the handsome, charming hero, starred in 144 episodes between 1955 and 1960; the Sheriff of Nottingham was a humourless villain; Maid Marian, one of the boys rather than Robin's girly girlfriend, put on her tights and mucked in with a bow and arrow instead of sitting around in a long gown, waiting to be rescued.

'There, that was the site of the Pavilion!'

I'm negotiating a roundabout on the outskirts of Barrhead. I haven't heard him so enthused.

'The cinema, the local fleapit, but as far as I was concerned it was the manifestation of heaven on earth. In the foyer there was a little booth, where the woman punched the lever and a little ticket came shooting out. It was 9d for down the stairs and 1s 3d for the balcony; I went for the balcony. The children's matinees, we'd all stamp our feet when the curtains parted and that famous tadadadadadadadadadadaa Pearl & Dean jingle started.

'And all those silly adverts, where people with English voices from another planet would announce, "MacDiarmid's Garage, Barrhead, East Renfrewshire, faw all yaw motoring requahments". And everybody's saying, "MacDiarmid's, whozat? Whit's that, y'now?" I mean, you could handle it if it was Kia-Ora or some other thing, but the local garage ... "faw all yaw motoring requahments ..."

'We'd watch anything, it didn't matter what; usually on a matinee there'd be something cut out for kids, fairly gory stuff like Three Hundred Spartans, where everybody ended up dead. There was a lot of that Greek thing going on then – Jason and the Argonauts, with lots of sword fighting and skeletons.'

He's lost in the dark: a small boy, wide-eyed at the big screen.

'Circus Boy with Micky Dolenz, later of Monkees' fame ... and sometimes some not terribly funny British film, Swallows and Amazons, which involved a lot of posh kids on a boat, saying things like, "Let's go home and have some cocoa." What are they talking about? Who are these people?'

I've pulled in at a lay-by. Outside, an old man crosses the road and ambles into the bookies.

'He probably went to the Pavilion with you,' I say.

But Gregor's not listening. He's too busy doing the important maths those Saturday afternoons demanded.

'Cis gave me two and six, half a crown. One and thruppence got me into the cinema. If I walked down to Barrhead, that meant I had one and thruppence on my tail. I didn't do that very often because usually it was raining. So, it was thruppence down on the bus and thruppence back on the bus, so how much did that leave? Ninepence – and that was spent on crisps and chocolate. Smith's crisps, thruppence a packet, with the little blue bag of salt, and a chocolate bar, not a very big one, it has to be said – they were obviously on the make.

'There was an old guy at the door – everyone was older because we were so young – saying, "Get your crisps and chocolate before you go in now. Get your crisps and chocolate before you go in now." Even that in itself was thrilling – all the little rituals that happened when you went to the pictures.

'I never quite recovered, you see, from when I was first taken to the cinema by Aunt Jean, who wasn't really an aunt but a great pal of Cis when they were young. We visited them and she took me on a special treat on a bus to a cinema in Dumfries and the first film I ever saw was Swiss Family Robinson.

'It was fabulous, I couldn't believe it – I'd never seen a film in my life. And I must've been quite wee – six, seven, eight, something like that. Anyway, fabulous!'

I've never seen him look so happy.

Some Saturdays, Gregor would get up and head for his best friend's house. Johnny Monaghan lived in the smart part of the village, down a pot-holed private road with a selection of big houses. '*Funny,*' the boys from the other side of the tracks thought, '*that rich people should have such a rough road.*' The Monaghans lived in a house called Barnfauld and Johnny went to private school – Belmont, and then Glasgow Academy. Johnny had lovely toys and – oh, bliss beyond dreams – a Scalextric set. Money brought other subtle class differences too. They had a drawing room, not a sitting room. And central heating – Gregor couldn't quite figure out what that was. Great clunky old-fashioned radiators, with a metal thing on top that you moved to let the heat out, and a boiler … and the best bit of all, an oil tank, which he found quite exotic. To have an oil tank of your own, that was like owning a garage. He thought it was pretty special.

Gregor and Johnny had been close since they were five years old. The first time they met, Gregor had gone to Johnny's house with another friend, Andrew Robinson. But Andrew had to go home for lunch and then Johnny was called in to have his. Gregor stood outside the imposing door, a very small boy in cheap plastic shoes, not quite sure what to do, thinking he'd better clear off. He remembers a woman coming out, Johnny's mother; remembers the posh Glasgow accent.

'"What's your name?"'

'"Gregor."'

'"Well, Gregor, you'd better come and have some lunch then."'

'So, I went in for lunch and I was a feature there every weekend for years to come.'

Those were wonderful times, another period in Gregor Fisher's life when the stars came into alignment. His happy little band of friends centred round the Monaghans' big, welcoming house. The friendship influenced his life hugely because they were a kind family, who had the money and wherewithal to show their son's friend a different world to that which Cis could provide for him. Gregor's eldest sister Margaret had once taken him to the theatre in Glasgow, but the Monaghans introduced him to much more: the excitement of performance on stage and the thrill of getting in a car and going somewhere as a family. It was almost as if, from that first day, Margaret Monaghan had read in Gregor's face the craving to belong, the fear of rejection, and in a way she adopted him too. She treated him and her son as equals. If Johnny got a tube of Smarties, Gregor got one too. He was included in family trips to the theatre, to the Pavilion in Glasgow to see shows such as *Beat the Clock*, starring Calum Kennedy. The boys would pile into the back of the family's old black Bentley – how Gregor loved that feeling of anticipation – and they would head out into a world of city lights and noise and fun, worlds away from watching John Leckie sit morosely by the fire and smoke Capstan.

Years later, as a teenager, some time after Gregor learnt of his adoption, Johnny Monaghan found out he had been adopted too. His reaction to the news was much the same as Gregor: he chose to put it to the back of his mind and move on. Life was good; he didn't want to upset his mother by asking questions. It was decades later, three years after her death, before her adoptive son started digging to find what was what and who he was. But it helps to explain something. Did Margaret Monaghan know the circumstances of the little boy with the curly hair, whom she invited in for lunch with her son? Had she guessed he was adopted too? Maybe she had seen Cis and drawn her own conclusions. Gregor does not know but in Mrs Monaghan he was lucky for he had found another good woman with a kind heart and space in it to offer to him. It would become a lifelong pattern.

He enjoyed primary school, mainly because he fell in love with his teacher, Miss Fay. He thought she was an angel, presiding over the safe little world where they made Easter cards for their mums and decorations for the Christmas tree. Everything started to fall apart, though, in his final year at primary. He was a bright child and it was assumed he would go to Paisley Grammar School, but like so many boys he was not ready for his 11 Plus.

I was a dreamer or a lazy bastard, whichever you prefer. I used to sit and look out of the window at the clouds and wonder what it was like, being a cloud.

Instead, he was consigned to the rough house of the local secondary modern, where the whole purpose seemed to be to teach the boys metalwork or woodwork (cookery for the girls) and then churn them out into the workplace. With hindsight, Gregor is extremely bitter at the way secondary modern pupils were treated like drones, second-class citizens, condemned for life for failing a single exam. That was the way it felt to him: a rejection, even if he did not articulate it at the time. Failing the 11 Plus was a self-fulfilling prophecy of further failure, and it meant that school became largely a waste of time for him.

Back then Barrhead High School was a tall, forbidding place, built in the 1920s in the shape of a courtyard, with separate entrances for boys and girls. Gregor caught the red Western SMT bus down the hill from Neilston and spent the day longing for the final bell. Going home was the best part, especially because it involved a bit of daredevil stuff, skipping off the bus while it was still moving. The bus stop was some way past his house, no point going that far and having to walk back, so he had it down to a fine art – waiting until the driver changed gear on the steep bit, then letting go of the pole at the back of the vehicle and springing off, knees bent, running. Everybody did it, if the bus was passing their house, but on a slippery day there might be trouble and pupils could end up with skinned knees. It was more fun than books, though.

> I was useless at school, worse than a man shot. The only things that interested me were cigarettes, gambling and sex, not necessarily in that order. The first two I did really quite well with: I was a world-class smoker, a very good card player, but the sex was just never forthcoming. Those were my obsessions and as for maths, science and arithmetic, I was utterly, utterly useless. I don't think I was particularly thick, it was just that at that time I wasn't interested.

Pupils were streamed by ability, from A to E. Gregor started off at C and moved swiftly down to D. School was tribal; a jungle. The A and B stream kids wore a collar and tie; they were always nicely turned out, leather shoes polished, with parents who cared. Not that Cis didn't care but that was the way the A and Bs made the other kids feel – like scruff. Gregor and his chums behaved according to the role expected of them. The head-master was Mr Burnett, a former Greek teacher, who gave the impression he would much rather have been head of a grammar school than a secondary modern and seemed bitter that he hadn't made the cut. Mr Burnett, nevertheless, made the most of his status. Every morning, at assembly, wearing his gown, he conducted a messianic entrance: there was a balcony all round the big assembly hall and he would walk right along the top corridor, very slowly down the stairs, with the entire school assembled beneath him, walk to the podium and take the morning service. The pupils sang rollicking great Christian hymns, and the A and B students would perform on their recorders. Often it was just too much pomp and ceremony for the reprobates to bear; it positively begged for a bit of disruption.

Laughter, Gregor was fast discovering, was a most subversive weapon. He was learning its power. There was one assembly in particular, he remembered vividly, when Mr Burnett stood at the podium and announced pompously that it had come to the attention of the janitor that someone had been blocking the toilets in the downstairs loo. One of Gregor's pals said – and he didn't mean it to be so loud – *'Oh, someone must have shit a brick'* – and his words echoed round the cavernous hall. Time stood still and then came the wave of suppressed giggling. Mr Burnett pointed his finger and the offender was hauled out for punishment, probably the belt. Discipline was still fierce in schools in the 1960s, and while Gregor and his friends headed towards a reputation, the A and B pupils headed towards success – *'Towards sainthood … Oh, they were probably lovely kids and nice people but school was tribal,'* he says.

With adolescence, Gregor had grown into a husky, strong young man. Not tall, but fairly broad. It changed the balance of power at home, up the hill in Neilston, where sometimes, inevitably, if there were less than happy memories, they were in the shape of John Leckie. The older man was not remotely interested in interacting with the boy who had invaded his house, usurping his wife's affections. Perhaps Mr Leckie might be forgiven his resentment at seeing his wife's attention switch to the cherubic little cuckoo in the nest, the child who made her laugh and brought her joy. Previously, her husband's welfare had been her main priority – suddenly he felt second in the pecking order.

There is a duty to understand and respect; and if Mr Leckie seemed a profoundly negative influence, especially towards children, perhaps those judging him needed to walk a mile in his shoes. Scotland in the 1950s was, for all but the very few, a grey landscape of hard graft. Since the Industrial Revolution, work in the heavy industries – mining, shipbuilding, steel-making, engineering – meant a lifetime of long hours, physical labour, the risk of frequent industrial accidents and low wages. It was just the way things were; there was no alternative. Men, both skilled and unskilled, toiled week-in, week-out, and hoped their sons would secure an apprenticeship to do the same.

John Leckie was a skilled man, an engineer at Weirs of Cathcart, where he had worked all his life – and mostly on the night shift, in itself a profoundly dislocating and unhealthy existence. Weirs, founded in Glasgow in 1871 – and in the twenty-first century still a global concern – were one of the powerhouses of the mechanical world. During the course of Mr Leckie's career at the factory their design engineers pioneered munitions for the First World War, developed the autogiro to enable the first helicopter flight and manufactured Frank Whittle's invention, the first jet engine. Mr Leckie was, in his day, one of up to 9,000 employees.

If his joylessness was oppressive, events in his early life can explain why. Born in 1901, John Leckie was a miner's son, with three younger brothers, Sam, Campbell and Hugh. When all four boys were small, their father died in an explosion in the shed where the mine explosives were kept. In those days compensation for such incidents did not exist. Not many years after that, their mother died – of a broken heart, it was said – and John was left to bring up his brothers on his apprentice's wage at Weirs. Given such burdens, perhaps it was clear why he did not laugh a lot. We can also guess why, in his late fifties, ground down by a lifetime of work, when he felt he had earned some peace, he resented the arrival of another dependent male child, another mouth to feed. It was history repeating itself.

Victorian by inclination, John Leckie had no apparent affection for, or interest in, Gregor – and the feeling was mutual. In this, there was nothing exceptional. Mr Leckie was typical of his era, his class and his locality. Scotland bred dogged working men who built an empire, but it was at a cost to their humanity. Such men were strict, intolerant, negative fathers, domestic tyrants light years from modern parenting ideals, because that was how their fathers, in turn, had raised them. Permanently tired and prematurely aged by the burdens of their role, they knew no other way. Being nice to children was women's work. Mr Leckie was not physically abusive but when roused he shouted and swore at the little boy and said some harsh things. On the plus side, his daughters adored their daddy. Growing up, they had seen a softer side of him. Plus, quite simply, they were his flesh and blood.

Gregor learnt to avoid him and to keep interaction to a minimum, but at mealtimes it was impossible to do so. There would be stupid arguments. If the boy did not finish his soup, Mr Leckie would lean forward and tap his plate with a spoon then say with heavy sarcasm, *'Same price as the rest.'* Or Gregor would play with the sugar, or take the wrong half of a slice of bread, and that would enrage him. One of John Leckie's peculiar *droits du seigneurs* was over the top part of the slices of pan loaf. He only liked the top half, the well-fired rounded bit. No one else could touch those bits; everyone else had to have the bottom half, with the square corners.

'You'll be good for bugger all but digging the roads,' he would tell Gregor. Other than that, there was little conversation. Gregor does not remember them talking civilly about anything. No guidance, no fatherly, let alone grandfatherly, chat.

Cis was always defensive – 'Ach, his bark's worse than his bite. He just says these things.'

Nothing in Leckie's behaviour gave any indication, as the 1950s drew to a close, that he perceived the younger generation as anything other than profligate. Young people were wasters. Literally. He and Cis would share a banana for lunch. On his days off, he withdrew into self-imposed isolation, staring at the fire. Today, we might diagnose over-work, clinical depression, seasonal affective disorder (SAD), a troubled mind, exhaustion, burnout, stress; unresolved post-traumatic stress disorder. Back then, Mr Leckie was simply a man with a hard life who found his rewards in silence and sitting still, doing nothing, his legs hard up against the hearth. He did not read books, the 1930s wireless was rarely on, and there was no working television in the house until later on, when Gregor bought the family a colour set with his early wages.

Nothing must disturb Mr Leckie's routine. There was calamity when, on one occasion, Cis was unable to prepare his lunchbox. The calamity wasn't that his wife had broken her leg – she slipped on some hen droppings in the sloping garden and had been hospitalised. It was that his daughter Margaret made up his lunch *wrongly*. Because he always had cheese, cheese, cheese, she thought she would ring the changes and bought some ham. How incorrect she was. Her father came home angry the next morning. Ham in his sandwiches, indeed! But that was the sort of man he was.

He was not a drinker, unlike the majority of men of his milieu for whom alcohol was a release, an excuse and a way to forget. The families of drinkers suffered cruelly and the problem was endemic. Gregor remembers the only time he ever saw John Leckie with a drink in him, after Aunt Babs's silver wedding celebrations. The Fisher family was travelling home on the train and Mr Leckie, by this time an old man, was in his cups.

'Do you still love me?' he blurted out to his wife as they sat with the family in the railway carriage, rattling past the Glasgow suburbs.

The teenaged Gregor was repulsed. He wanted the ground to swallow him up to escape the embarrassment. Witnessing such a display of emotion from a buttoned-up old man was unbearable. Getting off the train at Neilston, Mr Leckie slipped between train and platform and skinned his shin. The next day his daughter Margaret, returning to the station to go to work, was told by the stationmaster: 'I see you are keeping better company today.' Of the many unfairnesses in John Leckie's hard life, this seems one of the most gratuitous.

The family had no car. John Leckie would take the same train from Neilston to Cathcart for work at Weirs. Only latterly, as he neared retirement after 50 years at the plant, did he have the luxury of a lift in a car, sharing the petrol bill with somebody in the village who worked at the same place.

Gregor, older now than John Leckie was when he as the cuckoo entered the nest, holds real regrets. He would love another chance at the relationship and now thinks he understands the whole story, but by the time he found out the known unknowns, let alone the unknown unknowns, the old man was long dead.

When Gregor got some way into his teens, by which time John Leckie had retired, the boy was sent down to Langholm in Dumfriesshire during the summer holidays. Perhaps it was partly to keep him out of John Leckie's way. Aunt Agnes had a daughter, Carol, who had married a farmer called Billy Bell, with a place down there. They kept battery hens and she had a young family. A useful pair of hands, Gregor stayed on the farm for the entire holidays, collecting eggs, shovelling chicken manure and doing other chores. He enjoyed the country life; in his bones it suited him and he was perfectly happy there. Always there was a wheeze of some kind, either killing the rats that were nesting under last season's bales of hay or heading down to the Solway Firth to catch flounder.

Returning to Neilston for school in late August, though, after a summer of work and freedom, there were tensions. John Leckie, now home all day, sat by the fire and ordered his wife around.

Cis, a pensioner herself, was a slave to his needs and Gregor, watching, his body filling with testosterone, found it less easy to remain detached. He could cope with the old man's misanthropic ways in general, he just couldn't bear to see his mother talked to like that. One day, when Gregor was about 15 – and by which time Mr Leckie would have been nearly 70 – things came to a head.

Memories of family meltdowns are horrible to store – sour, embarrassing, guilt-inducing moments – so we try to forget them. Gregor cannot remember what had been said, just that the old man had shouted something nasty at Cis. Young lion provoked by very old, worn-out lion; fighting over the woman who sustained them both. In a flash of anger the teenager, determined to defend his mother against bullying, picked up a brush and struck him. Mr Leckie fell right to the floor and Gregor shouted at him, 'Don't you *ever* speak to my mother like that again!'

It was brief but nasty. John Leckie didn't say anything. He got up, walked back to the fire and resumed his position. Even today, nearly half a century on, Gregor squirms at the cruelty of his actions.

Young and stupid, not my proudest moment, I have to say. It's a relationship in my life that I would dearly like a re-run at. I hate not understanding ... You know, I don't mind if you don't get on with somebody and you think, well, you're not my cup of tea and that's fine and I'm not your cup of tea either and that's fine too – because we can't all be lovey-dovey creatures and that's just the way it is. But I just wish ... it's a regret. Always has been, always will be.

The relationship between Cis and John Leckie still puzzles him. Why did such a warm, vivacious woman, so lovely-looking when she was young, marry such a curmudgeon? They look happy and handsome in their wedding photos. Why did she let him treat her like that? Because you just don't know what happens in people's marriages, Gregor muses. He couldn't possibly have been an old grump for all his life, so what turned him into that? That was the fascination of John Leckie. Of course he'd had a lifetime of drudgery, and so had Cis, but she had remained warm and kind. What made him behave in that way to his wife?

Back at school, Gregor was expertly managing to waste six years of his life learning little but how to amuse his friends. The only subject to engage him in any way was art, so the sum total of his high school career was an O-Level in drawing still life and stitching embroidery. Big embroidery: collages, tapestries. And he was very good at doing paintings of plants. Again, this was down to luck and random connections. The art teacher, Mrs Burkett, saw something in the mixed-up boy and encouraged him. It was always fun to be in her class.

But something else had happened at school, when he was 13, which changed his life. It came in the shape of a teacher called Alan Ball. Mr Ball taught the A and B classes so Gregor didn't know him but things must have been said in the staffroom. The art teacher had spoken up for that silly but creative joker in fourth year, name of Fisher, who was heading for the factory floor unless someone got him interested in something. On the strength of such random conversations careers can hang. Mr Ball organised amateur dramatics and he was rather keen on Gilbert and Sullivan operettas. One day he passed Gregor in the corridor and spun on his heel, hailing him.

'"Fisher!" he said.

'And he gave me a little booklet and it was the Gilbert and Sullivan script of *The Mikado*.

'"You're playing Pooh-Bar," he said.

'"But sir," I said. "Sir, sir, sir! Why me? No, no, I haven't done anything!"

'And inside I was like, "Naw, why's he picking on me?" I couldn't believe it. It was punishment. I mean, you were in real trouble with your peers if you got involved with that kind of shit. It was only the As and Bs with their leather shoes polished that did that – and it was all right for that section of school to be involved in poncey things like am-dram, but not me.'

At break time Gregor went and knocked on the staffroom door and pleaded with Mr Ball. Told him he couldn't, wouldn't, didn't want to … any wild excuse he could grab out of the air, twisting and fidgeting in desperation. But Mr Ball refused to take no for an answer and was obviously gifted with natural psychology; he persuaded the aghast teenager that he'd be really good in the role. Flattery works for all actors and it worked for the boy who was yet to become one.

The reluctant player dodged his mocking mates, duly turned up at the hall for after-school rehearsal and started speaking his lines.

'Speak up, Fisher, for God's sake, we can't hear you!'

Mr Ball, at the back of the hall, appeared quite gruff, but as with a lot of big men he was actually a gentle person, sensitive enough to cajole and flatter and bully his unwilling star into

delivering his lines. The Grand Pooh-bar was a haughty character in this hugely popular comic opera, written in 1885, which
satirised the self-importance of British politics and the preten-
sions of the high-ranking establishment. Set in Japan, to avoid
censure, the operetta involved a lot of fun and farce dressing up
in kimonos. The Grand Pooh-Bar is designated Lord High
Everything Else and the name has survived in common parlance
for mocking those with huge self-regard. So too has the expression 'short, sharp shock' from one of Pooh-bar's jolly songs, just
made to be chanted by rowdy schoolboys with painted white
faces and chopsticks stuck in their hair.

> To sit in solemn silence in a dull, dark dock,
> In a pestilential prison, with a lifelong lock,
> Awaiting the sensation of a short, sharp shock,
> From a cheap and chippy chopper on a big black
> block!

Not only did Gregor enter into the spirit of the whole thing, he
made an extraordinary discovery: he could get a laugh. Not only
that, he could make *lots* of people laugh at one time; could have
a whole hall-full of grown-ups cheering for him, their faces split
wide open with pleasure. He remembers it still, the wave of
warmness that swept over him from the hall, that feeling of –
*'Oh, this is good, maybe I've found something I can do after all.'*
   An audience of about 300 turned up for the production in the
school hall – all the mums and dads and aunts and uncles of the
cast, plus Cis and his unofficial sisters, Una and Margaret. It was
obvious to everyone but Gregor that he was the star of the
performance; what he clearly remembers, however, is coming

on to take his bow and being annoyed when Mr Burnett, the pompous headmaster, stood up before everyone, the VIPs, school inspectors, councillors, and basked in his reflected glory.

'This boy,' he told them, 'is only 13.'

I thought, 'You don't even like me, you hardly know me, you two-faced little shit.' ... He really bugged me.

After *The Mikado*, he told himself, I'll be an actor, without a clue how difficult it would be. But that actually was the start of Gregor's career. His star quality was evident. He then acted the part of Reginald Bunthorne ('a Fleshly Poet') in Gilbert and Sullivan's *Patience*, soaking up the applause, loving that unfamiliar sense of, *'Oh, everyone wants me.'* The school also put on a production of a Noël Coward comic one-act play, *Hands Across the Sea* – how sedate and inappropriate were the 1960s am-dram choices of a tough secondary modern in working-class Scotland! In this Gregor was called upon to mimic a colonial English accent – 'How was India, old boy?' – 'Oh, very large' – and his power of mimicry was also given its first chance of an outing.

I was terrible at accents then, but I thought I was very good; it was amateur night out. I'm sure it was dreadful. There may have been, if I'm kind to myself, a talent there – but it was very raw, a diamond in the rough. Very rough.

Then, very swiftly, it was the summer of 1969, he was 15 and faced the shock of his life: on the other side of the school gates with an O-Level in art and apart from that no prospects, no future, no qualifications, no apprenticeship, no college to go to. He remembers thinking, quite seriously, *'You've messed that up, haven't you?'*

Before he left, he saw the careers officer. Gregor waited in the corridor outside his office in a queue of other gormless teenagers, picking their noses, counting their spots, facing the rest of their lives.

'Next!' shouted the teacher.

Someone had briefed the man.

'What are your interests? I hear you've been doing these school plays.'

'Yeah, yeah.'

Mumbling.

'Have you considered acting?'

'Dunno, sir.'

'Well, take this. It's the prospectus for the Royal Scottish Academy of Music and Drama.'

Gregor left the office with the prospectus, but it was the word 'Royal' that put the wind up him; put him right off. If it *was* Royal, especially with a capital 'R', they wouldn't want him. He took it home to show to Cis and told her the careers teacher had told him to apply – he didn't say *he* wanted to apply there. Hedging his bets, shielding himself, anticipating failure. His mother wasn't keen. He didn't blame her; she came not just from a different generation but a different world – one where working people said, get yourself an apprenticeship. The family were worried about the cost of further education, despite the fact there were full grants available. In the end, Cis came round a bit. She and Gregor agreed he should apply. But he couldn't do so until he was 18 and there was the small matter of finding work until then.

What followed was a succession of dead-end jobs. First, Thomas Thomson Tapes, a company now long gone, which made the equivalent of Elastoplast, which they shipped to Africa. For £9 a week he was a machine operator; and it was a simple fact that machine operators making Elastoplast in those days, long before Health & Safety, used to go home drunk every night from the fumes.

Even at 16 going on 17 he realised he didn't like it; he was also shrewd enough to see that it could go on for the rest of his life. Working lives were decided that way, if you let it happen. But there were enough jobs available in those days for young men to sample different industries before they committed. He decided to go for a more glamorous job at Shanks in Barrhead, a nearby town. John Shanks, a plumber, had patented the ball-cock and filling valve for a flushing toilet, and his company, which might be said to have helped change the world more than most, was internationally famous. But making loos had its limitations and for Gregor the U-bend was a dead end too.

His job was pot boy. The lavatory pans were made by pouring molten porcelain into a mould and the pot boy's role was to make sure the liquid didn't spill out of any of the holes, by blocking them with a little clay pot. And then he had to remove the pan and put the two parts of the mould back together again, making sure it was good and solid for the next go. He found it a pretty senseless task and didn't last very long – *'I don't know what I didn't like about it, I just knew from the minute I thought, "God, why am I here?" I mean, making lavvies the rest of your life?'*

The only good bit about being the bottom of the heap, job-wise, was being sent to the canteen, where the women fried copious eggs and bacon, which he carried back to the older men.

He seized upon the idea of getting a job in the open air and blagged his way into a post cutting grass, claiming to be experienced. Having lasted four days he was sacked on one of the world's less well-known grassy knolls, just off the new M8 between Glasgow and Edinburgh, when the boss turned up and Gregor was having an unscheduled fag break. Because he'd been sacked on the spot he couldn't get the van home, nor had he any money. He had to walk all the way from the other side of Paisley to Neilston, which took him a good three hours and was a bit of a shock to the system. History does not record what John Leckie thought of it. 'You'll be good for bugger-all but digging the roads,' hung in the air, unsaid.

At that point Gregor went back down to Billy Bell's farm in Langholm and got a job in a dye factory. His task was making the rainbow wool for the multi-coloured jumpers and tank tops of the 1970s. Everybody in that decade would wear one. One worker took the end of a pole with hanks of wool on it, someone else the other end, and together they would walk up and down the tank with the hank dipping in the dye between them. Then the hank would be turned round and trailed in other tanks with different dyes in them. The company was to become a vast retail empire called The Edinburgh Woollen Mill.

In every job, unbeknownst to him, Gregor was building his future. He listened and studied the people he worked with: the characters, the idiosyncrasies; the verbal tics. The Scottish working man – his grumbles, his pleasures, his chat, his put downs, his profanities, his mannerisms, his cynicism. Gregor soaked it all up like a sponge, filling the library in his head with voices and noises. As soon as he reached 18 he filled in the form for the Royal Scottish Academy of Music and Drama (RSAMD) in Glasgow and sent it off.

He was a young man with dreams, lacking in confidence in everything except the manufacture of rainbow wool. It was around that time, when what he didn't know was still far, far bigger than what he did know, that something happened.

Out of the blue he got a letter from someone called Maureen. She claimed to be his sister.

His real sister.

CHAPTER 3

# You Don't Know Me But I'm Your Sister

'When you laugh at something awful, it shrinks'
Joan Rivers

The letter arrived, out of the blue, at the farm near Langholm. It was summer, 1971. Gregor was still living down in the Borders, bouncing companionably around his Fisher relatives. He'd quit the wool factory and was doing bar work in the town, a goofy teenager killing time until he heard from drama school. The letter was brief:

Dear Gregor, I don't know if you remember me, I am your sister. Would you like to meet up at some point?

He was so taken aback that he didn't remember anything else it said. It was signed Maureen.

He was baffled, because this was obviously something to do with Jim Fisher, Cis's brother, whom he was convinced was

48

his father because he looked like him – or at least everyone said so.

They'd look at Jim and then me, and say, 'You cannae deny that yin.'

But he really didn't know anything about a sister. And he wasn't altogether sure he wanted to. In what was to become a lifelong habit when it came to turning over stones to see what was underneath, Gregor's initial reaction was wary. Suspicious. He didn't really know whether he was quite up to it or not. Emotion. Upset. Tears. *Stuff*. But then he thought, '*Why not?*', so he borrowed Billy Bell's best suit and cousin Carol put him gently on the train to Glasgow, where the rendezvous had been arranged.

Central Station, he'd suggested in his letter. But it's a huge concourse. Somehow, between the two of them, gauche teenagers, they chose to meet outside the lost property office. Well, every station has one, doesn't it? The pathos of it completely escaped them.

Gregor shakes his head. 'I'm not making this up, please believe me. Outside the lost property office! We, er, we … I dunno why, I dunno why we did this, it was just the way it happened.' He laughs, but it sounds a little hollow.

'I know, I know! It didn't seem symbolic at the time, but that's where we met, outside the bloody lost property office. I didn't have a clue about life, I didn't know which way was up in those days.'

49

So the short, stocky 18-year-old, in his borrowed farmer's suit and tie, green as the grass he'd watched from the train windows for the last 90 minutes, got off the train and made his way through the crowds to lost property. He hadn't a clue what she looked like, and they hadn't arranged to wear red roses, or carry rolled-up newspapers as a sign. So he stood there, awkward, self-conscious, looking at people, thinking, *'Maybe that's her there … Maybe that's … What does she look like? … No, she's walked past.'* Then a little skinny girl approached and he thought, *'That surely can't be her,'* because of all the things that Gregor Fisher never was, never has been, it was skinny.

'Are you Gregor?' asked the girl.

'Yup, right, that's me,' he said.

*Pause.*

'You must be Maureen.'

What followed was an awkward, messy sort-of-hug between the two: the young, daft, embarrassed boy and his slightly older and more emotional sister.

A mismatch of expectation and affection.

Gregor didn't like hugging anyone, let alone weepy girls who were complete strangers. Maureen was hugging the long-lost adored little brother she had been so cruelly separated from. She had recognised him instantly – he hadn't changed from when he was a boy.

They went for a cup of tea and started talking. Gregor felt awkward. He also felt immediately he was a disappointment to her.

These things are never how you expect them to be. I expected some sort of connection, but there wasn't, really. There was some kind of communality because she could remember when we were small, and once she mentioned things I vaguely remembered, but there was no instant bond. I once saw a documentary about two Japanese families whose children got swapped ... the ramifications of that were absolutely fascinating. It's to do with the time you spend together and the shared experiences.

Maureen and I have shared a lot since then, so it's changed, but at that time there was no instant potato about it, and as an 18-year-old stupid boy I don't think I coped with it particularly well. I just don't think I handled it very well and I don't think I was what she wanted me to be.

Story of my life.

But Gregor's life contained many stories and he was about to hear a completely new one. As well as getting to know each other again, he and his sister had a mystery to unravel. And Maureen knew far more about it than he did. The more she told him, the more unbelievable it all became, unfolding like a soap opera while their cups of tea grew cold between them.

Here was where the Fisher connection came from. Jim Fisher, brother of Cis, Agnes, Wull, Archie and Babs, was a pig breeder who lived in Lanarkshire. He had married a woman called Ellen Sellars and in 1948 they had a child called Linda. Five years later, when no more babies had arrived, the doctors told Ellen that she would be unable to conceive again. It was the days when very little could be done for fertility problems, so the couple accepted the verdict and decided to adopt. They wanted a sister for Linda. Formal adoption was a rather more lax affair in those days.

*'More a case of, how many do you want?'*

The Fishers' hunt took them to a children's home in Clackmannan in central Scotland, about an hour's drive away, where there was a girl of four available for adoption. Perfect. A lovely, healthy, well-behaved little girl called Maureen. But the only problem was, she came as a pair: she had a brother, Gregor, aged two and a half, and the two of them weren't to be parted. That was what the authorities had told the matron of the children's home. It was the family's wishes, whoever the family had been: Maureen and Gregor must be kept together as a package. The Fishers pondered it a while, then decided to take both children. After all, he was a lovely-looking boy too.

So, on 19 June 1956, Gregor and Maureen were wedged on the front seat of Jim Fisher's van, between their new father and mother, and driven to Closeburn, a house up a long track in the mining area called Cornsilloch, outside Larkhall in Lanarkshire. There was the dark mountain of a coal bing (a slag heap) nearby. Jim Fisher, who was 39, owned a piggery and cured bacon; the business brought in £500 a year and he also owned the house. *'A three apartment detached cottage, with kitchen and bathroom, found to be quite well furnished and in a clean and tidy condition,'* said the curator's report in the adoption papers Gregor Fisher was to read decades later. Ellen was 41 and Jim was her second husband: she had married in Derby in 1936 and then divorced at the end of the war on the grounds of desertion.

The story of Jim and Ellen Fisher came tumbling out of Maureen. She desperately wanted Gregor to remember, to bind him to her in the past. She told him she had memories, although very, very faint, of being in a children's home with him before they went off to live with the Fishers – just the two of them, in cots, alone in a room.

'Do you remember the red wellingtons?' she wanted to know.

And to his amazement, out of the fog something stirred. He was in a room somewhere and there was a pair of red wellingtons in front of him. And because he was a little boy, and he needed a pee, he pulled down his pants and piddled in both boots. The image was clear in his head, now she had brought it back: the supreme satisfaction of doing something so neatly and cleverly. But he also remembered, afterwards, the repercussions – the sense of trouble and harsh words. It was probably the first time he had ever been told off in his life and he recollected a bad feeling.

Maureen told him about her memories of what happened after they arrived at Cornsilloch. Ellen was very kind to them. The two of them had been treated very well, and she remembered being happy and content. They had toys to play with. A social worker used to come and visit them. Linda, their new big sister, was friendly to them. Their new dad had cut Maureen's straight hair; and then Maureen, getting the idea and envious of Gregor's white blond curls, had given her little brother a short back and sides. They went to Sunday school – and as she said it, Gregor realised he probably remembered that too – a vague sense of pitch pine floor and white walls.

In April 1957 the adoption was finalised and the papers lodged at Hamilton Sheriff Court. But by then, as can happen after adoption, Ellen Fisher had become pregnant, a surprise for everyone, including the doctors. She duly had the little girl she had always wanted, a baby they called Helen. But Ellen was, for those days, an extremely elderly mother; she had a tricky time and was unwell after the birth.

Quite what happened next remains opaque with horror. Ellen was recuperating at home. Gregor, prompted by Maureen, had the vaguest recollection of there being some other woman in the house at the time, someone kind, who was helping look after everyone while their adoptive mother spent most of her time upstairs in bed. They were all in the house the day Ellen had come downstairs, still in her nightgown. It was winter. Christmassy. The fire in the living room was stoked and roaring to heat the house. Maybe she had been drying nappies by the open fire in the living room, or perhaps she took a funny turn. Either way the flames caught her nightie and in her weakened state, screaming for help, she was terribly burnt.

As Maureen told Gregor the awful tale, images stirred in his head that fitted the jigsaw: of commotion. Upset. Shouts. He could, he believed, remember going to the hospital with Jim Fisher, presumably with Linda and Maureen and the baby too, for who was there to leave them with? He vaguely remembered the strange sight of a big grown man sobbing, and knowing that something very, very bad was happening.

Ellen Fisher died in early January 1958, in Glasgow Royal Infirmary, of multiple burns and pneumonia. She left two birth children, Linda and the new baby Helen, and two adoptive children, Gregor and Maureen. It was the second time in two years that Gregor and his sister had been left motherless in traumatic, bewildering circumstances. Were this fiction, you might suggest the author was trying too hard. But it was not, and you do not need to be a modern child psychologist to imagine the cumulative impact of such events on infants. The sudden loss of a second mother also managed to do what up until then the authorities had managed to prevent: it led to the separation of the little boy from his sister.

Those days, people dealt purely with practical things. For Jim Fisher – for any husband – the situation was impossible: a working man widowed with four young children and no one to care for them. How could he cope? Within hours of hearing the news, his sisters swooped into action. The authorities, those being the days before social work departments, did not seem to be involved at all. In the short term the children would have to be split up. Aunt Cis, the eldest sister, said she would take Gregor, and that's when he remembers being driven up the hill in the snow, making a pattern with his pee in the snow, seeing the lights of the city twinkling below him in the dark. Maureen was whipped away to Aunt Agnes the baker, in her flat opposite Queen's Park. The baby Helen went to Aunt Babs, who also lived on the south side of Glasgow, and Linda, the eldest girl, to her maternal grandparents in Derby.

These were to be temporary arrangements until things settled down and Jim had managed to organise childcare. He did this in the pragmatic way of many widowers. Not terribly long after Ellen was buried, within the year in fact, he had remarried to a policewoman called Flora. Once she was settled in at the pig farm, and had given up her job, the word went out that all the motherless children could now be gathered back into the Fisher fold at Cornsilloch for her to bring up.

The baby Helen went back, along with Maureen and Linda, but when it was suggested that Gregor joined them, the wise and feisty Cis, maybe unsure of her new sister-in-law, or perhaps just too much in love with her blue-eyed boy, refused. The child was staying with her. There was friction in the family as a result, hence the power struggle between the two women at the family party that Gregor vaguely remembered; and hence the fact he saw almost nothing of Jim Fisher from then on. Cis, gentle but fiery when called for, became his mother. He wanted that, she wanted that. End of story.

But not for Maureen, it wasn't. The judgement that Cis had implicitly passed on Flora's mothering skills, it seems, may have been correct. Flora and Maureen had a very difficult relationship. Not only was the little girl separated from her precious brother – and nobody explained to her where he'd gone or why he never came back – but she was now in the care of a stepmother she felt had little affection for her.

Sitting there, in the Glasgow cafe, Maureen struggled to explain to Gregor quite how bad it had been. Flora very quickly had two children of her own, Flora and Margaret, which made six altogether, a big family, and once she had her own family she no longer seemed interested in the children she had inherited with marriage. She may have left the police, but old habits died hard: Maureen remembered having to clean and tidy up the busy house to high standards. The minute she came in from school, she was told to start on the washing up and look after the wee ones. She could not remember any love or cuddles; she did not remember ever receiving praise. She remembers being shouted at and made to feel she was in the wrong all the time. Linda, the eldest child, left fairly soon afterwards to return to her grandparents but Maureen, entirely alone in the world, did not have that option. She also recalls being told by Flora that her real mother was dead, she was adopted, and that she, Flora, was all she had. Maureen met Gregor very occasionally at family parties but he didn't remember her, or need her; she could see he was totally wrapped up in Cis's happy, loving force field.

Sitting there talking to her brother again, now 18 and a stranger to her, Maureen recounted how she wore hand-me-down clothes while the others got new, and how she used to sit under the table hugging Helen, the motherless baby. And how she used to cry in the dark.

Jim Fisher wasn't in the house much, but occasionally, when he went out in his van collecting bread for the pigs, he took the older children with him, presumably to get them out from under Flora's feet. Maureen told Gregor that she thought Jim was a good father; she called him Dad.

And so the years went on. About the same time as Gregor was raking round the fields in Neilston and running home to indulgence and home baking from Cis, Jim Fisher gave up on the pigs and moved his family to nearby Motherwell. He could earn more money in a job at the Ravenscraig steelworks. This unfortunately meant he was out on shifts much of the time, and so there was no buffer between Maureen and her stepmother.

Gregor is pensive. 'Poor Maureen, she drew the short straw going back to Jim and Flora. She was that bit older than me, which I think makes a huge, huge, huge difference. If you're more knowing, it's harder. I think I've been the fortunate one here. I was at an age of, you know, this is where I am and this is what's happening and I've got a full belly and a warm bed and love and affection so I'm sorted. And no questions. I wasn't the questioning type.

'I think back to the red wellingtons and that feeling of being in trouble and the sense that there was no one who loved you despite what you'd done. I'm not saying I was beaten or anything because I've no memory of that – but the way you might treat other people's children is so different from the way you'd treat your own children if they did something like that. If they're your own, you'd be a bit grumpy and think, "Oh God, don't do that, I've got to clean those wellingtons now." But Maureen, she had no one on her side. It was positively feckin' Dickensian, some of the things that happened.'

Eventually Maureen, anchorless and unloved, went off the rails. She hated her stepmother. Her bad behaviour reached the point where, when she was 11, she was put back into the care system, this time with foster parents. That was not successful. In her own words she *'lost it completely'*, and when she was 12 years old she had a nervous breakdown and ended up in Bangour Psychiatric Hospital. Just beside the M8 motorway in West Lothian, Bangour was a villa-style campus originally built in 1906 to house Edinburgh's lunatic paupers and which stayed open until 2004, latterly one hopes with a rather more kindly mission statement. The little girl was to spend a year there, being treated as well as child psychiatry knew how in 1964, although one doubts if any satisfactory treatment has ever existed for abandonment and lack of love. Of all the many casualties in this story, Maureen's plight is at this point one of the most heart-rending.

Somewhere along the line, however, she became aware of one very big fact. As well as her little brother Gregor, she had an older sister. And it was during Maureen's spell in Bangour that a girl called Ann McKenzie, six years her senior, came to see her in another of those *'You-don't-know-me-but-I'm-your-sister'* moments. Ann filled in the momentous detail: that there had been the three of them, all born illegitimate, and they had lived near Menstrie, a village in the country near Stirling. They were taken away and split up from each other when they were little because their birth mother had become ill and died. Not because she didn't want them. Though how, the girls wondered, could anyone want illegitimate children, especially three of them? The very word 'illegitimate' cast a dark stain on them, made them lower their voices and feel deeply ashamed.

Ann told Maureen that they had different fathers. Ann's father had disappeared before she was born. She said that Maureen and Gregor's father was someone else, but she didn't know who he was. The two little ones had been separated from her after their mother died; Maureen and Gregor were put in a home, Ann taken in by a disapproving aunt. She too had been terribly unhappy, and had been thrown out of the house when she was 18 because her boyfriend was a Catholic.

Maybe it helped Maureen to know that she was not alone in the world. Perhaps it meant something, too, to learn that her mother had not chosen to abandon her. That she *had* been loved after all. Maureen recovered from her breakdown and was placed with foster parents. She went on to nursing college, married young, and then, when she was 19, decided to look for Gregor and at the same time settle some scores.

Maureen told Gregor how she had turned up at the door of the Fisher house in Motherwell and, ice-cold, driven with inner fury, confronted them. *How could they have treated her the way they did?* She also demanded to know where her brother was. Flora, she said, was hard as nails, but Jim drove Maureen back to the railway station and told her that Gregor was still with Aunt Cis. He was very contrite and apologetic for all the bad times.

Thus Maureen had written the letter and found Gregor; and so here they were, lost property, brother and sister, strangers to each other. Suddenly, what had been a taboo subject, a large, unwieldy mystery in their past, was no longer secret. Oh, there was still mystery, but illegitimacy was their new, unwelcome label. The stigma was still profound. Now, for the first time, they were forced to address a whole new raft of questions. Who were they? No, who were they *really*? Why Menstrie? Where *was* Menstrie? *Why had they been split up?* wondered Maureen bitterly. Why had Cis been allowed to keep Gregor, and he be loved and happy? Why had Maureen ended up with a step-mother whose perceived lack of kindness haunted her for most of her life?

Gregor got on a train back to Langholm with lots to think about and plenty of judgements to pass. Illegitimate, huh? Father unknown. Mother a bit of a tramp, perhaps? Not quite what a naïve teenage boy wants to hear. He and Maureen had decided that they wanted to find out a bit more. They would meet up with their big sister Ann, for a start. A few weeks and several letters later, and it was all arranged – the sisters would come down to their little brother. Gregor was still dodging about the Borders, staying either at the farm or Uncle Archie

Fisher's council house near the old station in Langholm – it was handy for the bar work.

> I was always itinerant – funnily enough, it's been like that most of my life, actually. Yeah, I'd lay my head anywhere and be quite content. I don't know why that is, it's still that way. Used to it, I suppose, from early doors. It was just normal kind of behaviour.

So it was in Uncle Archie's small front room that Ann, Maureen and Gregor were reunited for the first time since their mother had died, 15 years before. It wasn't the easiest of meetings: the room was crowded with strangers and fractured with emotion. The sisters had hired a car and driven down from Glasgow with their husbands. Gregor's Fisher family was represented too, in the shape of cousin Carol, to give him moral support. Archie, a retired farm worker, wisely made himself scarce.

But the sisters didn't feel like sisters to the gallus 18-year-old boy, and they wanted to talk about things he had sealed away quite successfully and didn't want to address. Gregor was not, at that age, blessed with any kind of tact or finesse. He listened to them pondering what little they knew of their mother's circumstances and the riddle of their illegitimacy. Ann told them their mother was called Catherine McKenzie (some people called her Kit McKenzie). She had been ill for a long time. Ann used to have to come home from school at lunchtime to give baby Gregor his bottle. Mum had died and they had been split up.

And that's when Gregor said the awful thing about his mother. He remembered saying it, not knowing whether it was to hurt

Ann, the bringer of all this difficult information, or whether it was a general expression of his own anger.

> Well, you could forgive somebody one, couldn't ye?
> Two at a push but three? Come on!

The words came out of his mouth and hung, harsh, cocky, in the air.

Nearly 45 years later and several centuries wiser, he squirms with discomfort. He knew immediately he had cut Ann deep. But their childhood was a mess, something that could never be righted. Ann's loneliness, Maureen's troubled behaviour, Clackmannanshire social service's decision to split them up … No wonder the sudden ugliness of his feelings towards a mother he never knew.

> You could blame this, that and the other. That's why my first idea of a title for this book was *Nobody's Perfect*. And nobody is perfect. I don't know what the perfect scenario would have been.

Gregor admits to an ingrained sense of distance – pushing back if anyone expects too much or comes too close. There's a line, and if someone crosses it, uninvited, they've gone too far. He didn't want to feel obliged to feel emotion for a woman, a mother, who meant nothing to him; whom he felt had let him down.

The minute somebody comes over the line I go:
What is it? What do you want, you expecting
something? I don't know where this comes from. I've
never worked it out. I'm fine, I'll give and I'll share and
all the rest of it, but once somebody gets too needy
I'm really no good at it. Maybe it's because I think if
they get in too close, it's all going to go tits up or
something. Because everything else always has.

After the meeting in Langholm, he saw little of Ann, who
retired, hurt. She had always been the most isolated of the three
in the sense that she had a different father; the other two at least
shared the same parentage, even if they didn't know who he
was. Gregor and Maureen built a friendship and went on to
discover one significant thing: they could make each other
laugh uncontrollably to the point where everyone else in their
company, looking on from the sidelines, would say, 'Strange
people, don't know what they're laughing at, it's not even funny.'
There was the time, years later, during a church service they had
been invited to, when Gregor and Maureen disgraced themselves by taking a fit of the giggles at a priest swinging the
incense, two middle-aged people who should have known
better, corpsing, stuffing their fists in their mouths, laughing to
the point where they thought they were going to have to leave
– 'It was like some kind of fit.'

   If he's honest, Gregor always felt there was a bit of tension
between himself and his sisters. He was the lucky one, the blue-
eyed boy; the one who found a new mother to love him. They,
by comparison, had been thrown to the wolves, left to survive,
desperately alone and unloved. There is of course another way to

look through the prism. He was luckier, yes, but Gregor by no means got off scot-free. And had he not been saved by Cis, it is debatable where he might have ended up, possibly worse off than his sisters. Arguably, it is because of Cis that everything else that subsequently happened in his life happened because she put so much love into him, nourished the laughter and the confidence. Certainly, right then, as he waved a horribly awkward goodbye to his blood family on the doorstep, Gregor knew which way to turn: enough of being a bastard, enough of having some poor wretch for a mother. He didn't fancy these unwelcome realities about his origins; he didn't want to find out any more.

His great allies in the Fisher family, Cis, Carol and Agnes, understood. And if, as they shut the front door, Carol whispered, *'It's OK, don't worry about them. That's in the past, you're one of us now,'* she was speaking for all of them. In the Fishers he was blessed with a family that, give or take the usual nip and snide comment to be had in every household, always gave him the feeling that he was loved and wanted. They made that obvious, and they also made it obvious that they thought it would be easier if he let it go. His life was working out fine with them, why complicate things?

Oh, just put the blinkers on, put it away back there, lock it away. That's fine.

And so he did. He pretended none of it was true and that he really was Cis's child. Yes, she was his real mother. Because she was the woman who only once, in the 30-odd years he was with her, withdrew her life-giving love. And that was a moment that shaped him for life.

We're exploring Neilston in the car.

'Down here,' he says. 'I'll show you where Johnny Monaghan used to live.'

The narrow lane winds around and down the hill. Lots of expensive houses with gates and walls and private gardens behind high hedges; the posh end of the village.

It's a leafy dead end, a cul-de-sac of class. I turn the car in Johnny Monaghan's former drive, wondering whether anyone will suspect us of being burglars casing the joint, and jot down the numberplate. Probably. It's a Neighbourhood Watch sort of street.

'So you and Johnny and Andrew Robinson used to play here, in this gateway, did you?'

'That was Andrew's house, there.'

He points.

Pause.

'Andrew had lots of Dinky cars. I didn't have any so I stole one. But I couldn't take it home because Cis would know immediately.'

'So what did you do?'

We're heading back up the hill towards scruffier climes.

'There, just there, in the wall.' He's turning in his seat, jerking the seat belt. 'There was a loose stone. I used to take out the stone and hide the Dinky car behind it.'

'Then what happened?'

'Andrew Robinson's mother never let me play with him again.'

I'm digesting it. Children may steal if, subconsciously, deep down, they feel they've been deprived of love. Maybe it happens with some adopted children, I think – but I can't remember where I heard this stuff and I don't want to offend him with half-baked armchair psychology.

*'Did I tell you about the Burdall's Gravy Salts?' he asks.*

*I shake my head.*

*And he begins to talk.*

It came about because the sweet shop in the village, just up here by the junction we're coming to, used to be run by a little woman called Miss Gilmour. Occasionally Gregor was given a penny, an old penny, to spend en route to school. That worked well until he saw that other children had slightly more than a penny and were getting more sweets than he was. When you're small, and you like sweets, as he did, such injustices burn deep. Gregor was aware his mother had a tin, a Burdall's gravy salt tin. Burdall's gravy salt was a thing of the early twentieth century, a forerunner to Bisto or Oxo; a potent black mixture of salt and caramel that housewives stirred into their mince to darken and flavour it. Inside the Leckie household, however, this particular Burdall's tin was used to store shillings specifically for the gas meter. Gregor cunningly decided to take just one shilling for sweets, reckoning it wouldn't be missed, and sure enough, it wasn't.

But, in the manner of urchins, he got greedy. He decided to treat his friends and himself to Mars bars so he took three shillings, which he didn't think would be missed, but he entirely overlooked the fact that his mother and Miss Gilmour were very chummy. Nor did he consider for a minute the fact that he had form with Miss Gilmour, who had never quite forgiven him for pinching a small box of Omo out of her shop. Gregor had needed the Omo, of course, because with the unalienable logic of a small boy, he thought it a very good wheeze to put it into the waterfall in the local burn, down in the valley, and watch the bubbles. All in the interests of science ...

He was about seven or so, because from that age he always walked home from school by himself. On that particular day his mother, however, unusually, was standing waiting for him at the school gate. Whether she had come po-faced from a conversation with Miss Gilmour, he knew not; all he knew was that she took him by the arm in silence and frogmarched him home.

'What's wrong?' he asked plaintively.

She never said a word.

He knew exactly what was wrong: he had been found out. Cis's punishment was devastating. She didn't hit him, she didn't shout, she didn't scream, she just ignored him, unless speech was absolutely necessary, then she would speak briefly, communicate what was needed, and she would place food for him on the table. Her silence lasted three weeks; and for the child utterly hooked on her love and affection, whose very existence depended on her, it was a lesson he never forgot. She taught him honour and the difference between right and wrong.

Gregor visibly softens round the edges, smiling at the memory.

'I can never forget because it had a direct bearing on another event in my life, 50 years later. Cis is long dead and I'm married, I've got three children, we're living in Lincolnshire. In fact, it's my daughter's 21st and it's a big affair – there's a tent, a marquee, in the garden, there are 150 guests, there's the whole jingbang. So that takes place and it's all very jolly, the house is moving with people, everybody's using the toilets up the stairs, this, that and everything.

'Anyway, about two weeks later we were going out to a do and my wife Vicki said: "I can't find my diamond earrings."

'"Oh," I said, "they'll be there somewhere, just look."

'And I went upstairs to help search and no, they're not there, and by this time everyone was involved and there's a bounty on these bloody earrings.

'"Come to think of it, I can't find any of my jewellery," Vicki said.

'The house was turned upside down looking for the damned jewellery. After three days of searching we remembered the party. There had been caterers here, strangers in the house, and you think, "Oh, please don't say ..." Anyway, I phoned the insurance company and they told me to get a crime number. I phoned the police and got a crime number; and then receipts had to be found, because the whole issue was deadly serious. So the cheque for the jewellery, something like £12,000, arrived, and was put in the bank and forgotten about.

'Anyway, about three months passed. In that house we had one of those closets where you store shirts in drawers, mine on one side and Vicki's on the other. And I mean there are shirts you just never bloody wear, aren't there? But on this particular occasion for some reason I thought, "I'm going to put that shirt on, that's a jolly shirt," and I'm reaching up to get it and I think, "Oh, what's that? Oh, it's a box ... What's in here? Jewellery! Ah ha ..."

'You know when you're in a situation like that, and you suddenly think, "Oh, I remember now, I saw her jewellery on the bedroom mantelpiece, and I thought that shouldn't be left there so I put it up on the shelf behind the shirts."

'It was me all along, I just had a brain freeze.

'But that's when the Burdall's gravy salt tin came back. I heard my mother at that point, heard her saying, "Gregor!"

'Whereupon I phoned the insurance company.

'"There's been a bit of an incident ... where do I return the cheque to?"

'The guy sounded nonplussed. "What, are you going to send the money back?"

'"Well, I've found the jewellery so, you know, yeah, I'm sending the money back."

'And he said, and I found this really sad, he said: "D'you know, I've been 30-odd years in this game; you're the second person that I've ever dealt with that sent the money back?"

'"No, tell me that's not true."

'"It's true."

'"By way of interest, who's the other person?"

'"She was an old lady who had dropped a sapphire – she'd been cleaning out a drain or something – and she'd dropped a ring down a drain and it had been rediscovered when somebody was doing work. It was a couple of years after the event and she sent the money back."

'I think he thought I was slightly loony, because I said: "Well, I heard my mother in my ear and I couldn't get away with that. She'd come back and visit me if I didn't return the money."

'"Oh well, right," he said, obviously thinking he had a right nutter on the end of the phone.

'But that's the power of the Burdall's gravy salt tin and it's just one of the many things that Cis gave me.'

She instilled her values in him. Because Cis, says her heart-son, if not her birth son, was the best: a good, kind, do-anything-for-anybody woman; the sort who would go round the parish quietly dishing out home baking to old ladies living on their own. She'd turn up with a couple of scones or a cake. One of life's givers, some might say she gave the ultimate: taking in a lost child to her home, opening her heart to him and giving him life. The point is, without Cis, this story could not be told.

Later that summer another letter had arrived, this time from the Royal Scottish Academy of Music and Drama. He read it in surprise, delight and terror – and it said, in nice flowery language, we'd be delighted to offer you a place. About an hour later he was still staring at it, and it still said the same thing, although he was convinced there must have been some mistake, and he would turn up and they'd say, *'Oh, no, it wasn't you, it was that fellow there, not you. Never mind, nice to see you but this isn't for you.'*

Gregor couldn't believe he had got into drama school, against competition from hundreds of other young people from all over the country, because he'd been lazy and bored and perverse at school, and wasted his opportunities. This time, he realised, he'd been given a break. He wasn't someone to get overjoyed at anything, he'd had too many knocks, but Cis and the girls were overjoyed for him. With his mother's encouragement, he accepted the place that autumn.

Little did he know what was yet to come.

# CHAPTER 4

# I'd Like You to Move
# to the Colour Blue

'Who ever loved that loved not at first sight?'
*As You Like It*: Act III, Scene V

Gregor walked up Glasgow's Buchanan Street for his first day at drama school, checking out his reflection surreptitiously in the shop windows. He was looking as smart as Cis could make him. It wasn't quite the borrowed farmer's suit, but as near as: a navy blazer, grey flannels and a white shirt with a tie. On this occasion she had washed the whole shirt, not just the collar.

He was feeling reasonably good about himself until he entered the portals of the grand old Royal Scottish Academy of Music and Drama, where in an instant he knew he'd blown it.

Catastrophe.

*'Spot the arse.'*

Everyone else was wearing loon jeans and Afghan coats; had long hair and mascara. It was 1972 and anything went. They said 'Hi' in breathy posh voices. 'Hullo,' he replied defensively, in his gruffest, roughest West of Scotland man voice.

*'You know, I couldn't have been more out of place than a side of ham at a halal butcher.'*

It was a steep learning curve. Needless to say the next day he ditched the blazer and flannels, but the trouble was, he didn't possess any trendy stuff either. The best he could manage was to look dirty and interesting, a bit grubby. Gregor never felt he fitted in. It was a re-run of school, that was the trouble; reawakening old insecurities, that tribal thing again. His fellow students were all A and B stream kids, with slightly arty parents who lived in the smart suburbs of Milngavie or Bearsden, where people's horizons were wider and the world was their oyster, whereas, with his lot, it was more a case of *'Keep your head below the parapet, get a job, get your wages, don't get ideas above your station.'*

Here, quite simply, was another planet. The movement classes, for instance.

'I'd like you to move to the colour blue,' said the teacher.

*'Well, I mean, Jesus, how could you let me go now because I can't do this?'* Gregor was silently, internally, huffing and puffing.

'OK, now move to the colour black.'

*'Well, I can do that. Black's hellish! I'll pretend I'm at a funeral.'*

The next class required students to wear leotards and tights. And here was Gregor, the husky 18-year-old who didn't feel he looked good in ordinary clothes, let alone …

Leotard and tights. I mean, you're talking about a sex-starved virginal boy who's not at all happy about his rolls of fat in a leotard. It's not good; it's like a panic attack, all of us in leotards and tights, all the boys, all the girls. It was decided the boys should be trees and the girls would be vines growing up the trees. Oh, the whole thing's not good, the girls wrapping themselves around us, and I'm thinking, 'Oh no, help, I can't handle this!'

But he survived and went back the next day ... and the day after that. The main drama school was then in the old St George's Place, in the centre of Glasgow, later to be renamed Nelson Mandela Square, but first-year classes were held in a little annexe to the school in Atholl Gardens, in the West End. To get to it from his village home Gregor had to travel into the city by train, then negotiate the quirky little Glasgow Underground, where the distinctive smell was an entirely new experience to him. He'd never done anything like that before – cross the city, find the place and turn up, on his own – *'I was a bit of a yokel.'*

He began to get to know his fellow students, realising to his surprise they were in as much of a state of anxiety as he was. Lifelong friendships were formed, and he started to explore an entirely different culture. Voice classes, for instance; lessons in how to put on make-up. Fencing, but not like on Billy Bell's farm, with posts and a mallet – these were lessons in sword fighting. His épée work was not very good but his lunges grew better. He learnt how to prepare for parts in plays, modern and classical. Most of these works were completely unknown to a boy without O-Level English who had cut his teeth on Gilbert and Sullivan. Gregor didn't have a clue about Shakespeare either. He remembers his first foray – *Macbeth* – and the words still roll richly off his tongue: *'If it were done when 'tis done, then 'twere well it were done quickly'.*

Drama school was an odd place, he decided. It took him a long time to be confident enough to grow into his potential. He kept his head down, terrified he'd be found out. In those days there was a state of affairs that would be unthinkable now under a Scottish nationalist government: the RSAMD taught their students to speak proper English. It was drummed into them that in their normal daily lives they must adopt the standard middle-class southern English way of speaking otherwise they simply wouldn't get work. Voice classes were there to knock any accent and identity out of them. Gregor was happy to practise Received Pronunciation at home but paled – uh-oh – at the thought of walking into a pub in Neilston and trying it.

*'Ah, a pint of your best bitter, please, old chap. I've popped in to meet my good friends, Timothy and Nigel.'*

Besides, there was no comic acting in the course. In fact there wasn't much room for humour at all. There was Shakespeare, naturally, and something called a Christmas show, which was much more upmarket than a pantomime and held in the Athenaeum. This, now long gone, was the school's old theatre, a fantastic, atmospheric place with gaslights, which had once hosted Charles Dickens. The first time his unofficial adoptive sister Margaret Leckie took him to the theatre as a little boy it was to the Athenaeum. He vividly remembered it – a production of *The Soldier's Tale*, and as the gaslights went down there was a fan blowing silk on the stage and he thought it was a real fire. Enthralled by the magic, little did he know ten years later he would be on that very stage acting his first roles.

One of the lecturers, a drama teacher called Margaret Gordon, was not a fan of Gregor's, though. At the end of every term the students got report cards, little slips of paper stapled together. Margaret never wrote anything good about him and the first time it happened he found her criticism quite devastating, and afterwards it simply became a bit wearying. What she wrote confirmed his worst fears: that he wasn't that good at acting, and was certainly not as good as the posh kids. They seemed to have a better handle on it, especially when it came to Shakespeare. It was Margaret who did a lot of the productions and she would usually cast him in some lowly part, like the neighbour who appeared infrequently, or in the chorus. Gregor was fast learning one of the great truisms of adult life, and especially of the acting world – that not everyone likes you.

Another drama teacher, however, an exuberant, slightly manic man called Peter de Souza, thought well of him and gave him some good stuff to do. He trusted Gregor. The comic Shakespearean role of Falstaff was one such casting, which showed foresight for Gregor's future talent. In hindsight, he thinks much of the work was completely unsuited to the young students, but that was drama school and they had to learn their trade, acting little scenes in front of the whole class.

Cis's gauche boy, then, had very mixed feelings about drama school. Part of him was in love with it – the mystery of the art, the thrill of performing. He was drawn instinctively to theatricality. It felt natural, and he felt very comfortable with all the crazy people. But at the same time he felt he was distanced from them; that he was outside looking in. He didn't feel he was one of them.

Part of this dissatisfaction, of course, lay in his persistent and preoccupying failure to lose his virginity. Sex just wasn't happening for him, no matter how much he thought about it and how much he practised. For this, he could blame a religious upbringing, a lack of sex education and a rejection by a girl called Patricia Smith. Particularly Patricia Smith. To tell this story, we must rewind to the days of Neilston Primary School, where Gregor, aged 10 or 11, was a member of the Life Boys, the junior section of the Boys' Brigade. The Life Boys had Christmas parties, and Gregor, who was achingly – *achingly* – fond of a girl called Patricia Smith, managed to pluck up the courage to ask her to go to the party with him. It was a good party, with games, for which there were prizes, and Gregor won a smart propelling pencil and pen set. He remembers presenting it to the new love of his life with great ceremony and then he ran home, happy, to Cis. As far as he was concerned, the romance was going to run and run, they'd probably get married and everything would be happy ever after. Nothing else mattered in the world; he was as far gone in love as it is possible for a small boy to be.

And the next day Patricia Smith went to the Scout Christmas party with someone else. Gregor was devastated. Only twice in his life did he fall in love as profoundly like that: once with Patricia, and then, many years later, with Vicki, the soulmate who became his wife. He took Patricia's rejection deeply to heart, to the extent that Cis twigged that something was wrong. Valentine's Day was coming and he got even gloomier because in those days Valentine's cards were a big thing – you wrote things like 'S.W.A.L.K' (Sealed With A Loving Kiss) on the flap and put a secret message under the stamp. Unlike the smarter boys in class, who'd boast about how many cards they received, Gregor wasn't the type of boy the girls sent cards to. But that year, he got some. It didn't quite make up for Patricia but he was chuffed.

Only much later in life, when he had come home on a trip and was going through a drawer, did he come across the Valentine's cards again.

'Whoever was it that sent these cards? I never found out ...'
*Pause.*

And then he looked up and saw the look on dear honest Cis's face.

'*MUM!* God!'

She had got one of her friends to do the writing on them so he wouldn't guess, and had posted them to him.

At Barrhead High School sex and girls had remained a total mystery to him. He was very keen on them but terrified at the same time, and acknowledges it might have been unconscious fear of yet more rejection in his life that caused him to be so reticent. When the stirrings came upon him, when like all boys he realised that an erection was not just for peeing over high walls, he remembers thinking it was something rather odd and filthy.

'*Basically, I used to go to church too much.*'

Because this was Scotland in the 1960s; the sexual revolution had not reached Neilston and it was long before the days of proper sex education in schools, let alone Internet pornography. Gregor could only learn from the family around him, who never spoke about it – '*John Leckie? Are you kidding?*' – or from people at school. Enter Newton Darroch, a maths teacher, who was the only member of staff brave enough to give any kind of sex education. It was usually an all-male class and a boy was positioned next to the blackboard under strict instruction, should anyone of the female persuasion come in the door, to roll the board round instantly to hide any offending diagrams.

And so Gregor's schooldays passed in a haze of unrequited lust and guilt. The only thing that made him feel better was the fact his best friend Johnny Monaghan was just as obsessed and frustrated. At drama school the conflict continued, all mixed up with the tug of his stern Church of Scotland upbringing. His church attendance began to tail off when he passed 18, mainly because it was regarded as pretty uncool to be seen to be going to church at that age – although he still had a bit of faith.

There were some very strange people in drama school because theatre bred a more eccentric environment than most places of study. It was a funny hotbed of knowingness and naïvety. He remembered one-to-one interviews with Grace Matchett, one of the lecturers, who had an office in a little Edwardian-style conservatory at the top of the stairs in Atholl Gardens. Grace would ask him all kinds of quite personal questions and sometimes, with his buttoned-up background, he convinced himself she might be asking him about his sex life – or lack of it. She was genuine, he was convinced, but drama school was all a bit strange like that, with illicit affairs between some of the other lecturers and the students. The drama students mixed with the music students, also highly sensitive young people, and Gregor remembers one sizzling anecdote that summed it all up. One of the music students had been playing some kind of Chopin nocturne on the piano, and his teacher suddenly interrupted him.

'Have you ever been to bed with anyone?' he asked.

The poor student, just out of school, sat at the piano stool, frozen.

'Well, go and get laid and come back and play that.'

And it's true. It's true. You know it was that, it was raw. He was right to say that because that's what the music is about. And it was the same at drama school. I should've gone away and got laid too – you know what I mean? In a funny way I'd like to go to drama school now; I'd be more prepared for it, I'd get more out of it. You hear about all these Hollywood actors going to acting lessons, and you think, but they've made 49 films. Yeah, but you know, you have to keep scratching it.

Glasgow, circa 1975: the curtains were swishing back and all kinds of things were happening. This was real life, in neon; rich with possibilities. Soon Gregor was off to a place where even John Knox could not rescue him. And it all happened when he ran away to join the theatre.

He never graduated from the Royal Academy of Music and Drama. Halfway through his third and final year, out of the blue he was offered an acting job and an Equity card. The timing was unfortunate because it was during a production of *Leonardo's Last Supper*, about Leonardo da Vinci, with Gregor in the lead. So there was upset when he said he was leaving, but the director of the play, the kindly Callum Mill, told him not to worry and encouraged him to go. In those days acting was a tightly closed shop and an Equity card was like gold dust. If you didn't have a union card, you didn't work.

So he seized his next lucky break. It was all down to chance and a young actress called Maureen Beattie, who had been a year ahead of Gregor at drama school. She knew the man who was running a company called TRYP, The Rep for Young People in Dundee, where a venture was planned to take a show round schools to encourage children to write, paint, act or get involved in history. The company needed a young actor and Maureen recommended Gregor.

Before he knew it, he was an employee of Dundee Repertory Theatre and the proud owner of Equity card No. 78633, a number on a card he carries in his wallet to this day. He was not sorry to leave RSAMD without finishing. There had been a lack of encouragement, he felt. Plenty of criticism, but not enough positive suggestions.

> It's a terrible thing to do to a drama student, to keep squashing them all the time. And I thought there was a bit too much squashing and not enough watering, so I was pleased to leave.

Thus Gregor stepped off a train at Dundee station on a Saturday night, ready for first rehearsals on Monday, in a city where he knew no one and nothing. Other than to stay with one of the numerous Fisher clan he had never been away from home before. It was a shock to him, that autumn evening, with the east wind whipping off the North Sea and no friendly face to welcome him. Dundee was not a sophisticated metropolis in the mid-1970s; it was a tough working-class city, like Glasgow, only colder, tighter and much smaller, where tiny, malnourished old ladies still spat phlegm from the jute mills in the street and the natives in general tended to be six inches smaller than the incomers. A new Dundee was emerging, in the concrete city centre, but the tenement slums and the gap sites of Hawkhill persisted close by, gaping raw around the new high-rise university buildings above the Perth Road.

By chance his friends Alan Waters and Maureen Beattie were elsewhere the night he arrived, and he remembers making his lonely way, carrying his bags, towards his digs. But it wasn't far. Magdalen Yard Road was at the bottom of the city, the prosperous bit near the river. Above were the prestigious mansions on the Perth Road, and lots of parallel steep lanes with names like Strawberry Bank ran down to Magdalen Yard Road. It was a big old house that reminded him immediately of the one where Norman Bates's mother had lived in *Psycho*. '*Oh God,*' he thought, '*how did I choose this?*'

A strange little man let him in and showed him his room, which contained a camp-bed and little else. The cooking facilities were on an electric ring, which was plugged into the wall by a silk twist electric cable. It looked bare. There was a loo with a bath outside on the landing and nicotine stains on the walls. At the petrol station on the Perth Road, the only place that stayed open after 5pm, they sold milk in plastic bags, like goldfish at the fairground.

'*Very peculiar, like an udder. You needed a jug to put it in. Never seen that before or since.*'

Yes, that first weekend Dundee felt like a foreign country and Gregor was very unsure.

Ooh, ooh! Naw, I don't like this. It was a shocker and I thought, 'D'y'know? I think I'll just go home. I don't like this.' I'd never been away before, never had to properly fend for myself. I mean, I could stot about, I could go into Glasgow or I could get a bus down to Pollokshaws, but you knew when you got there there'd be a meal on the table from Aunt Agnes. I'd always been looked after. Dundee was a major shocker for me – major.

But he didn't go home. He managed to last out until Monday, when he turned up for his first day's work at Dundee Repertory Theatre, at that time based in a converted church in the Lochee Road. He got his precious Equity card and very soon moved into better digs offered by Julie Sturridge, one of the administrators at the theatre. She was married to a schoolteacher, George, and they gave Gregor a room in their Castle Street flat, right in the middle of Dundee. And life immediately got better. In fact it didn't just get better, it exploded, encompassing him in a whirl of fun and colour and friendship and performance. He even felt rich for the first time – he was paid £35 a week, which was a fortune for him in those days, plus another £5 a week for his digs.

And then there was the acting, which was a romp. Gregor Fisher's first ever professional acting job was in a performance called *The Fiery Cross of the Clans*, which involved running about with claymores, shouting and having a lot of fun, many years before Mel Gibson ever dreamt of *Braveheart*. Under the Theatre in Education scheme he performed in school halls up and down the East Coast around Dundee, trundling around the countryside in a big van. There were four of them in the team and they played multiple parts, changing their hats to change roles. It was fast, frenetic and designed to enthuse schoolchildren with short attention spans. The drama was deadly serious, drama with a capital 'D', even verging on high tragedy, but it is impossible to believe that even then Gregor, discovering how physically funny he could be as an actor, did not make them laugh. He remembers playing the part of a clan chief who, sliced by a claymore, had in his dying moments to make a terrible speech, much to the entertainment of the children.

When they weren't doing the *The Fiery Cross of the Clans* they did a mime show called *Clowns*. This being educational theatre, there always had to be audience participation. In speak-when-you're-spoken-to Scotland in the 1970s, when teaching was still repressively authoritarian, sometimes it was hard to get the children to express themselves. The headmasters of the time didn't help: before the start of the show they would invariably lecture the assembled kids, sitting cross-legged on the floor, to the effect that anybody who misbehaved would be in serious trouble. The youngsters were told they were to sit up, pay attention and keep quiet. And the actors would catch each other's eye ruefully, because it made the task of getting the children to stand up and be involved even more difficult.

In general, though, Gregor had to pinch himself to believe how lucky he was, playing cowboys and Indians *and* getting paid to do it. Dundee was a great place after all. There was Mennie's Bar on the Perth Road, which the Rep actors frequented, and after it shut at 10pm, as all pubs did, they walked up to Hawkhill, to the taxi rank and the all-night bakery, where they queued with the students and the drunks for hot fresh steak rolls.

*'And bloody good rolls they were too!'*

After about a year, though, just when he thought he couldn't have been happier, things improved even more: he was asked to join the main company of Dundee Rep. He had found his permanent niche in the enthralling, over-the-top world of greasepaint and performance. He was learning stagecraft – he liked the style of Robert Robertson, the director in Rep, who would come into dressing room when they were doing something subtle like Chekhov and exclaim: 'I want you to grab it by the balls, kick it into touch!'

He was also forging lifelong friendships with people such as Juliet Cadzow, Tony Roper, Lindy Whiteford and Bill Lindsay; and, with the freedom, shaking off some of the repressions of his upbringing. Which included getting laid. The sexual revolution may have missed his home village, but it caught up with him in Dundee by the mid-1970s.

Alcohol was fun; drugs impressed him less. He tried cannabis – someone at the Rep gave him his first joint – but he went to sleep and never bothered with it again, which is quite lucky really, because, again, where narcotics were concerned, in theatre and TV-land any combination of anything was freely available. They never interested him in any way.

All this was a very long way indeed from attending church with Cis every Sunday. The Reverend Whiteford would have been horrified. In that regard too, Gregor's unworldliness was being blown to smithereens. He couldn't explain exactly what he believed; he found the whole thing far too confusing. The Buddhists thought they were right, the Muslims thought *they* were right and the Christians too. Everybody thought they were right – so maybe none of them were right, or maybe all of them were, he reasoned. As a child he had believed his mother's blind faith because if she believed it, it must be true. But now, with the glory of being young and free, his horizons were opening up and he began to see Cis's generation for what they were: deferent, well-behaved citizens who believed that if they read something in the *Express* or the *Sunday Post*, it must be right. And if the Minister told them the Bible was the ultimate word, they believed that too. Theirs was an age of authority, and if you sinned you would go to the bad fire.

Gregor was fast learning to see the world through tolerant, cultured, arty, liberal eyes. He'd found an expressive job, which he loved. Now, he was being freed, not just from an upbringing by a much older family, but from the narrow ethos of a Calvinist West of Scotland society where the only permitted form of self-expression was heavy drinking. He certainly didn't believe people went to hell any more.

But then something happened to him. He went to St Andrews one evening and his life was turned upside down.

There was a problem: Dundee Rep didn't have anyone to play the part of Helena. They were going to tour the north of Scotland with *A Midsummer Night's Dream* and hadn't found anyone for the role of the lovesick young beauty. The other parts in the play had been cast from within the company and most of them were actors Gregor already knew. He himself, his comic physicality already noted, had got one of the leading parts, as Bottom, the ridiculous, self-important weaver whose head is turned into an ass's. Despite his inexperience with Shakespeare, he had that magic ability to make an audience laugh even when he wasn't saying anything.

A young actor called Tony Roper had turned up, cast as one of the mechanicals in the play. He was just back from a tour of Canada and arrived in Dundee wearing all sorts of Indian jewellery. Gregor's first impression was, 'Who's this gadgey?' They were to become lifelong friends. But still, what to do about Helena? Eventually the cast heard that an actress had been found; she was joining them from St Andrews, where she was performing. Curious to see how good she was, the young actors from Dundee trooped over the Tay Bridge to the Byre Theatre to have a sneaky peek at a young Englishwoman called Victoria Burton.

Vicki was acting in *Equus*, a graphic new play by Peter Shaffer about a boy who blinds six horses by gouging out their eyes. It was notorious for its goriness and its nudity. Which is why it came to be that the first time Gregor clapped eyes on the next important woman in his life, she was, as he delicately puts it, stark buttock naked on the stage in front of him – and looking really rather splendid.

But it was nothing he hadn't seen before, not by that time, and he didn't give the new girl another thought until the read-through on the first day. The cast were to assemble at the theatre on Lochee Road. To get in, you climbed the stairs from the main road, turned sharp right and there were the doors. On the day in question Gregor was standing at the top of the steps, about to turn to go in, when Vicki rounded the corner straight in front of him. She had a long grey coat, Annie Hall long before Annie Hall, striped fingerless gloves, possibly striped socks as well, dark brown hair, blue-grey eyes and a smile to make one's heart skip a beat, and, well, quite simply, that was it: a *coup de foudre*. *Coup de coeur*. A thunderbolt.

A strike direct to his heart.

Up to now, Gregor has tried to pretend to me he's the least romantic man that ever walked. Here he is now, leaning forward, hugely sincere, a curious mixture of droll and dignified, reliving that moment at the top of the steps when he was annihilated. He was 23 years old.

'And I remember thinking, "That's the one." I've told this story before and I think people think I make it up, but that was it, then and there. Whether this is total nonsense on my part, I don't know, and it's a claim for which I have no evidence, but I do truly believe that we have been here before, Mrs F and I. It was as certain as that, it wasn't anything other than an absolute ... I can't even describe it, it was an optionless situation, that was the way it was. As sure as I had to take my next breath, she had to be part of my life.

'But, having said that, she didn't think that. Didn't think that for many long and weary months ... years.'

The theatre company went on tour, to many far-flung places, including Orkney and Shetland. Vicki was playing the lovesick character, but it was Gregor who was quietly dying. He had found out several things. For a start, Vicki was heavily committed to another romance and had no interest in him, especially someone who spent most of his time perspiring heavily under a donkey's head and making a complete ass of himself on stage. Secondly, she seemed oblivious of the crush he had on her, and simply didn't notice that sometimes, when he was next to her, he could hardly breathe, so deeply and silently was he afflicted. Acting alongside someone you were in love with was torture. And frankly, he was a bit miffed that she had come along and ruined his fantastic carefree lifestyle. By this time he was renting a flat in Rosevale Street, owned by an Italian landlord, Mr Sovi. He was sharing with Alan Wands, a friend from drama school, who was Dundee Rep's lighting designer. They had some wild times, lots of parties, and were very happy. Gregor liked Dundee a lot. He felt settled and was now earning the fabulous sum of £50 a week. If that wasn't enough, as it often wasn't, for Gregor tended always to be a bit behind, he could chat up Ken Keeling, the theatre administrator, and get a £10 advance on next week to see him through.

And now this hedonistic, unthinking existence had been turned on its head by his inner turmoil over Victoria Burton. And that was the other thing about her: they weren't suited, chalk and cheese. She sounded posh and English although she claimed to be half and half – English father, Scottish mother. She was exceedingly middle-class too. But none of this dented his unrequited devotion to her, which endured throughout the season they spent at Dundee Rep together.

His heart may have been broken but his career was forged there. After *A Midsummer Night's Dream* came more opportunities. That was the very nature of rep: as part of a core team with half a dozen plays to be done, the likelihood was that you would get to play roles you would never in normal circumstances be considered for.

He ended up playing Max in the Pinter play, *The Homecoming*, who was just about as far removed from Gregor as it was possible to be. But that's what improvisation was about. Max was a much older East London hard man, who ruled the roost in his house and whose sexual powers were over the hill. Gregor was 24, so adjustments had to be made, but they all had challenges like this and made brave, brave efforts, not least with the make-up, which they had to do themselves. For Max, he whitened his hair with the same product people used to whiten their plimsolls with, and to look older he would tear Kleenex tissues in half and stick them on his face with Copydex glue. That would look a bit crinkly and lumpy, not to say ghostly, and so then he'd get some Five and Nine, a theatrical staple of two sticks of make-up, one paler, one redder, mix it and apply it on top as skin cover.

*In the car, Gregor and me again, on the road to Dundee: spring 2015, and it has been 36 years since Gregor last appeared on stage at Dundee Rep. Make-up and costume have come a long way in the intervening years. Very soon he will be coming this way again, playing the part of a 100-year-old granny in the National Theatre of Scotland production,* Yer Granny, *and it involves a metamorphosis with a pale, straggly wig, enormous false boobs and wrinkled stockings.*

'And a pair of carpet slippers to get the walk right …' he says.

*The old dual carriageway is now a hundred times faster than it used to be.*

*A magpie floats lazily over the hedge on the passenger side.*

'Magpie,' he says, starting to scan the passing countryside. 'We have a thing about magpies in our family, we always count magpies.'

'It's a superstition, isn't it?'

'A single one's supposed to be bad luck. So in our family, it's a case of, "Oh, bugger, there's a single magpie!" and then we have to look out for more. I have to count them and I often see seven.'

'Was it Cis taught you that?'

'It probably comes from me, I think. Remember the TV show, Magpie, *in the sixties? The signature tune was:*

*One for sorrow*
*Two for joy*
*Three for a girl*
*Four for a boy*
*Five for silver*
*Six for gold*
*Seven for a story never to be told.*

*'So if I see one I have to count them and I often see seven.'*

CHAPTER 5

# Eat the Ice Cream While It's on Your Plate, Ladies and Gentlemen

'We are such stuff as dreams are made on'
*The Tempest*: Act IV, Scene I

Dark and stately Edinburgh, in the latter half of the 1970s, was an austere place. Change was coming, but not just yet; the city was like a judge contemplating hitching up his robes and skipping a little. Gregor, after a long spell in which he had been far too preoccupied with the present to think about the less-than-enticing mystery of his past, decided to go looking for himself for the first time.

He was sharing a flat in the city with a couple of people, one of them a girl called Lorna, who was adopted. The pair occasionally burnt the midnight oil talking about their shared experiences. Lorna had been to Register House to search for answers and she encouraged Gregor to do the same. He couldn't claim to be bothered either way, but all he had ever seen of his birth certificate was the shortened version, which simply said 'Gregor

Fisher, male, born December 1953'. That was it, no details about anything. It would be interesting, he thought, to discover more.

Register House was imposing, as only Edinburgh's Georgian public buildings can be: a vast, Robert Adam-designed archive at the east end of Princes Street in Edinburgh, complete with a 10-metre-high bronze of the Duke of Wellington on a rearing horse out front. Inside, in those days, long before genealogy became one of the nation's favourite hobbies, was a pretty faceless, heartless governmental place. Or so it seemed to Gregor, who wandered in off the street, on spec, and approached the woman behind the desk. She seemed to him pure East of Scotland tightness, twinset and pearls, and although he couldn't see over the desk he guessed she was wearing stockings with seams up the back. East, West … such women were always tight, he thought.

He said what he was looking for.

'You'll have to take a seat,' she told him.

Then another woman appeared.

'Would you like counselling of some kind, Mr Fisher? These things can be upsetting.'

Gregor didn't quite understand. Didn't know what the hell she was talking about, in fact.

'Counselling? What does that mean?'

'Well, somebody will come and speak to you, and if you have any issues or you're upset in any way they'll help you.'

'No, not really, no, I'm all right.'

'Well,' she said, 'I can show you your birth certificate but your adoption was dealt with in Hamilton, and they'll hold the documents there.'

'Oh, right, OK … So I have to go there to see the details?'

'Yes, but it's up to them whether you'll get to see them or not.'

'Really?'

His hackles were up; he felt he was being condescended to. Although now, in remembering the story, he freely admits he may have imagined the slight. Acknowledges his own touchiness. Anger, even. They produced a book and he saw his original birth certificate and his entry in the adoption register, but of course no details of anything, no whys or wherefores. Just the bald facts. His existence processed, possessed and filed away by the authorities.

> You know it's like looking at somebody's death in the ledger. You know, so and so died such and such. Bang. Next! And they fill in the next one, and the next one. There's nothing to say who you really are. There's nothing personal about it. You're just a number, really.

There, for the first time written down, he saw his birth name: Gregor McKenzie, born 22 December 1953, at Airthrey Castle, Bridge of Allan, son of Catherine McGregor McKenzie, housekeeper, of 20 Glenochil Terrace, Menstrie. There was no mention of any father. His birth had been registered by his mother three weeks afterwards. 'Airthrey Castle,' he pondered. 'Well, there *was a thought!*' Maybe he was the illegitimate son of some minor nobility. '*Christ, there might be a couple of quid in this!*' He might be able to walk up to the big house and say, 'Actually, some of this is mine.' Announce, 'You'll never believe who I am.'

Forty years later, he chuckles, taking the sting out of it; mocking himself. 'I think every adopted person thinks that – that they are from a better class than the people they grew up with. Not that I think people who live in castles are a better class, you understand.'

The bold Gregor tumbled out onto Princes Street again, asked himself what that was all about, and decided he didn't really know the answer. Why had he done that? Oh, well … onward and upward! He put the whole thing to the back of his mind and trotted off to the theatre, or whatever he was doing that particular day. In fact he was beginning the long-term process of learning that bare facts, entries in a ledger, waymarkers through a human life, are always unsatisfactory. You can see them, stare at them as much as you like, listen to various interpretations about the whys, the wherefores and the outs and ins of what actually happened but you will never, ever know what the truth is. Because you can never fill in the spaces between the facts – and it is those that make the difference. He had seen, in print, more or less what Maureen and Ann had already told him; and he had seen confirmed his adoption by the Fishers. That was it, nothing more had come out of it – there was no flesh on the bones.

Even if he had wanted to, he couldn't take it any further. Not while Cis was alive, out of love and respect for her. Besides, it would be some years before people like him were entitled, by law, to go and examine the documents that shaped their lives. In the meantime, he had lots of living to do.

After the 1976/77 season at Dundee Rep ended, everybody went their separate ways. Vicki travelled back down south, where she was to become a stalwart on the soap, *General Hospital*, while Gregor barricaded his heart. Lovelorn he might be, but his career was on an upward trajectory. Talent-spotted, he moved to Edinburgh to join the thriving Royal Lyceum Theatre Company, which after a refurbishment and a Royal gala opening was thriving. That first season he did everything from Shakespeare to Chekhov to Ibsen. He was learning his trade – *Entertaining Mr Sloane*, *As You Like It* (in which he played the court jester, Touchstone), *The Cherry Orchard*, alongside the legend that was Moira Shearer. Stephen McDonald, the theatre director, had a penchant for Russian plays and the company did Ostrovsky's *Diary of a Scoundrel*. Gregor played Rikki Fulton's servant, which was brilliant in more ways than one, because Rikki, who he'd never met before, told him he would be very good in a show he was doing for BBC Scotland television called *Scotch and Wry*. Which is precisely how Gregor Fisher's TV career started.

He remembers Edinburgh fondly for another reason. Cis, his mum, had come to see him in Gilbert and Sullivan productions at Barrhead High School, but Dundee had been too far away for her to travel. Edinburgh was much easier to get to, and so he organised tickets for Cis and his Aunt Agnes to watch him perform on a proper stage. She was never impressed by the big names acting alongside him; it was Gregor she wanted to see. On one classic occasion, Cis came to see the panto *Babes in the Wood* at the King's Theatre, Edinburgh, where Gregor was appearing with Rikki Fulton. When he and Rikki came out together she was waiting at the stage door, a proud little old woman in her best coat. She collared Rikki, who at that time was second only to Billy Connolly as the biggest entertainment star in Scotland, and said: 'Oh hello, how are you? Isn't he good?' [gesturing at Gregor].

Rikki took it in good part, as well he might, and from then on Cis was in the habit, if Gregor went home at the weekend, to send him away with some potato scones – *'Give those to Rikki, please, he said he liked them.'* By now she was getting used to the idea her unofficially adopted son was going to make his career on stage, for she had stopped asking him, could he not get a proper job, get a trade? Besides, she was fairly recently widowed – John Leckie had died in 1978 – and she could enjoy Gregor's success more freely.

Those were busy years, first with the Lyceum and then the Borderline Theatre, who were based in Irvine, Ayrshire. Gregor had digs down by the water of the ancient port and he would walk along Harbour Street to get to the theatre. A few years later, knowing then where he came from, he would think back to that street, that route, remember the houses he passed, and shake his head at the coincidences almost too oppressive to accept.

Borderline took performances to the Edinburgh Festival Fringe. Gregor, who could sing, did stomping shows like *Guys and Dolls* and the musical comedy, *The Threepenny Opera*. With them he also did his first comedy review, a hit show called *Play It Again, Tam*, written and created by Morag Fullerton, the girl-friend of Alan Wands, his former flatmate from Dundee. If Scotland was a village, the theatre world was a hamlet. *Play It Again, Tam* won the company its first prestigious Fringe First award.

Gregor was ambitious but had no grand plan. He was always highly delighted if somebody phoned and asked him to do a job. One minute he was in *Play It Again, Tam* and then somebody

offered him six lines in a television show, and he would immediately say, I'm your man. He was wise enough to know that
what he needed to do was work because nothing could quite
teach you like experience. There was nothing like standing on a
stage and knowing it was not working to make him remember,
don't do that again. The act of doing that was also the act of
learning.

He was offered plentiful theatre parts in London, including
several subsequent West End hits, but turned them down. And
he also rejected a role in the TV film *Conspiracy*, for which
Kenneth Branagh won an Emmy. He freely admits, 'I've made
some real bummers of decisions in my career, usually for all the
wrong reasons, terror being the main one.'

In 1981 the radical Tom McGrath wrote a play called *1-2-3*
for the Traverse Theatre, in which he was cast – it was a success
in Scotland but less so in London; and then they took it to the
Toronto Theatre Festival, where it went down a storm and he
won the Best Actor Award.

Around this time came his first foray into TV, which was
memorable for all the wrong reasons. He was cast as a glorified
extra on a production of *Rob Roy* for BBC Scotland, starring
Andrew Faulds and Rikki Fulton. This was also Gregor's first
meeting with a very young assistant floor manager called Colin
Gilbert, later to become a key figure in his career. Gregor had
been cast as one of a band of raucous brothers, a late-1700s wild
bunch, who, mounted on film horses, had to gallop in style over
the set at Bardjar, in Dumfriesshire. There were about ten of
them, in frockcoats and wigs and tricorn hats, and armed to the
teeth with flintlock pistols and swords. All this *and* they had to
ride horses at speed.

Gregor's agent at the time was Ruth Tarko, who had received a call from the BBC, looking for actors who could ride.

'Oh yes, darling, of course! Gregor's a very good rider, *very* accomplished.'

She then phoned Gregor and said: 'I've got you up for this part, *Rob Roy*, horse riding.'

'Well, my sum total of horse riding has been at Langholm Common Riding a few years ago on …'

'Oh, that's fine, darling, you'll be perfect!'

The Common Ridings in Langholm, in which townsfolk ceremonially ride the boundaries of their territory, are annual showpieces, with participants mounted on hired horses, which had seen and done it all before. By the time the animals got to Langholm they were tired out; they'd already done Selkirk, Hawick and Jedburgh. Novice riders turned up, got on, rode around the hill looked after by the horse and came back, which is exactly what happened to Gregor as a young man. He had been handed the reins of a big horse, broad of beam, more of a Clydesdale than anything, with what one of Billy Bell's children called 'furry feet'.

It was a very solid affair and it didn't matter how much you kicked it, it was for going at its own pace because it had done it before, knew what the game was. There was only one tricky bit at Langholm Common Riding as far as a novice horse rider like myself was concerned, and that was gallop up a backstreet at a kind of 33-degree incline and then onto the hill. I managed that, although there were one or two tricky moments, especially coming down

again when I was, 'Ooh, trouble!' Anyway, that was
the extent of my horse-riding experience.

Desperate for the job, equally desperate to make his way in the
world of television, he agreed to do it. But film horses, especially
on this occasion, were a bit more skittish than the Common
Riding ones, and Gregor's beast had a mind of its own. The wild
band of brothers, fresh from carousing, had to charge up the
drive to the big house, jump off their horses and run inside.
They included a young actor called David Hayman – a better
rider than Gregor as it turned out.

First take.

'ACTION!'

*'Anyway, this damn thing that I was on, well, when I kicked it
went off like an effing rocket, so for the first go I was in the wrong
position.'*

'CUT!' shouted the young assistant floor manager, the boy at
the bottom of the drive with the walkie-talkie, who was relaying
instructions from the director, who was with the camera up at
the house.

They reassembled.

'ACTION!'

On the second go, Gregor fell off, crump, sword going one
way, flintlocks flying up in the air. He landed at the feet of the
young assistant floor manager.

'CUT!' cried Colin Gilbert, for it was he.

'Oh, bloody hell! Sorry, it's the … I dunno, what's wrong with
this horse?'

He was hoisted back on, tricorn adjusted, and they lined up
once more.

And it happened again. He fell off the horse. Gregor, mortified, lying there on his back with his highwayman's boots waving in the air, wished the ground would open up and swallow him. Little did he know that he and Colin Gilbert would play such significant parts in each other's working lives – or that Colin would tease him mercilessly about that first meeting for years on end.

*'Which incidentally, I think, is very unkind of him.'*

After that humiliating start, and the realisation he would never be cast in a starring role in *The Three Musketeers* astride a black stallion, Gregor's TV career began to flourish with *Scotch and Wry*. The comedy sketch show, which ran from 1978 to 1992, had started off as a series and then became a New Year staple, shown every Hogmanay before midnight. Anyone who was anyone in Scottish comedy acting was on it – Fulton, Fisher, Tony Roper, Claire Nielson ... Their voices and faces were becoming well known, making it inevitable that several of them would be asked at some point to join a BBC Radio Scotland comedy called *Naked Radio*, a weekly satire of topical events that started in 1981. *Naked Radio*'s producer, as is the way of these things, turned out to be Colin Gilbert, and the show was a huge hit.

This was to be the decade of alternative comedy. Mimicry was essential, and Gregor was good at accents. Politicians or punters, actors had to play whoever the sketch writers came up with. Everyone had character voices they were better at. Tony Roper was good at American presidents and Gregor excelled at the rough end of the scale, but also had a knack for doddery old judges and suchlike. For the actors it was fun stuff to do: silly voices and a quick turnaround.

Meanwhile, he had been cast in a comedy show called *Foxy Lady* for Granada TV and was commuting up and down to London. *Foxy Lady* was a sitcom set in a newspaper office and Gregor, as a man, was playing the woman's editor and therefore ripe for laughs. But 30-year-old sitcom jokes rarely bear retelling and *Foxy Lady* figures in this story only because it brought him back in contact with Victoria Burton. Granada had rehearsal rooms in Stockwell and Gregor found a room in Clapham with an old friend from Dundee, Billy Lindsay. He got the Tube in the morning to rehearsals and, with a certain painful inevitability, bumped into Vicki again. She was sharing a flat with fellow actress Lindy Whiteford on the other side of Clapham Common, was romantically involved with someone else and had lots of TV work to keep her busy.

And the minute Gregor saw her the barricades around his heart crumbled. Billy Lindsay was always a great party giver and at that point in the wild, brash 1980s he was fond of what he called 'Swedish nights' – he would serve Swedish rye bread with an onion ring with herring and an egg yolk in it, which everyone would chase down with vodka out of the freezer.

*'We thought we were very smart and trendy. It was actually vile, come to think of it.'*

Lots of their circle of friends from Scottish theatre days were around and came to the parties; and finally, amid those tangled, crazy days, Gregor and Vicki fell into each other's arms. He repeats that favourite line: 'It was one of the things in my life that was meant to be.'

Depending on where work took them, the new couple sustained a long-distance relationship dotting between Glasgow and London. Vicki bought a basement flat in Brixton with her earnings from television, supplemented by waitressing jobs in her spare time. Gregor, technically, he says, was the lodger. Meanwhile, north of the border things were hotting up. In 1985 Colin Gilbert put the *Naked Radio* show on stage at the Edinburgh Festival Fringe, where it was a great success. By now the idea of transferring it to TV had been mooted, so Gilbert created *Naked Video*, using much the same cast. A golden age was beckoning, for Scottish comedy in general, and Gregor Fisher in particular.

This memoir is not about show business but a few words are needed here to acknowledge the sharpness of *Naked Video*'s cutting edge. It was commissioned by Alan Yentob for BBC Two and made by the newly formed Comedy Unit in Glasgow. The show was a series of anarchic, edgy, rude, silly sketches, written by up-and-coming stars like Harry Enfield, Nigel Planer, Helen Lederer, Steve Coogan, Jennifer Saunders, Ian Pattison, Phil Differ and Rik Mayall. The old type of TV humour was dead and *Naked Video* was part of the new wave, along with *Not the Nine O'Clock News*, *The Young Ones* and *The Comedy Store*. *Naked Video* was where Gregor Fisher, Colin Gilbert and writer Ian Pattison, whose alchemy together was soon to create *Rab C. Nesbitt*, first met. The *Naked Video* attitude was that anything went as long as it was funny. They were up for doing stuff more surreal than the land of Harry Lauder had ever seen before.

One of Gregor's characters was a jolly yokel of a Gaelic TV presenter who, 30 years before the birth of the immensely worthy and politically correct BBC Alba, relentlessly took the mickey out of incomprehensible Gaels and their habits. Even now, on YouTube, it is gloriously subversive.

'Hallo, hallo, hallo, this is the Outer Hebrides Broadcasting Corporation calling civilisation!

'Tonight, it's time for our brand new quiz, *Come On Now Out With It!* First prize, a lovely big bag of nails. Look at that, some lovely big six inchers in there.

'Sadie, you're our first caller. Now, what's the weather like with you? Now, your question! On average, how many eggs can a hen lay in a week? Is it a) 7, (b) 46 or (c) 97?'

In another *Naked Video* sketch, mocking the West of Scotland's sectarian weaknesses, Gregor played the bass drummer in an Orange flute band. The band met Paul Simon's agent in a pub. He was scouting for ethnic musicians.

Agent: Paul would like you to record an album with him.
Gregor: When would that be?
Agent: Oh, early July sometime.
Gregor: Ooh, that's a bad time for us, we've a lot of marches on in Wishaw then, you know.
Tony Roper (a flautist): This Paul Simon, he's not a Catholic, is he?
Agent: No, he's Jewish.
Roper: Ah, but is he a Catholic Jew or a Protestant Jew?

Gregor remembers a sketch where he stood outside Gartnavel General Hospital holding a huge bunch of purple grape-like spheres that the costume department had come up with, under a sign saying 'HAEMORRHOID CLINIC THIS WAY'.

'And you'd think, "Good God, are we doing this? Really?"'

From this fertile anarchy sprang the persona of Baldy Man. Written by Phil Differ and Colin Gilbert, 'Baldy Man' was the timeless parody of the frailties of men who try and conceal their hair loss under a comb-over. The character was a vain halfwit who never spoke; he just spent his life trying to keep those precious strands of hair glued over his bald bits. To play him, Gregor, a man with a low boredom threshold, had to endure many tedious hours in make-up – 'It took forever.'

First, a rubber bald cap, like a bathing cap, was put on his head and then the join had to be meticulously blended with his face. Long strands of hair were attached above his left ear, which took ages; and then it was time to face the cameras, where the filming had to be done in a frantic rush because the lights would melt the make-up in a matter of minutes. It tried his patience but he knew it was funny: he remembered one particular scene in which Baldy Man was looking in the mirror and discovered a hair in his nose. It was classic silent comedy, at which Gregor, master of the eternally thwarted but ever-optimistic face, was unbeatable.

'Oh God,' you could see Baldy Man think to himself, 'it's a hair in my nose.'

And he started pulling the hair, and as he did so, the hair on his head started to disappear until he had pulled the whole strand through his nose.

The hapless Baldy Man, surely partly inspired by Gregor's observations of Uncle Wull all those decades ago, was a hit with a lot of people, including the advertising agency that had the account for Hamlet cigars. Gregor agreed to make an ad for them, a re-make of the sketch in which Baldy Man went into a photo-booth (this being before the age of mobile phones with cameras, as well as a time when tobacco advertising was allowed on TV) and tried to get his pictures taken.

I said, 'This is just a rule of three, this. It's got to be.' He goes in. He looks. He preens. He puts the money in, he preens, bang!, the seat goes down – that's it. And we did it that way. And the Hamlet ad was the same. They lifted that sketch, except at the end when he puts the money in and bang!, the seat collapses, you just see the top of his head with the strand and the puff of cigar smoke.

There was a second Hamlet ad made, and spin-offs too. Gregor's then agent Steve Kenis, a British-based American, got him two hugely lucrative ads for Swissair, filmed in Mexico with Geraldine Chaplin, actress and daughter of Charlie Chaplin and Oona O'Neill. It didn't get much better than that. He also made commercials for Dry Blackthorn Cider. Later on, in the 1990s, when Baldy Man became an institution and got his own series on ITV, Gregor gave up on the hours in make-up and the rubber cap, and took to shaving his head. Back home in Ayrshire, his children were appalled and banned their father from picking them up after school.

Gregor Fisher sits in my living room, drinking tea. He touches his hair, grimaces.

'If we were doing six episodes of *Baldy Man*, it had to be a shaved head every day. I got ringworm as well, terrible.'

'Oh, no!'

'I bloody did.'

'It was actually something to do with the shaving thing, I don't know why. Of course that didn't stop filming.'

'That comes from cows, ringworm; it's a fungal infection. Big round patches.'

'Yeah, it was a kind of purple thing. God! Imagine, ringworm on your head.'

There is a strange footnote to *Baldy Man*, for it did not amuse everyone. After the character had been on the go for a number of years, a letter arrived. All mail from the public was filtered out by his agent, but for some reason this particular correspondence reached Gregor. It was angry:

Do you think that *Baldy Man* character is funny? Because I effing don't. And I know where your children go to school and if you don't stop that immediately I'm going to effing do them in.

'*Nutter*,' Gregor thought, and promptly put it in the bin.

Then another one arrived. Reluctantly, he got in touch with the local police.

'Oh right, don't you worry, Mr Fisher, it'll be all right. Leave it with us. Do you want us to have somebody meet your children at the school?'

'No, no, no, I don't want the children to know anything about it, I just want to get to the bottom of it.'

The police took the letter away and found the culprit, who was living in a caravan park in Ayrshire. And he was indeed challenged in the hair department and a bit of an oddball. But it showed the power of a comedy sketch.

*Naked Video* was so harum-scarum, dashing in and out of the bus to change, making it up as they went along, Gregor can't remember half of it. The sketch in which they acted out a cartoon from *The Broons* sticks in his head, for he was dressed up as Maw Broon, with a big roomy bosom, while Tony Roper played Paw Broon – that one was especially fun. And he recalls another sketch that challenged the make-up department.

I can remember distinctly playing a sumo wrestler in one of those loin cloths that they tie round you, you know, with the bit that goes up your crack at the back? And of course I had this huge rump. I can remember Julie Dorrit, poor make-up girl, painting DANISH – you know, the bacon stamp – on my rear end. I can remember things like that, things that were uncomfortable; a lot of sitting up to the neck in a bath full of beans and gunge and crap, and you think, 'Oh, dear heavens! This isn't funny anymore. It's COLD!'

Gregor embraced his career. He hadn't forgotten the issue of where he had – or *hadn't* – come from, and he didn't know where he was going either, but he liked the journey. He loved to laugh and he loved the fact he could make others laugh too. In a funny way, maybe because the past was so hard to pin down, he trusted in the future. He was open to change and uncertainty, to events moving swiftly. One minute he was living in one place, the next being looked after by some other people, then the next someone else, and then, in yet another situation, Cis was taking him round the outside of a house to go for a pee and he could see the lights of Glasgow. This was normal; this was what happens. Similarly, whatever the performing business had thrown up at him, he'd thought, *'Oh well, might try that, might be good – educational theatre in Dundee, might be good … Oh, here's another job here, might be good too.'* He'd do this, he'd do that, he'd do this. At the same time he had fantasies about joining the Royal Shakespeare Company but he had no grand scheme.

Mine is not the business for grand schemes, you know. Eat the ice cream while it's on your plate, ladies and gentlemen. Thank you very much. One minute you're doing this, the next minute you're doing that. Which is fine.

And he has remained in demand throughout a long, fruitful career on TV, film and in the theatre. He was the star of the acclaimed *The Tales of Para Handy* and other TV dramas such as *Blood Red Roses*, *Kidnapped*, *Gormenghast*, *Oliver Twist*, *Empty*, *The Railway Children* and *Nicholas Nickleby*. His film credits include acting alongside the likes of Al Pacino (*The Merchant of Venice*), John Hurt (*Nineteen Eighty-Four*) and Phyllis Logan (*Another Time, Another Place*), as well as *White Mischief* and Richard Curtis's *Love Actually*.

He has battled the contradictions embedded in his background, his temperament and his chosen career. The Church of Scotland, which shaped him, was not a showy place, and he is similarly self-effacing about his achievements. He remembers how, as a 13-year-old with a good singing voice, he was part of the Neilston church choir but he embarrassed his family by showing off. The choir sat on a platform in front of the pulpit and for some reason, consciously or otherwise, he crossed his leg and struck a pose. He saw his sister Margaret Leckie, his elder by 25 years, in the family pew and took in the withering glance she drew him. As far she was concerned he was obviously showing off. His family were very much the kind who believed you didn't stick your head above the parapet; you didn't grandstand. Countless other incidents with teachers taught him the same message: keep your head down, don't be a show-off. It gave him a total aversion to boasting and he feels the same about actors' biographies listing success after success, award after award.

*'It just goes against the grain, that. It makes my stomach go into some sort of bleuurgh!'*

But the same man chose to become a professional show-off, a performer. Push him, and he reluctantly concedes there were certain things he knew he could do well. He knew he had an honest relationship with an audience, and he knew there were a lot of times in his early career in the theatre when the audience went with him, when the precious connection was made and he knew that what he was doing worked. They liked it. He instinctively felt that – and the challenge was always to try to repeat that connection.

The most joyous moments he ever had as a performer were not necessarily the ones that the audience would know anything about. They were the times when the two-way thing between him and another actor gelled, or when every single person on the stage connected and knew for an exquisite two minutes, or however long it lasted, that what they were doing was magic. Knowing you had scored a goal, that you'd found the sweet spot on the tennis racquet or hit the hole in one. The feeling never lasted long, but it was what kept him going.

> For the joy of that; for the joy of the few occasions when you get it right, because you're always looking for that next fix. Even a telly show's like that. You play a scene with somebody and, ooof, it's not right. Can we go again? Yep, and we go again. Suddenly, suddenly, z-z-z-zip – that was it! That was it; that was it! And the director knows that was it and even the cameraman goes, 'Yup'. And sometimes I think to myself, 'Well, maybe it's just my mind playing tricks on me,' but then you get confirmation from somebody else and you know you're not conning yourself.

When it came to the critics, Gregor had long ago stopped bothering about them. This cynicism dated from a 1976 performance he gave in a Restoration comedy called *The Recruiting Officer* by George Farquhar. He was cast as a country bumpkin and the running joke in the play was that he had bad breath. The critic Cordelia Oliver dismissed him – 'We have seen Mr Fisher's type of country bumpkin before, many times, with and without halitosis.' About three or four months later he found himself at the Royal Lyceum in Edinburgh, in a play, *Il Servatore de Duo*, which was translated into Scots as *The Servant O' Twa Maisters*, and he was once again cast as a country bumpkin. Ms Oliver this time hailed him as a comic genius.

*'Pass me the salt, critics! Take a large pinch of it.'*

A role was coming, however, that would win him some of the greatest critical comment ever lavished on an actor. But first there were deeper personal mysteries to navigate, for Gregor had yet to find out how he came into the world.

# CHAPTER 6

# Aunt Ruby and the Red-Chip Gravel Drive

'I grow; I prosper/Now, gods, stand up for bastards!'
*King Lear*, Act I, Scene II

The decision to go hunting for his birth parents could only happen after Cis had died, for to have done so earlier would have been a betrayal. Cis lived long enough to hear Gregor on the radio and to see him on telly, and then, in 1983, she slipped away, quite quickly, dying of bowel cancer. Being of the generation that didn't complain, she had left it too late to seek medical help. Gregor was in Glasgow at the time, filming at the old BBC building in Queen Margaret Drive. He stayed with Aunt Agnes in Shawlands, who didn't want to visit the hospital towards the end, so Gregor, Margaret and Una would take it in turns to go and sit with Cis, by then reduced to a rickle of bones, and hold her hand. The last thing she said to him before she lost consciousness was, 'That's it, son, I've had enough now. I want away.'

After she had gone, he remembered a feeling of total dislocation with the rest of the world. He drove through Barrhead and as he passed the bus stop near the roundabout there was a gaggle of teenagers messing around, laughing. Kissing. He couldn't believe everything was still normal, that the world was still turning.

I'm sure it must be quite a common feeling. That sense of, don't you know? Does anybody realise what's just happened? That this person, who had lived what I thought was a remarkable life, was gone. Did you realise Mrs Leckie was away? Why were there no news reports or anything? Yet why would there be?

People would tell me I'd never forget the day. And of course I do. But I don't forget her, mind. I often, you know, have a little chat. I think of my mother ... we used to walk to church and she'd have had a reasonable tidy up and put on a hat ... We'd be walking up the street and she'd see an apple core on the ground and she'd bend down and she'd pick it up, open the handbag, put it in – for the hens. Oh, I was just so embarrassed. But I'd give a king's ransom now to walk up the street with my mother, picking up apple cores. In fact, I'd help her.

Weird, isn't it?

Cis's death had a profound impact on Gregor. After all, she had rescued him after his two former mothers had been wrenched away. She had shaped him and taught him about love and laughter. They had adored each other. Mary Jane, that was her proper

Sunday name. Folklore has it that her little brother couldn't say Mary Jane, just used to say *'my sis-ter'* and it stuck. Gregor never once had a conversation with Cis about where he came from because he didn't want her to think that he didn't consider her his mother. Losing her fractured him a little, inside.

But he had much to take his mind off things, commuting up and down to London, juggling work. In Scotland he was doing *Scotch and Wry* and *Naked Radio*, in London there was work with Granada and in Brixton there was home with Vicki, who was expecting their first child.

He was in the BBC studio in Glasgow, just about to do a recording of *Scotch and Wry* before a live studio audience, when the unexpected phone call came. Vicki wasn't due for another four weeks, but he was told she had been taken into St Thomas' Hospital and the baby was imminent. Swallowing the shock, he went out in front of the audience and did his stuff, kicking into a kind of professional overdrive. But it wasn't easy. Then came another call to say things weren't that imminent after all and Vicki was fine, but he was warned not to leave his journey until the morning. There was no quick way to get to London at 10pm at night in those days. His friend and fellow actor Claire Nielson was due to fly down in the morning and Gregor had a car. After conferring, they decided to travel together through the night, sharing the driving. They bundled their cases in the back of the car and got on the M8 out of Glasgow, heading south, keeping each other awake.

Gregor dropped Claire at her home in Highgate in the early morning and got to St Thomas', where he made a dramatic entrance to find a peaceful Vicki padding around, still pregnant, and perfectly fine and dandy.

'I've just driven through the night!'

'Darling,' she said, 'don't worry about it. I've spoken to the midwife, and she says you can just go home and get yourself organised, there's no rush.'

So he headed for their flat in Brixton, and just as he got in the door the phone rang.

'Get yourself in here right now!' the nurse commanded.

The whole event had kicked off. At the beginning Gregor spent a certain amount of time feeling pleased, in fact very, very, *very* happy, that the powers that be, if indeed there were any, had decided he was a man and not a woman. Vicki had wanted a drug-free delivery and their beloved first son duly arrived, a little wrinkled because he was early, but fine. The nurses took him away and tidied him up before placing him in his father's arms. Gregor looked down at his son and had the feeling that nothing like this had ever happened before.

Ever.

Well, this is ... Wow, this is my first-born child! I didn't ever think this was possible, that this was going to happen to us. Like most things in life like that it just takes you by surprise, takes your breath away.

And I remember Vicki being taken away and I was left with him, this little baby, and I suppose it just felt complete ... that sense of, well, nothing else matters. It was one of those moments in life when things click into place and you just think, this is the way it should be, everything is right with the world; nothing could spoil this.

I felt a vague bit of terror too, in the background, sort of 'I hope I don't break him,' because they're little, babies. I mean, every other animal on the planet – you see a horse having a foal and minutes later it's up and running, but this wee thing can't run, can't do anything ... It's down to you to look after him and you feel very, very protective.

They were now a happy new family of three. Everything was great, fine, tickety-boo. Alexander was placed in a cot next to Vicki, and she and Gregor spent two or three hours together billing and cooing over him before Gregor was sent home with the usual list of things to bring in the next day.

But the next day turned into a terrible one. Halfway through afternoon visiting time, with quite a few visitors round the bed, Vicki suddenly said: 'I've got an awfully sore head.'

'You want something for it then?' Gregor asked.

He got the nurse. But within a very short space of time the headache became quite unbearable, the doctor was called, visitors were cleared and it became evident that something serious was happening. Things moved fast. Alexander was taken away and put in a nursery, and then, very suddenly, Vicki started having some kind of seizure. Fitting. Gregor was ushered away and told, in the usual reassuring way, everything was under control; they'd give her some medication. But it *wasn't* under control – the doctors couldn't get Vicki stabilised. They decided to sedate her heavily and eventually she was diagnosed with postpartum pre-eclampsia, a rare condition that occurs when a woman has high blood pressure after birth. Both Vicki's mother and her twin sister had had pre-eclampsia, but this was different and potentially much more serious.

Gregor's voice crackles with emotion as he recounts the nightmare: 'All the doctors were rather baffled and I didn't realise how baffled until a man called Dr Auld, a nice young fellow, he couldn't have been much older than me, must have known I was a smoker, took me down the back fire escape at St Thomas's and said: "Have you got any fags?"

'I thought it was a strange thing for a doctor to say.

'"Why? Do you want one? I've always got fags."

'"Yes, why don't we have a fag on the stairs?"

'And I thought, "What's the sketch here?" I'm getting a bit panicked by this time.

'We lit our fags and he said: "You know, we aren't quite sure what's happening here and it's all a bit touch and go. And I think you should be aware of that."

'And I remember not quite taking that in, because you think – this is a hospital, this is where they fix people, isn't it? You have faith in that.'

And he needed that faith through the long and harrowing night to come. Hours slowly passed as he sat by Vicki's bedside in intensive care. The doctors kept her knocked out, waiting to see if the cocktail of drugs they had given her would work. Somehow it made it worse for him, seeing her just lying there, unconscious; a lump of flesh. At one point in the night he visited the nursery to see Alexander and gazed down at his sleeping child, his emotions a blur. History could not repeat itself, there could be no more motherless children – surely not? Already he had endured more than his fair share of tragedy. Gregor remained on automatic, in some parallel place, throughout that night and for most of the next day as Vicki's life hung in the balance. Eventually, he cannot remember when because of the state he was in, the team of nurses and doctors, those total, blessed strangers, managed to save her.

Whether they did so with skill or good luck or a mixture of both he knew not and cared not. Things could have gone one way and they went the other; and he learnt above all else that life hangs on a thread, that there is a moment when everything changes. When he realised Vicki was going to be OK, the feeling of relief flooded him: he now knew what precious meant.

Later on, the tragi-comedy of life reasserted itself. When Vicki had come round a bit, but was still drowsy with drugs, Dr Auld came to see her. Immediately Vicki saw him, she said: 'Oh, Dr Auld, you've come to examine me,' and whipped up her nightie for inspection of her nether regions. She didn't have a clue what had happened over the last 36 hours. The time was lost to her. She just thought she'd had a baby, fallen asleep and everything was routine.

'No, no, it's fine, Mrs Fisher. Just here to see how you are, I don't need to see down there, that's fine,' said Dr Auld.

He paused.

'It's nice to see you. We thought we had lost you.'

Both Vicki and Alexander left the hospital perfectly fine. The new parents decided the baby was the most beautiful thing they'd ever seen. He was theirs, they were both there for him.

Perhaps, holding his precious son in his arms had made Gregor, consciously or otherwise, more curious about his own beginnings. Perhaps it was something to do with the huge emotion it awoke in him, that he now wanted to find out who had brought him into the world. To discover, if he could, exactly why they hadn't wanted him, hadn't cherished him; hadn't felt about him the way he felt about Alexander. Hadn't someone once felt like this about him? And if they had, how could they have abandoned him?

When Alexander was about a year old, when Gregor was doing pantomime in Glasgow and had a free day on his hands, he and his birth sister Maureen decided, finally, to get a stick and prod the past. Together, they set off on an expedition to try to track down their mother's relatives, their unknown family, and find out what had happened. Maureen had got an address for an Aunt Ruby, who they believed was the elder sister of their mother, and they hatched the idea to go and see her. Gregor by this time was driving an ancient powder-blue Mercedes, which he thought was simply the business. He picked up Maureen and in their naïvety they simply drove to Alloa, in Clackmannanshire, to say hello. Unannounced.

It was the way Gregor preferred to do things.

Together they went in the hope that Ruby, whoever she was, could maybe fill in some of the blanks. They weren't trying to get written into any will, they just wanted to find out the circumstances of their births. By now they had a sense of a basic human right to know what everyone else took for granted – who their parents were.

Gregor pulled up outside what he regarded as one of those Scottish 'haven't-we-done-well?' kind of houses – a semi, but granite, with a porch and pink gravel chips on the drive. He hated those pink chips then, and he hated them even more afterwards.

Their feet crunched up the path. There was somebody working up a ladder outside.

'Christ, maybe that's our uncle,' Gregor thought.

They knocked on the door and a woman answered – smart, tweed skirt, twinset and pearls, sensible shoes with Cuban heels and a gold bar across the front. There were two or three steps up to the door, so they got the impression she was tall, but then both he and Maureen were quite short. They were looking up at her.

'Yes, can I help you?'

Well-spoken.

'Er, perhaps you can. We're not here to disturb you in any way but I'm Gregor and this is Maureen. We're, erm, we're Catherine's, er, Kit's children.'

He saw immediately this was a mistake. Across his aunt's face everything registered, everything from shock, horror, guilt, sadness to 'what will the neighbours think?'

'Well, I'm terribly sorry but, ah, I have workmen in the house,' she said and promptly shut the door.

The encounter was over in seconds.

'So obviously, that wasn't Uncle up a ladder,' thought Gregor drily as the two of them trailed back down the red chips.

Maureen burst into tears.

'Get in the car, it doesn't matter, in the car, in the car!' he said, shepherding her, chivvying her.

He helped her in and as he walked round to the driver's side, he glanced up at the house. The curtains twitched. They drove away, clocking up yet one more rejection in lives already shaped by such things.

A little while later a letter arrived for Gregor at the King's Theatre, Glasgow, where he was performing in the pantomime *Sleeping Beauty*. It was from Aunt Ruby, saying she was sorry but she had been busy that day, and would he like to go and have some tea? She gave a date two or three weeks later. By chance, Gregor could fit it in before his performance, so he went back by himself. It was a very stiff, cup-and-saucer type of tea party. Ruby was there, with her daughter, Rena, for moral support, and the three of them perched uncomfortably on the edges of their chairs. Gregor couldn't read what Ruby was thinking, but he could recognise a very unwelcoming welcome when he received one. For sure, this was not a relationship that was going to run and run.

Any questions he asked were given polite but clipped responses. Yes, Catherine, or 'Kit' as she was sometimes known, had been Ruby's younger sister. Yes, Kit had had a daughter Ann, then two more babies when she lived near Menstrie. Ruby did not give him or show him a picture of his mother. She informed him their father was a man called Bill Kerr.

'Oh yes, he was your father. But did you know he was an alcoholic? Perhaps that's something you should watch in your own personality,' said Ruby coldly. Doing her best, it seemed, to poison everything for everyone.

'What?' thought Gregor, incredulous, his mouth gaping open.

He heard very little after that. It wasn't a long visit; the minute he got in, he couldn't wait to get out again. Ruby's discomfort and hostility were evident. He came out feeling bewildered, angry and dissatisfied, and decided to give the whole thing up as a dead loss. He never wanted to see Ruby again – indeed, he never would – and she had put him off searching. Why would he want to get in touch with any more of his mother's relatives if that was the kind of reception he could expect? Perhaps it would be better if he concentrated on his father's side.

And now they had a name: Bill Kerr, William Kerr.

Before Gregor and Maureen finally gave up on the mystery of their mother, however, Maureen persuaded him to go with her to visit a woman called Mrs McAdam, who lived in Menstrie. Their older half-sister Ann had told her about Mrs McAdam. An elderly lady, she had been a friend of their mother – indeed, she may have been her only friend. When they sat down with her, they found her palpably good, kind and honest, but very reticent too. Gregor got the impression she didn't want to tarnish the memory of someone to whom she had always been loyal. It was frustrating. The old lady didn't know what Gregor and Maureen had or hadn't been told about their origins, and she skirted round their questions.

Gregor decided to be direct.

'Would you happen to know who our father was?'

'Ooh, I … no, I don't. Nooo, I don't!'

But her face had come over hazy, glassy; the way it does when people are hopeless liars.

'Was it, erm, William … Bill Kerr?'

'Oh, well … Oh, you knew, uh-huh.'

And she looked relieved, as if she'd been let off the hook in a funny kind of way, because if anybody asked she could say she wasn't to blame; she didn't tell them. She didn't say any more about him but she gave Gregor something very precious: the first picture of his mother he ever possessed. It was a small black and white print of a pleasant, round-faced young woman in a tailored suit walking along a city street, probably Glasgow or Stirling. She was holding a little girl, Mrs McAdam's daughter, by the hand. There were two buttons missing on the jacket, hinting of poverty, but she held herself proudly and had a smile for the street photographer, the men who snapped the 1940s crowds on high days and holidays, and handed out tickets so people could purchase a print. Few old photographs can have mattered as much as that one did to Gregor and Maureen. It was taken before they were born, but they didn't care. Now, at last, they knew what their mother looked like. And her face was like their faces: broad, open, with friendly, amused eyes and a plain nose. There was an unmistakable similarity.

Before they left, Mrs McAdam gave them another nugget of information. She smiled as she said it: 'Oh, your mother was always quite, well, show-offy. Put it this way, if she went to the bakers to get something, all the cakes always had to be put in a box. A posh box.'

It left Gregor with an amusing, if poignant image to store away in his head. More than that, for him it had real resonance. Once he'd been able to afford it, he'd always had a taste for the high life. Why was that? He'd always assumed cakes should go in a box too. Maybe it was a genetic thing. When you know none of the bigger things about who you are, who made you, you will peck at any scraps you can find.

Their final visit, that trip, was to Menstrie, where they wandered around a bit pointlessly, looking for traces of Catherine. They also drifted around Logie churchyard, the beautiful ancient graveyard at the foot of Dumyat Hill, the place where many folk from Menstrie were buried, but couldn't find her name on any of the headstones.

Around that time, a rather odd thing happened. One evening at the King's Theatre, at the end of the performance, the manager came into the dressing room Gregor shared with Tony Roper (the two of them always shared).

'There was a man asking after you,' the manager told Gregor. 'He came in and had his tea with us in the interval … some fellow called McKenzie. He left his card.'

'Why me? What was he asking about?'

'He asked a funny question … what was it? Oh yes, he said, "That guy, Gregor Fisher, has his name always been Fisher?" I said, "Yes, as far as I know." There's his card.'

On the card it said 'Gregor McKenzie, Member of Parliament for Rutherglen'. Gregor wondered what all that was about, but he never followed it up. The ripples in that particular pool fell still. To be honest, he was no longer very keen on the McKenzie side of his parentage. He'd decided to give up on them; Ruby had done for him. Not that long afterwards, he went back to the hunt to see what he could uncover about his father. The desire to find out more about his past never really went away, but the funny thing was the lack of urgency he felt.

I didn't go, 'Whamwhamwhamwham, I've got to find out all about this!' I did a wee bit here and there and you know, life took over, and I was doing this and that and I forgot about it. And then something else happened to set me off, like talking to people on the bus or whatever.

He was sitting on the *Naked Video* bus with some of the crew, sometime in 1986, somewhere north of Glasgow, watching the raindrops running down the windows and bemoaning the West of Scotland weather. There was invariably lots of sitting around, interspersed with periods of frantic, ant-like activity when it stopped raining and they tried to get as much filming as possible done before it started again. On set, a film unit was like the circus. There was their bus and then the other bus, rigged up for make-up and costumes, and then the trucks with all the film equipment and vast paraphernalia that went with filming. Like a travelling troupe of players, both actors and crew lounged on the seats and amused themselves with idle chat. It was a strange relationship: they were a tight-knit band of brothers who spent long working days together and told each other about their hopes and their fears, their families, their highs and their lows. They talked about things that would not ordinarily be talked about with people who were in many ways total strangers.

That day, for some reason, adoption came into the conversation and it transpired that three of them, the bus driver, a young woman assistant floor manager (the lowest but most essential member of the crew), plus Gregor, were all adopted. The bus driver was convinced he was a lost scion of one of the great shipbuilding dynasties on the Clyde – somebody had got someone below stairs pregnant, the classic story, and he, the baby, had been adopted. Although fascinated with her status, the young woman hadn't done anything to find her birth family. And that left Gregor, most of whose story was a total mystery to him. It brought the whole thing back into his head. He mused on how many people there were in his life, including Johnny Monaghan, now the nearest thing he had to a brother, who were all adopted. Was it coincidence, or did adopted people some-how find each other?

He resolved to do what it had not crossed his mind to do several years ago when he had gone to Register House; he would do as the woman there had suggested and go and look up his adoption records at Hamilton Sheriff Court, a few miles south of Glasgow in Lanarkshire. The next free day he had he headed out there. He didn't make an appointment; he was still like that – appointments annoyed him because it meant putting things off. He liked it when he did stuff on impulse and things went bang-bang-bang.

He went on his own. The reception area at the Sheriff Court had a tall wooden counter, and behind it sat an officious-looking woman of middling years who obviously had to deal with the pretty mixed clientele who attended the court. Gregor got the firm impression she considered him one of them.

'Ah, I believe I was adopted and the adoption was dealt with at Hamilton Sheriff Court ...'

She looked at him. Maybe it was his imagination, but he got the idea she was less than impressed that some little illegitimate chappie had walked in.

And she probably went twice to church on Sunday, but maybe that was just me making more of it than what it was, but I didn't get a friendly kind of, 'Oh, come in, we'll get you a cup of tea,' there was none of that.

'And I believe it's now possible for me to see my, eh, file. Can you help me in this matter?' he added.

'Well,' she said, 'it's not up to me whether you can or can't see the file. I'll have to ask the Duty Sheriff and he's in court just now.'

It was his turn to stay silent.

'But if you care to wait, I'll try and catch his eye.'

She gave him a form to fill in. He remembered her chubby fingers – soft, unnaturally soft hands. But he appreciated that she could have told him that without an appointment he would have to go away and come back another time, so he waited obediently. After a long time the Sheriff appeared at the back of the office, and Gregor watched as she went and spoke to him. The Sheriff looked up and glanced over at Gregor, appraising. Then he flew out of the room again, back into court. The woman returned.

'He says that's fine but you cannot take photographs of the documents, or photocopy them. I can give you a pencil and a piece of paper if you want to copy anything down.'

'OK.'

'Now you do realise this might be upsetting, but we could have a counsellor with you, if you want.'

'Oh no, I don't need a counsellor. But thanks, anyway.'

She ushered him into a little anteroom that to him felt a bit like a headmaster's office and an envelope was laid out on the table in front of him. It was one of those special legal envelopes with a metal catch with string round it and he remembered feeling suddenly – irrationally – furious because the metal was rusty.

An internal flare of anger.

*'For God's sake, this is my stuff in here! Rust? Could they not have put it in a new envelope? See the state of that!'*

Like nobody cared. Like he was forgotten. Then he swiftly chided himself.

'What difference does it make? Let's be honest, it doesn't.'
The woman unravelled the string and laid out the papers.
'I'll leave you to it now, you can take some notes.'

And with that she gave him a pad with a pencil. He decided she was not unkind.

Most of it was legal bumf, documents giving details about the couple who had adopted him, Jim and Ellen Fisher. He skipped that to begin with; he wanted a name. And what stopped him, pinned him to his seat, in a moment that remains crystal clear with him to this day, was the sight of a single sheet of blue Basildon Bond notepaper.

I never liked Basildon Bond. It signifies the worst tightness and conformity of the bloody Scottish aspiring working class, you know – as in 'Basildon Bond, it's got a watermark on it.'

And on the blue paper were two short lines, written in fountain pen. It was dated March 1956, and said, 'I, William Blake Kerr, do hereby promise to pay the sum of £3 per month towards the keep of Gregor McKenzie in the care of Clackmannanshire County Council until such time as he is adopted.' It was signed W. B. Kerr.

The writing was deliberate, clear – a very well-practised signature. An educated hand, but Gregor got the impression of somebody who was trying very hard to keep it steady. The signature was a big 'W', in that old-fashioned way with a flourish, then a big, pregnant 'B': W. B. Kerr. It was very definitely not a hurried, scratchy, indecipherable signature. His address was 2 Park Terrace, Tullibody, a village adjacent to Menstrie. There were no medical signatures there, nothing. Just the lawyer's name: Victor E. Cuthbert.

Gregor stared at it for a very long time: William Blake Kerr, his father's name.

But it would only have taken a minute for him to sign that bit of Basildon Bond. To sign away his son.

He thought about it for a bit more; thought of his own son, Alexander.

Three pounds a month – that's £1 6s a fortnight. Nine shillings a week. Nine shillings. Not a whole lot more than me and my pals used to spend on crisps and chocolate at the Pavilion on a Saturday. Nine shillings for my keep. For me.

Gregor turned to the other documents. W. B. Kerr had been back at his solicitors in November 1956. Here was the official legal document giving his consent for James and Ellen Fisher to adopt Gregor McKenzie: 'I, William Blake Kerr, Officer of Customs and Excise, 2 Park Terrace, Tullibody, being the father of said child, hereby state that I understand the nature and effect of the Adoption Order for which application is made and that I understand that the effect of the order will permanently deprive me of my parental rights.' The line where he was asked to specify what religion the child should be raised in was left blank. He had signed it, a larger signature – W. B. Kerr – with a certain authoritative flourish in the slanting line he drew under the 'Kerr'.

It would only have taken a minute to sign that too. To sign away his son. To sign away ... me.

The Curator's report, contained within the document, said the mother of the child applied for was unmarried and had died in March 1956. Paternity was established by verbal admission and the father was 62 years old, married, a Protestant by religion, a British subject and in employment as a Customs and Excise officer. In the course of the interview the father declared that, as he had never had custody of the child and did not now wish to assume this responsibility, he felt it would be in the child's best interests if arrangements were made for his adoption. In consenting to the adoption the father understood the effect of the Adoption Order was to permanently deprive him of all parental rights.

The child, Gregor McKenzie – *'Is that really me?'* – had been taken into the care of the County of Clackmannan under the Children's Act 1948 on 21 February 1956 and was boarded out with the petitioners, the Fishers, on 19 June 1956, and had been continuously in their care since. The child appeared happy in his new environment, and was receiving much care and affection.

The Fishers, wrote the Curator, had said they intended as and when a suitable opportunity arose, to inform the child that they were not his natural parents. This course commended itself to the Curator as a wise precaution against possible difficulties or misunderstandings arising in later years. In the course of his investigation, the Curator elicited that the father of the child had been contributing the sum of £3 a month to the County Council of Clackmannanshire. The child himself had no right to, or interest in, any property. There was no insurance over his life.

*'In other words, he's penniless.'*

William Kerr went back to his solicitor in Bank Street, Alloa, one more time, on 22 March 1957, to fill in the blanks on the final document consenting to permanent adoption and giving up his parental rights. This time his writing is a little more crunched, less deliberate, more hurried. 'I, William B. Kerr,' it begins, but in the space 'being the ......... of the child', the space where he should have written 'father', he wrote nothing. The word has been added later in the handwriting of the lawyer. Was William Kerr in a hurry that day, or simply agitated? Or did he just want the whole embarrassment over and done with, couldn't bear to be dragged back once again? And couldn't bring himself to acknowledge paternity one last time.

*'You weren't hanging around that time, W. B., were you?'*

The only other things in the file were the final document authorising Gregor McKenzie's name to be changed to Gregor Fisher, and an amended birth certificate.

And that was it.

Gregor walked out of Hamilton Sheriff Court into the fresh air. He felt peculiar. It was another of those moments, just as when Cis died. Normal life was going on all round him, but everything had changed – that sense of dislocation again. Didn't people realise what had happened? The world had slipped a bit, shifted, but nobody realised.

Now he had proof of who his father was. He knew his name. Knew where he lived and what his job was. But somehow he felt even emptier, and knew even less.

# CHAPTER 7

# The Poem in the Wallet

'One touch of nature makes the whole world kin'
*Troilus and Cressida*: Act III, Scene III

It was an April evening, 1994. The children were in bed, and Vicki and Gregor were relaxing in the sitting room of their renovated house, Kennox, in Ayrshire. Doing up nice old houses was fast becoming a hobby of theirs. Gregor's sister Maureen had come down for the weekend and the three of them were chatting over a gin. As was often the way of it, when Maureen was there, talk turned to the mystery from which neither of them could ever escape. Their father's name came up: W. B. Kerr, the man without a face. Gregor expressed a recurring fantasy.

'You know, I don't even know what he looked like. It would be quite nice, wouldn't it, just to walk into a bar or a restaurant or something and say, "There he is, see that, see that, second to the left, there? That's him. Really? God, he doesn't look like me, does he? Oh, taller than I thought. I don't want to go and speak, I don't want to do anything, just a look, that's all I wanted.'

He didn't want any emotional engagement. No more Auntie Ruby incidents. He'd rather just live in his little daydream that he and Maureen were the products of some great hidden love affair. He now had three children of his own, he was quite happy. But he did want to know what the old man looked like.

'Why don't we try and get a picture of him?' suggested Vicki, out of the blue.

By this time, with the help of an old friend, Sheila Duffy, radio presenter-turned-professional-genealogist, they had found out from Register House that W. B. Kerr was dead, but there was remaining family. William Kerr apparently had had three legitimate children, two daughters and a son – half-sisters and brothers, in other words, to Gregor and Maureen.

'There's someone called Margaret, who lives in Bearsden. I've got an address. Why don't I phone up and see if they've got a picture?' said Vicki.

Margaret was William Kerr's granddaughter; Gregor's unknown niece.

'Oh, oh, oh, OH! Cold call … You *can't* do that, what would you say? That could cause trouble,' Gregor said.

Another gin was taken and Vicki disappeared for a while. Then she reappeared.

'I've phoned that number.'

'You *didn't*! Was that wise?'

'She seemed perfectly pleasant and she's going to send you a picture. I just said we thought there was a family connection and would she mind sending a picture of William Kerr, if she had such a thing. And she said she'd be more than happy to do that, but the only thing she asked was not to get in touch with her Aunt Dorothy because she was of a very delicate disposition.'

Two pictures duly arrived – one of W. B. Kerr playing golf, the other of him standing by the corner of his house. An elderly, balding man, wearing glasses and an open-necked shirt, behind him was a garden gate and an expanse of parkland. He had a benign half-smile and perhaps a certain quiet authority. Given his secret life, it was possible to read something enigmatic into his expression. In the other picture he was squaring up to tee off on a golf course. Gregor thought he looked a bit like his grandfather, far less his father. But somehow the images were neutral. They showed nothing more than pleasant respectability, which only deepened the mystery.

The next day Gregor sent Margaret a bouquet of flowers with a little note attached, saying thank you very much, it was very sweet of you to do that and he really appreciated it. And that was the end of that.

Except it wasn't, because of course the news that an unknown relative had turned up in the family, *and* the fact it was that famous chap who was everywhere on the television, Gregor Fisher, aka Rab C. Nesbitt, must have reverberated like a small nuclear bomb amongst W. B. Kerr's children. Gregor later found out that Margaret had immediately phoned John Kerr.

But for years and years and years, nothing more happened. Twelve years, in fact. The trail went cold. The mystery of Gregor's identity retreated to a dark corner and he was content to shut the door on it because a new door had opened for him – he had his own, very happy family to attend to, one that belonged to him. Alexander, born in 1985, had been joined by Jamie in 1987 and then Cissie in 1989; now he and Vicki had their hands full bringing them up.

> People might think this was a bit odd. You think, 'Well, here's a mystery, let's solve it, let's get on to the next bit.' But the fact I didn't, I think, that was more of an indication that I was in a happy, contented, smiley life. I had my wife and kids and friends, and everything was normal – whatever the hell 'normal' means – but everything was just OK. Maybe when life isn't treating you very kindly and you're confused about something, maybe that's when all these things matter more. But because there were kids and meals to be cooked and walks to be walked, well, life was full.

It was 12 February 2006, a rainy afternoon near Langholm in the Scottish Borders, where the Fishers were now living in a farmhouse called The Middleholms. Vicki had taken the children out somewhere, and Gregor and his sister Maureen were on their own, drinking tea. And the itch, once again, required to be scratched.

Gregor said: 'I've got one of those big green sheets, to set out your family tree. It might be a laugh, let's fill it in.'

So they spread the sheet and all the scraps of information gathered over the years out on the kitchen table.

'You'd better write this because you're a neater writer than me, Maureen, and I'll shout them out and we'll see how far we can get.'

Partway through the jumble of dates and names of the mysterious Kerrs – *our ancestors* – they took another short pause for
tea, discussing who was who and what was what. That was when
they noticed that their half-brother, John Kerr, was in his eight-
ies. Thirty years older than they were.

'Funny that, isn't it, that we've never heard from this chap or
seen a picture of him or anything?' said Gregor. 'Time marches
on and if we don't do something about it we might never get to
meet him, say hello.'

They had found an address for him, near Grantown-on-Spey
in the Highlands, and so they determined to write to him. Even
as they did so, they were preparing for rejection. Their experience in Alloa, on the pink gravel chip driveway, had taught
them that. They weren't expecting very much to come of it,
but they thought they'd do it anyway. So they sat and composed
a letter.

Dear John Kerr
I am at present researching my family tree and it
would seem from my investigations that we have a
connection.

Let me tell you what little I know. William
Blake Kerr had two illegitimate children with
Catherine McGregor McKenzie. Myself born in 1953
and my sister born in 1952. Catherine died in 1956
and we were subsequently adopted by the Fisher
family.

We have some photographs of William and
Catherine but what we don't have is any knowledge
of our father and what kind of man he was. I was

wondering if you would be prepared to share any
information on the Kerr family history.

Both my sister and I appreciate that this letter may
not be a welcome one. However, over the years we
have tried to piece together a picture of our family
without causing any distress to the Kerr family by a
direct approach. Please accept our sincere apologies
if these revelations have upset you in any way and
we quite understand if you decide not to take this
any further.

Yours sincerely

Gregor and Maureen Fisher

At least, they thought, the letter gave him an out, because it wasn't his fault. It wasn't anybody's fault, really, but they knew something like that dropping through the letterbox would come as a shock. What would he think? The reply came by return of post.

Dear Gregor and Maureen

Thank you for your letter, which elaborated on some
fragmentary details that I came by at third hand a
year or so ago.

Certainly I would be glad to help in any way I can to
provide family background, which would best be done
in person. You would be most welcome to call on us
here if you were to be in the Highlands. On the other
hand, my wife and I will be in the Borders in May.

In the meantime I enclose an old print of the Kerr
family as it was during the 1914–18 war.

I hope this will make a start to a fuller exchange in
due course, and I shall look forward to hearing from
you.
	Yours
	John Kerr

After further correspondence, it was decided that Gregor and
Maureen would go to visit him in the Highlands. John and his
wife Jane sounded very friendly; they offered to pick them up at
Inverness airport and give them a bed for the night, but Gregor
thought it best to remain independent – Aunt Ruby still haunted
him. He and Maureen decided to drive up and stay nearby.

So at least after whatever happened we could
retreat; we could talk, drink tea. Which I was quite
pleased about because I didn't know how Maureen
was going to react – and to be perfectly frank, I
didn't know how I was, either, if I was being totally
honest.

They left the car in Dulnain Bridge in Grantown-on-Spey and
on the appointed day, at the appointed hour, they walked up the
road. Maureen was jumpy. Gregor wasn't jumpy at all but he still
felt unsure. They turned up the drive and happily there were no
pink gravel chips, just a substantial Arts and Crafts style of
house; a genteel residence in the Highlands.

The door was opened and there stood John Kerr, their half-
brother, an older man of very precise speech, the sort of precision that meant that he chose every word carefully and then
uttered it even more carefully. But the wonderful thing about

John was that he had a twinkle in his eye. There was an unmistakable joy about him, expressed even on first meeting. Jane, his wife, was of that upper-class Scottish tribe beloved by Gregor for their posh eccentricity: tartan skirt, knitted tights, dancing pumps. She reminded him of Johnny Monaghan's Great-Aunt Nelly, who had been a nurse in the Great War. Great-Aunt Nelly wore knitted tights and if she was making the boys a salad with olive oil, and if any oil spilled on her hands, she would just run it through her hair – 'It's terribly good for it,' she'd say.

Gregor took to them immediately. Their welcome was warm; they were lovely people. For a first meeting, of a particularly loaded kind, it went off well: they had a gin and politely sized each other up, trying to get to know, understand, interpret, scan each other's faces for sibling likeness. There was little possibility of finding much family resemblance, Gregor felt, because their new half-brother was a generation older than they were. Rather sensibly, John Kerr steered the conversation onto common ground. He was a journalist, in an era when journalism was still a respectable trade, and had at one point many years earlier been the drama critic of the *Glasgow Herald*, so he and Gregor had shared interests. Much to his surprise his half-brother was quite theatrical, actorish, luvvie-ish. A bit 'Dear Boy!' It made him feel quite at home.

As they chatted, it was clear John had known for some time of his relationship with Gregor, ever since Vicki had phoned Margaret in Bearsden and asked for a picture of William Blake Kerr, their father. Gregor wondered why, as the years had passed, he had never chosen to get in touch with him. He would never know the answer, but he put it down to John's unswerving loyalty to his sister Dorothy. She was, it appeared, especially sensitive about her father's legacy of illegitimate children and perhaps there was a family understanding that nothing would be said about it; a tacit agreement that doing nothing was better than doing something, and John had respected that. On first meeting Gregor found his half-brother gracious, interested and charming, although he personally could not get over a sense of dislocation. Gregor had felt exactly the same when he first encountered Maureen and Ann as an 18-year-old – sitting with people who were total strangers but with whom he shared the same genes. There was a blood connection, but what did it really mean? He never shook off the vague sense of disappointment that he didn't feel more affected by these momentous reunions, that they didn't cure the sense of emptiness.

And Gregor being Gregor, there was always the shadow of self-doubt. It all came back to that question of identity: was he being accepted by these good people just because he was famous and not because of who he himself was? Was that why John was being so welcoming, because he was Gregor Fisher, one of Scotland's favourite actors?

*Nearly a decade after the visit to Grantown-on-Spey, Gregor lights another fag, frowns at both the horizon and the memory. 'I couldn't help thinking that maybe our meeting was coloured slightly by who I was, by me the actor. It always strikes me as irritating, but understandable, when people see me that way. But irritating nonetheless because you think, "Well, who the hell am I anyway? I just happen to have been in your living room."'*

*He laughs a mirthless laugh.*

*'But people go very peculiar about that, Mel. They just go very peculiar, even sane people go relatively peculiar. I'm not saying John did that, I'm not saying they went, "Ooh, come in, come in! Can I have your autograph?" No, it wasn't remotely like that. It was just there was 1 per cent of me felt that if I'd turned up at their front door, going, "Howuryegettinon? Ah'm yer relative by the way, ye know whit ah'm sayin? Come, we'll go get and getch ye a pint," then they might not have been so impressed.'*

*The cameo is spontaneous, tragi-comedy gold. I explode with laughter but even as I cackle I feel desperately sorry for him. Because he knows, and I know, there is an absolute truth in his words. Very few families would welcome that.*

*'You know what I'm saying? I put it very crudely, but that's the bottom line of this sometimes. It bloody well is.'*

Whatever Gregor's insecurities, the fact was that John and Jane Kerr were kind people, delighted to meet him and far too sophisticated to have their heads turned by his fame. The meeting ended with promises to meet for lunch the next day. William Kerr had not been mentioned and the expression 'our father' not used by either brother. For the rest of John Kerr's life, if they talked about him (which was fleetingly), they called him 'WBK'. Things were just easier that way.

If the meeting was polite, tactful and unemotional, then instinct told Gregor that was the best way. This had been the time to say hallo, to stay reserved. He went to bed and mulled it over. John was very good company, a man to sit in a bar with, a bloody good teller of tales. He was a journalist, a wordsmith, a talker, a communicator; a studier of people. They had common acquaintances and common interests. Maureen too was delighted to have found real family and to have been accepted.

And there was an ever so slightly spooky coincidence, one of many stalking this story. In the early 1980s, as John Kerr's journalism career was ending, Gregor's career at BBC Scotland was blossoming. Both men frequented the BBC's old headquarters in Queen Street, Edinburgh, at that time, and both used the canteen high up on the top floor of the old building. There, unaware, they had been in the same room, sitting a few feet away from each other, drinking cups of infamously bad BBC tea.

Lunch was restrained but chatty and as they left, John told Gregor and Maureen that they must keep in touch. He floated the idea that, as he had a son in Melrose in the Scottish Borders, it would be a good idea if they had a bit of a family gathering there. He emphasised the word.

*'Good heavens,' thought Gregor. 'Us? Family? How strange.'*

Yes, said John, it would give us all an opportunity to meet each other's children and the extended clan. *'Clan?'* Yes, and perhaps they could share a glass or two.

John Kerr had a talent for writing excellent letters. Very soon after the trip to Grantown-on-Spey, he wrote:

Dear Gregor

I wanted to write to say how much Jane and I appreciated your visit, with the clarification it brought of our shared parentage. We both enjoyed meeting you and Maureen, and for us particularly unravelling at least some of our mutual family history, thanks to your research.

I enclose a few mementoes of our father, which sister Dorothy passed on to me a year or so ago, saying they were found in Dad's wallet after his death. They would seem to reflect a sidelight of his character which many of his acquaintances in life might not necessarily have been aware of.

We have already written to our children to let them know of their newfound extended family.

Yours aye

John

The words he had chosen to use were oblique, dignified and deliberate, but they spoke volumes, as did the enclosures from W. B. Kerr's wallet.

\* \* \*

Unexpectedly, another letter arrived for Gregor, a hesitant note from an address in Cumbernauld, Lanarkshire, written in a different, precise hand. This time there was no 'Dear Gregor', just:

> How do I start?
>    What can I say?
>    Here goes ...
>    To hear that you and Maureen had met John and Jane recently was good.
>    And I hope that some day you may both want to meet your younger half-sister.
>    Dorothy

It was becoming very obvious to Gregor that the hurt inflicted by the past was not confined to him and Maureen.

The new extended Kerr family had their first gathering at a farm outside Melrose later that summer. It did indeed amount to a clan. John and Jane's three children and grandchildren were there, along with Maureen, her husband Michael Doonan, Gregor, Vicki and the teenaged Jamie and Cissie. Although John and Gregor were brothers, the gap in ages meant Gregor was a contemporary of his children. John and Jane, wed early in 1955, had a baby, Nick, born in 1956 – which meant he and Gregor were in nappies at the same time.

The timing was extraordinary but it seemed polite not to discuss such things.

There was a notable absentee at the party: Dorothy had declined. She would rather, she had told John, meet her newfound brother and sister privately for the first time. But it was a great party – there was a big long table groaning with food, the sun warmed the Eildon Hills and John Kerr, resplendent in his tartan trews, stood up in the middle of it all and made a sweet speech, saying how pleased he was to welcome Gregor and Maureen and their families. He then produced an anthology of poetry, which W. B. Kerr had given him and which, he said, he thought appropriate to pass on to Gregor – W. B. Kerr had been keen on poetry.

'And I remember when I got it, somebody said round the table, "Why don't you read us one of the poems?"

'And it opened at "She Was Poor But She Was Honest". It's a great fun poem, actually. There's a filthy version of it, but of course this wasn't it. And I thought, why not? I'd had a couple of sherberts by then. And so I read it at the first gathering in Melrose.'

Perhaps, not for the first time, it can be said that you couldn't make this up. Of all the poems, why should William Kerr's poetry book fall open at this one? And what movements of the stars should decree that Gregor, son of the fallen woman, should come to proclaim the rollicking words in his great, rich, precise performer's voice to his father's family?

She was poor but she was honest,
Victim of a rich man's whim,
First he loved her, then he left her,
And she lost her honest name.

Chorus: 'It's the same the whole world over;
It's the poor that gets the blame,
It's the rich that get the pleasure.
Isn't it a blooming shame?'

It went down a storm, to laughter and clapping. Maureen was also given a memento of her father, his cigarette case; and everybody was of the opinion that the day had been a great success, and that they would reconvene for the next annual gathering at Gregor and Vicki's house in Langholm.

Later that summer, Gregor and Maureen were invited to meet Dorothy at her little house in Cumbernauld. Elderly and childless, Dorothy had worked most of her life in the administration of the Cumbernauld Development Corporation and married late. She was the youngest of W. B. Kerr's children and the most affected by the revelation of his relationship with another woman, not least because she had still been at home when it was going on. It was clear she had been shattered by her father's betrayal and had sided with her mother, burying the hurtful secret very deep. She got emotional when, over tea and sandwiches, the matter was raised by Gregor and Maureen; and it was apparent she had known about it most of her life but had shared it with nobody. She had obviously lived in dread that one day something like this would come out of the woodwork. They tried to be as tactful as they could. Gregor perceived that she

*Left:* Cis. She was the first mum I ever knew and the woman I adored all my life.

*Right:* This is me, aged about four, wearing a very smart pair of Ladybird trousers with Cis (right), and her daughters – my big sisters – Una (middle) and Margaret (left).

*Right:* My first year at Neilston Primary School. Clock the bitten nails.

*Above:* The marriage of Jim Fisher and Ellen Sellars, who originally adopted me. Everyone thought I looked like Jim Fisher.

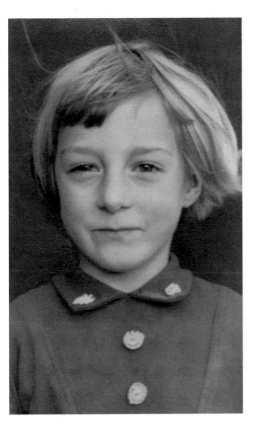

*Left:* Maureen McKenzie, my full sister. Nice haircut, eh?

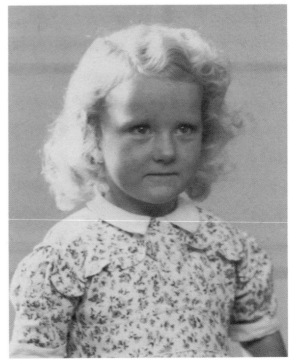

*Right:* Ann McKenzie, my half-sister, with a rather nicer haircut.

*Left:* My grandfather Matthew McKenzie, with his wife Catherine and two daughters, *c.* 1915. Little Catherine (Kit), my mother, was yet to be born.

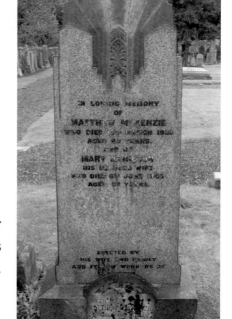

*Right:* My grandfather Matthew McKenzie's gravestone.

*Right:* Catherine (Kit) McKenzie, my mother, doing an impersonation of me – and doing it rather well.

*Left:* Kit McKenzie with a friend, *c.* 1940s. My only picture of my mother until recently. A happy day in Stirling, I think, with highly polished shoes.

*Above:* Catherine (Kit) McKenzie (front row, fifth from right in satin dress) at the DCL staff dance, Golden Lion Hotel, Stirling, February 1951.

*Right:* The houses under the hills. We got very excited when we found this. Easily pleased, eh?

*Above:* An aerial view of the distillery in Menstrie. Clock the full picture of Glenochil Terrace, nos 2–20, at the top of the picture. This was my first home – on the wrong side of the railway lines.

*Left:* The Kerr family, 1917. Back row: my father's brother John; his stepmother Margaret; William Blake Kerr, my father; his sister Jean. Sitting: W. B. K.'s father, my grandfather William; my great-grandfather John. Front row: my father's half-brother David. Complicated, eh?

*Above:* My father William Blake Kerr as a young exciseman, 1920s.

*Right:* My father William Blake Kerr, his wife Margaret and daughter Dorothy at the wedding of my half-brother John to Jane, February 1955.

was a precise, sensitive, reticent person, very different from her extrovert brother. She did not reveal much; they did not probe for fear of upsetting her. But she was a kindly soul; she seemed genuinely enchanted when Gregor gave her a copy of an impish picture of himself at Neilston Primary School. Maureen and Dorothy also began what was to be a lasting relationship.

The siblings sent their new sister flowers afterwards, and she was very touched to receive them. She replied with a note, signed with love. And so they constructed a careful friendship. Later that year, when Gregor was performing in *Chitty Chitty Bang Bang* in Edinburgh, he organised – *'typical show-off, me'* – for Maureen to go and pick up Dorothy in a chauffeur-driven Mercedes to take her to see the show. Dorothy was not someone who went out much, and they were later to discover from John just how much the evening meant to her.

Fond as he became of both John and Dorothy Kerr, though, Gregor never felt intimate with them. It was that old thing: the lack of connection. Much as he wanted to, he didn't really feel as if he had come home to a brother and a sister.

An interesting thing happened one day, however, with one of his new nieces, John and Jane's daughter Barbara: a flash of undeniable connection. Gregor was staying in a flat in North Castle Street in Edinburgh while performing at the Playhouse, and he invited Barbara and one of her sons to come for supper after the show. He preferred eating at home to going to some restaurant or other, where strangers would come up and say, 'It's you – how are you?' So he scuttled around and made some food. While he was serving, he rested his hands on the table. Barbara stared at his hands and started to weep.

'Oh, God! What's the matter? You OK?' he said.

She took his hand. 'You've got Grandpa's fingers. His hands were just like yours.'

Startled, Gregor examined afresh what he calls his little 'prehensile' fingers.

'They're not sort of … piano player's hands, are they? They're wee, fat kind of …'

'They're Grandpa's.'

For him, it was a bit of a shocker. But that really was the only emotional thing that happened. Fairly typically, Gregor underplayed the impact he had made upon the family, but in their dignified way the Kerrs were charmed. John Kerr wrote to him:

Dear Gregor

A word of thanks for all the fun and pleasure you have bestowed on Family Kerr via *Chitty Chitty Bang Bang* on-stage and backstage. In particular I was charmed to hear at first hand how much Dorothy had enjoyed her visit. Her verdict was unequivocal – 'the greatest show on earth'. She was thrilled with the whole occasion and last heard of was proposing a follow-up with a night at the ballet. I thought you should know that the result was a total conquest, for which I am most grateful.

Yours

John

Because of the bad weather in Inverness, John and Jane had been unable to get down from Grantown-on-Spey to see the show for themselves, but so successful was *Chitty Chitty Bang*

*Bang* that an extended six-week run was put on in Bristol and the family organised for the senior Kerrs to fly down, see the performance and spend three or four nights in a rented flat there. It was an opportunity for Gregor to get to know his half-brother better and he took it, going up to visit them every night. Hendrick's Gin was all the rage then, so Gregor brought with him a bottle of Hendrick's with some Fever-Tree tonic, just for a treat. He poured a gin for his older brother and sloshed in a whole bottle of tonic. There was a communality between them; John Kerr was great fun and very jolly. He loved the theatrical gossip and they began chatting.

'Another one?' Gregor asked.

'Perhaps we should, that would be very nice, but perhaps a little less tonic this time,' said John in his rich voice, chortling.

It was here for the first time that John spoke about their father. He offered the briefest of sketch portraits of him: W. B. Kerr was a man who very much wanted his family to do well and was keen on education. Aunt Ruby's slur that he was a drinker appeared to be sheer nastiness. John remained oblique about the affair. He took the view that the revelations about Maureen and Gregor's existence had rather opened up a whole side of W. B. Kerr's personality that they weren't aware of. Beyond that, he was too loyal and protective of his father to comment. Out of love and respect, he would not engage in anything that was even slightly critical. He and his legitimate siblings had a good opinion of him and wanted to protect his memory. It was perfectly understandable.

John didn't want to go there. And why should he?
Damn all to do with him. It was, yet again, stupidity
on my part to even try to get any information,
because he couldn't give me any. I guess I was also
asking for his opinion, but it was wrong to do so.
John Kerr was a good man – he didn't know anything
about his father's secret relationship and he wasn't
prepared to hypothesise. He was old enough and
wise enough to know that I didn't know; and old
enough and wise enough to know that he didn't
know, so what was the point? It was a case of, let's
just enjoy this now, why are we talking about it? And
I took that on board.

Gregor understood that his half-brother was, in a way, trying to
protect him as well. He didn't want him to have a bad opinion
of their father or to add to his own feelings of hurt. Gregor felt
obliged to give John and Jane a brief sketch of his own childhood and what had happened to him, and they listened politely.
But if the conversation touched upon the details of Maureen's
intense suffering, John Kerr would steer away from it and they
would quickly move on. Both men were aware it was a loaded
situation and that their father's actions had caused pain. It was
awkward and much easier for everybody to handle if the lid was
kept pretty tightly shut.

Meanwhile the relationship between the two flourished.
John's letters were beautifully written; he sent news, quoted
Shakespeare and Robert Burns, and followed Gregor's career
with interest. Jane dug out family photos of W. B. Kerr and sent
them to Gregor, filling him in on who everybody was. Gregor

genuinely enjoyed his half-brother's company and always looked forward to hearing from him. It made him sharpen up his act; he had never been a great letter writer himself, too impatient and his hand too messy, but when it came to replying to John, he took time and always made an effort.

Sometimes if he was on a film set he would phone because he knew the older man loved to hear the gossip. He'd call the number in Grantown-on Spey.

'Well, I'll tell you what's happening today, you're not going to believe this one, but I'm standing here with blood dripping off my chin and ...'

And John would gasp with pleasure.

'Oh! Heaven's sakes! And then what happened?'

Their friendship lasted until John died, aged 86, in 2012. The sad phone call came from Nick to say his father had passed away. Gregor, by then living in Lincolnshire, drove north to Speyside for the funeral, picking up Maureen en route. The weather was wintery. It was a big funeral; and because John Kerr was well connected, as a journalist and as a big Labour Party supporter, some of the great and the good had turned out. They assembled in the snow at the graveyard and one of John's grandsons played the pipes. Gregor found it very moving, even more so when, much to his surprise, he was called forward to take a cord to lower the coffin into its final resting place.

It really touched me. I just thought, 'You really didn't have to do that.' I'm sure that was Jane and I just thought that was such a sweet thing to do.

The generosity of the gesture, the sense that he was included in such an inner family sanctum, meant an extraordinary amount to him – *'The sheer classiness of asking me'*. Not to mention the powerful symbolism of the cord, the long-lost link re-established between the two men. Strangely enough it had stopped snowing when they came to lower him, the clouds had broken and they could see the snow-covered mountains all around them, a beautiful, sombre scene. After the brief service, the minister asked everyone to join them in the local hotel. Gregor and Maureen felt slightly uncomfortable, because although they knew the immediate Kerr family, there were many people there who were strangers to them. Gregor's spirits dipped at the thought of the explanations he'd have to make.

A family member who he did not know stood up and addressed the funeral party as they took refreshments. The man spoke about John and his life, and then said how latterly John had been so *happy* to have met Gregor and Maureen. 'Oh God,' thought Gregor, swallowing hard, and he looked at Maureen, worried this would set her off. He grabbed her and hissed, 'Steady, steady, public display here, behave yourself!' and the moment passed.

The speaker had not revealed what the connection was. He'd just said how delighted John was to know them. But somebody else came up afterwards and said: 'Now what is the … are you connected to the family at all, to John?'

'Yes … yes, I am,' said Gregor.

There was an expectant pause. He thought about it a bit; decided to express his pride.

'Erm, well … yes. I think you could call me his brother.'

'Oh!' she said, but not in a nasty way. 'Anyway, I'm glad the weather cleared up, it turned out nice.'

'*Move on,*' thought Gregor.

He left shortly afterwards because he didn't know what to say to people. But it occurred to him that it was a measure of John Kerr and his family that they had effectively said to him: 'Here's a cord, here you are, you are important enough to do this, you are a part of us.' That a family grieving a father, husband and grandfather could take the time to include him and Maureen, and mention them in the speech, he found really touching. The Kerr family had given them recognition. Amid that familiar jumble of feelings – connection, disconnection, fear and dislocation – it meant a considerable amount to both of them.

It was, quite simply, a nice end to Gregor's relationship with his brother.

Cold, late spring, Glasgow 2015. We've been talking about the Kerrs all day.

'You do remember the other huge coincidence in all this, don't you?' I say.

'About your pal?'

'Yes, my good friend Angie … Jane Kerr is her aunt. She had told me that before we started writing this book. And she had already told me, before I met you, how delighted they were that you were in their family now. And it's not because you're famous, it's just that they think it's a wonderful, wonderful story. They think you're great because you're you.'

'I don't know how you divorce the two.'

'Of course you can.'

'If I had fallen by the wayside, some drug addict, a poor wee drunk from Govan or something, I wonder what they'd have thought then.'

'Gregor, stop it! Please stop it. Just remember what was in the wallet. Just remember what they gave you. The poem, the clue … That explains something.'

# THE BOY FROM NOWHERE

In the second letter that John Kerr wrote to his newfound brother he had enclosed an envelope with a little bit of dynamite in it. When the old man had died, the Kerr family had found in his wallet newspaper cuttings of the war poems, 'In Flanders Fields' and 'The Anxious Dead'. But in there too was a scrap of paper on which he had copied, in fountain pen, in a precise hand, the lyrics of the Victorian parlour song, 'Just A-wearying for You'. A song about lost love, it was made famous by Paul Robeson, the American singer, who recorded it in 1935.

All the time I'm feeling blue,
Wishing for you, wond'ring when
You'll be coming home again.
Restless, don't know what to do,
Just a-wearying for you.

Morning comes, the birds awake,
Used to sing so for your sake,
But there's sadness in the notes
That come trilling from their throats.
Seems they feel your absence too,
Just a-wearying for you.

Evening comes I miss you more
When the dark glooms round the door,
Seems just like you ought to be
There to open it for me.
Latch goes tinkling, thrills me through,
Sets me wearying for you.
Just a-wearying for you.

The family were a little puzzled by it because the words were not, let's put it this way, what a man married 40 years would keep out of sentiment for a very much alive wife. But then, years later, after Gregor and Maureen made contact, things began to fall into place.

# CHAPTER 8

# Kit

'... to suffer/The slings and arrows of outrageous fortune,/Or to take arms against a sea of troubles ...'
*Hamlet*: Act III, Scene I

Little Kit McKenzie's start in life was not an auspicious one. She came into the world on 8 April 1917, in what was, even with the kindest spin put upon it, single-roomed squalor. Number 2b, Long Row, was part of the infamous 'row' workers' housing built around the iron factories and coalmines of Coatbridge, Lanarkshire.

Some local woman with midwifery experience may have assisted, but the circumstances of life, let alone birth, in these hovels were uniformly harsh. The room in Long Row had no running water, sanitation or gas lighting, just two beds and a fire, with the coal stored under the bed. A wooden floor if they were lucky, otherwise mud. At the time there were at least four adults living in the room – the baby's mother and father, the father's sister and brother-in-law, whose home it was – and we may presume some other children too. Outside the only window, across the street, smoke and sparks belched from the Dundyvan Iron Works seven days and nights a week, like some scene from Hades, and immediately behind the Row was a sprawl of rail lines, where the coal and ironstone trains shunted and rattled. This was normal; everybody in the town lived much like this. In fact there were worse places.

The baby was born healthy, the one joyous thing amid the reek of despair. Her mother, Catherine, was just 31 but desperately ill with a heart condition. It must have been clear for some time that she might not survive the birth and for support she had gone to stay with her sister-in-law at Coatbridge. The baby's father, Matthew McKenzie, had been granted compassionate leave and had rushed home from the Western Front in time to be there for his wife and baby.

It is doubtful whether the young woman ever rose from the bed after giving birth, or indeed was able to hold or nurse her baby. Two and a half days later, the mitral valves of her heart, irretrievably damaged by rheumatic fever, finally gave up the fight. Every baby she had had – she and Matthew had two older daughters – weakened her heart a little. This third and final one was too much for her body. She died quietly, uneventfully, as women were wont to do in those disease-ravaged days.

Late January 2015, and Gregor and I are on the road again. Destination, Coatbridge, because the Lanarkshire town, which became one of the industrial powerhouses of the world in the 1830s, boasts the Summerlee Museum of Scottish Industrial Life, a serious testament to the glory and the cruelty of its heritage. And this is where his real mother had entered the world.

I've warned him that the circumstances of Kit's birth were unremittingly grim. A single-roomed miner's cottage, in an area notorious for some of the worst, overcrowded hovels in the UK. So bad, in fact, that one drawing of the Rows was used as an illustration for George Orwell's famous book, The Road to Wigan Pier.

'They've got a reconstruction of a row of cottages, similar to where she was born,' I say. 'Except that they had to sanitise it, because if they'd made it totally lifelike they'd have turned people off – the public can't take too much reality. So there are no ash-pits for toilets, or open sewers, or seven kids in a bed, or mud floors, or rain running down the inside walls.'

'You're going all Angela's Ashes on me,' says Gregor, uneasily.

His dreams of being the offspring of nobility, bastard son of the Lord of Airthrey Castle, are long gone.

'I'm afraid so,' I say.

What chance did someone as ill as Kit's mother have? There were no hospitals for people like her, no NHS, no antibiotics, no heart monitors, no surgery. The concept of training and registering midwives had only just been advanced in Parliament. And how to thrive in living conditions we would now forbid for animals? Long Row had originally been a straight run of terraced cottages, a third of a mile long, for workers at the Dundyvan malleable iron foundry. In the second half of the nineteenth century, as if to demonstrate how little they prioritised the welfare of their workforce, the mine owners cleared a space in the middle of the Row and sank a coal shaft, slap bang between two cottage gable ends.

It is impossible now to imagine the living conditions. Evidence given prior to the Mines and Collieries Act 1842 revealed that in Coatbridge some families with only two rooms took in 14 single men as lodgers. The clerk at the Dundyvan Iron Foundry claimed some one-roomed houses at Long Row had up to 18 occupants, half working day shift, the other half the night shift. In 1864 the local paper published a report headlined 'The Filthiest Puddle in the World', describing a vast open cesspit in an area close by.

By 1917, not a lot appeared to have improved. Evidence presented to the Royal Commission on Industrial Housing in Scotland that same year described the situation in parts of Coatbridge thus: 'The rows are a wilderness of single- and double- (mostly single-) roomed houses. They cannot be described justly, and to do so unjustly would flatter the owners … they consist of rows of single-storey hovels; most of them have not even rhones to carry the rain from the roofs. Rainwater simply runs down the roof and then runs down the walls, or falls off as chance or the wind decides. There are no coal-cellars; coals are kept below the beds. There are no washhouses. Water is supplied from stands in the alleys. The closet accommodation is hideous. The closets outside are not used by the women. In some of the rows 7 or 8 people occupy a single room. The sanitary conveniences are in a state of revolting filth … The whole place is an eyesore, and positively disgraceful.'

The typical miners' rows, said the inspectors, were dreary, featureless, dismal; arranged in monotonous lines. The open spaces were cluttered with washhouses and privies, often out of repair, and in wet weather they became churned up into a morass of semi-liquid mud, with little in the way of road or footpath – 'a fact which adds greatly to the burdens of the over-wrought housewife'.

The Royal Commission concluded working people lived in conditions no modern community should be expected to tolerate and the scandal was such that within a few short years much of the housing in Coatbridge had been demolished and Acts of Parliament were passed to make local councils in Scotland responsible for building houses. In the meantime, people had no option but to lead short, brutish lives in squalor. Small wonder, at one point, that of Coatbridge's 126 shops, 66 sold drink.

'You read out aloud this bit from the Royal Commission,' I say to Gregor. 'I'll give you *Angela's Ashes*. This is about privy-middens.'

'Privy-middens?'

'Read it.'

He starts to read. 'The dreary and unkempt surroundings of many rows have already been referred to, but a word must be said as to the nature of the outhouses. Occasionally there is a properly constructed common washhouse, but in the older villages more often only such makeshift and ramshackle washhouses as the miners have run up for themselves. But the chief of these unsightly structures are the privies. In the West of Scotland this often is a "privy-midden", which has only in comparatively recent times been expelled from the cities and still unhappily retains its place in the mining villages.

'It is a large erection, open on one side, where ashes and all other household refuse are thrown in, and closed (though often not adequately closed) on the side which serves as a latrine. It is the only sanitary convenience in many rows; and it is so impossible to keep clean, so foul-smelling, and so littered with filth of all sorts, that no decent woman can use it, while if children do so, it is at grave risk to their health of body and mind.'

He pauses. Sighs.

'Shit seems to follow me, doesn't it? It's never too far away.'

We're talking about a time less than 100 years ago. We've gone from open cesspits and privy-middens to ensuite bathrooms for every bedroom in a house.

'By the way,' I ask. 'Do you have a jacuzzi in your house in France?'

'No.'

'Good.'

Amid such abominations, we can only guess what Matthew Donaldson McKenzie felt as he bowed his head over the body of his wife and his mewling newborn. His were difficult circumstances. Shivering with trench fever (an influenza-like infection) and smitten with grief, he had no home and three motherless children to look after. His sister Helen Weir tried to comfort him. He was too sick to perform the sad job of notifying the authorities of Catherine's death, and Helen's husband Alexander registered it instead.

Matthew named the baby Catherine after her dead mother, soon shortened to 'Kit'.

The cruel thing was, he had not been away for long. Just three months earlier he had been passed fit for Foreign Service and ordered to embark on the troop ship for France. Up until then, because of his slightly deformed feet, his war had been spent in a reserve unit in the UK, guarding his country. For the call for reinforcements to come when it did, was, for him, the worst time of all.

This is not to suggest cowardice. All foot soldiers knew their destination was likely to be the Western Front, from where devastating tales of the Battle of the Somme had filtered back, but personal fear was not the issue. He had not wanted to leave Britain when Catherine, sick as she was, was within weeks of giving birth. However, go he must. He disembarked in France on 3 March 1917 and on 23 March joined the infantry of the 3rd Battalion of the Highland Light Infantry, regrouping in the aftermath of the Somme. We are all familiar with the story, but still it defies comprehension, this most dreadful battle in history, brought to a halt only by the winter of 1916–17, and the foot soldiers were still mired in a landscape of rain-filled trenches and acres of liquid mud. An estimated one million men, from both sides, had died. In the lingering squalor Matthew almost immediately succumbed to trench fever.

After a few days in the field came word that he was needed urgently at home: his wife had taken a turn for the worse. In what was very rare for private soldiers at the front, Matthew was granted compassionate leave and within less than two weeks of arriving in France had turned around and was heading home. It was a slow, anxious journey by train to Glasgow; and he reached his sister and brother-in-law's cottage in Long Row just in time. There, next to the railway sidings and opposite the iron works, amid the noise and filth, he witnessed a more personal war of life and death.

How different things were from nearly two years before – June 1915, when, as a 26-year-old millworker at Paton's of Alloa, in central Scotland, Matthew had signed up in the prevailing spirit of patriotism. He was an honourable man, a talented pianist, who in life tried always to do the right thing. His enlistment papers describe someone of 5ft 8in, 153 lbs, 38.5in chest, with good physical development, no congenital illness, and scars on the index and ring fingers of his right hand. He had, it was noted, deformity of the feet, but not bad enough to make him unfit for some kind of service. Initially he was sent to join the 3rd Battalion Royal Scots, a reserve unit that served in the UK throughout the war, which meant he got regular leave to see his wife and two young children and, in the summer of 1916, another baby was conceived.

Matthew's war was not ended by the sad events in Coatbridge. After his wife's funeral, he was due to return to the trenches, had not his health intervened. On 15 May, when the baby was five weeks old, he was recalled to the Highland Light Infantry depot in Glasgow, for posting to France. His physical state must have deteriorated, for he was ordered straight to Stobhill Hospital and admitted on the same day.

Some men were hit particularly hard by trench fever and it appears Matthew was one of them. The blood-borne illness, caused by the bacterium *Bartonella quintana*, debilitated up to a third of men in the trenches. It was not until later, in 1918, that doctors discovered the infection came from the lice that invaded every crevice of the soldiers' bodies. All that the sufferers knew about it was a high fever, relapsing on five-day cycles, with severe headache, inflamed eyes and pains in the back, legs and particularly the shins – it was sometimes called shin bone fever. Lethal cases were rare, and it was not a reason to be returned to the UK, but the fever could reoccur as many as eight times. Recovery could take several months, often leaving an unwelcome legacy of heart problems, fatigue, anxiety and depression.

From May until October, Matthew remained at Stobhill. It had opened as a Poor Law hospital in 1904 and was requisitioned by the Royal Army Medical Corps in 1914, with wounded men brought by hospital trains to a specially built station inside the grounds. Patricia R. Andrew, in *A Chasm in Time*, her book on Scottish war art, features a painting, 'Ward 12B – Stobhill: 5am' by the artist Francis Martin, who had been injured in France and brought there. He portrays the entire ward floor packed with beds, stark walls and a young injured soldier with a thousand-yard stare, up and dressed as if it were daytime. Here, Matthew was treated, particularly for pain in his shins. He was briefly recalled to the infantry depot, but was plainly still unwell and in December 1917 was officially classified unfit for field duty due to a wasting of his left leg, caused by trench fever. He was transferred into the Royal Army Medical Corps and for the next 14 months was posted – presumably performing auxiliary, portering and sanitary duties – to hospitals in York, Bradford and Blackpool. Finally, in February 1919, he was sent for final examination and demobilisation.

And what of his baby daughter during this time? Who was to care for her? In an age when people routinely died by their early fifties, her maternal grandparents were already dead and gone. She may initially have stayed with her aunt and uncle in the abysmal overcrowding of Coatbridge. At some point, though, according to her father's military records, she joined her older sisters, all effectively orphaned while their father remained away in service, under the care of a Mrs Taylor in a rented house in Alloa. Family memories suggest this may have been a woman Kit called Auntie Nellie – an aunt or a family friend, we know not.

Matthew the handsome widower was evidently still a man: from January to March 1918 he was treated at the Royal Military Hospital, Kirkham, near Blackpool, for gonorrhoea. He was in good company; it was one of the most common diseases of war. In what amounted to a moral panic in 1917, the authorities had declared venereal disease a national emergency and one of the treatments was to irrigate the soldiers' penises, painfully, with the chemical Protargol. If Matthew had snatched some brief happiness he later paid for it; and who would now judge him, but in those days the community, not to mention the Church of Scotland, where he would later become a stalwart, would have been appalled.

He kept his shame deadly secret.

Compassion of any kind was in short supply in a broke, and broken, Britain immediately after the war. In York, in February 1919, an examining medical officer, Captain K. Morrison, ruled in most elegant copperplate that Matthew's leg was 20 per cent congenital and 10 per cent aggravated by service in France. His degree of disablement was therefore 30 per cent. Captain Morrison noted Pte McKenzie complained of intense pain when his knee-cap was tapped. Matthew duly left the British Army with a paltry disability pension, which expired after six months.

On 24 March 1919 he was finally demobbed and caught the train back to Scotland, returning to Clackmannanshire in time for Kit's second birthday, though he was presumably a complete stranger to the toddler. How many children across Britain screamed in terror at the gaunt, strange men who suddenly appeared in their home, and whom they had to call 'father'? For Matthew, though, how welcome his old haunts must have seemed, in the small industrial villages scattered beneath the Ochil Hills. Now he could breathe, could seek to rebuild.

In this part of Scotland, one of the Industrial Revolution's oldest factory floors, small-scale weaving, mining and brewing survived. There were also several distilleries, using local grain and hill water. Matthew got a job as a journeyman machinist in a mill. As soon as he could, he did what any 30-year-old widower desperate for a mother for his children would do: he sought another wife.

By 1920 he had found a 24-year-old dressmaker, Mary Jamieson, herself already widowed. Her husband, a cabinet-maker, may have died in France or of the Spanish flu epidemic post-1918, we do not know. Mary lived with her parents in

Menstrie, tucked hard in beneath the mountains. The village was a tough, hard-working place, with primitive housing and little sanitation. There were stories of families who routinely drove their pig through the house as the only way to get it into the back garden. Matthew and Mary married at Menstrie Parish Church in 1921 and settled in the village, where she took on his ready-made family and very soon had a baby of her own, called Elizabeth. Meanwhile, her father, a maltman at the nearby Glenochil Distillery, may have helped his new son-in-law find a better job. Soon Matthew took on a post as maintenance fitter in the Glenochil yeast factory, next to the distillery, on the outskirts of the village.

Scotland did like its drink. At the turn of the century Glenochil Distillery was churning out a million gallons of whisky a year. But the production of pure culture yeast, which had started almost as a by-product on the same site in 1878, was growing dramatically. In 1920 three giant generators had been installed to create electricity for the yeast plant. Distillers Company Limited had founded their vast whisky conglomerate upon the distillery and others nearby, but now this special DCL brand yeast had become the Rolls-Royce for baking, as well as distilling, and it was in high demand all over the British Isles. The yeast factory even had its own special rail siding to send out its product.

For a few years Kit and her sisters lived in the village. Later in the 1920s they were lucky to move to a tied flat on the distillery site – their first sight of the houses under the hills. Numbers 2–12 Glenochil Terrace were flats in a proud, two-storey stone tenement built in the 1880s and tenanted by the Board of Works for resident excisemen. Now some were being returned to DCL for workers' housing. The flats, for their day, were luxurious. They were better built than many, with sanitation, running water and big sash windows. To the south, the factory side, there was a generous walled garden, with allotments, a washhouse and a drying green. On the north side ran the railway, and beyond that an open field until the hills reared up, a backdrop to a child's dreams.

Just next door there was another tenement building, Numbers 14–20, which had been hurriedly put up by DCL to house more workers. The four flats in this block were one-roomed, without sanitation or running water. They are important to our story, but more of them later.

In this corner of the countryside Kit grew up with her older sisters, Ruby and Isabella, her stepmother Mary and baby Elizabeth. They played games on the drying green or on the external stone steps to the upper flats; they threw pebbles in the nearby burn. They lived in Number 6. In other flats on the block lived factory workers, but some were still used by visiting excise-men, the government officials, lawmen, who came to supervise the production, taxation and storage of alcohol. Some of these men were in uniform, but the higher-ranking ones dressed in plain clothes. Matthew's little girls would watch them come and go, greet them with a shy, polite hallo. Is it possible this was where Kit and William Kerr first met, in 1929 – she a child, he her father's age? It is both possible and probable.

At primary school in Menstrie, Kit was an adept pupil, good enough later to keep other people's books. Church attendance and music were staples of her life. Her father worked long hours, and sometimes night shifts, in the yeast factory, but he and his wife devoted their leisure time to church and to music. Music was in Matthew's veins and he longed to get back to the ivories; in 1920, even before marriage, he had become the organist at Menstrie Parish Church. A devout, responsible man, he was also choir-master, taught the junior choir and took the Sunday school.

*'At once he became the close friend of the Choir and especially of the children who were his care,'* effused the parish records.

Menstrie's social life was of its time. The village had three pubs, a weekly Robert Burns Club, a Reading Club and whist evenings; and there was gambling on an outside game called 'bats', similar to quoits, in which metal hoops were thrown towards a stake. Matthew was a member of the British Legion and a Freemason, but it was as a music maker that he was prominent socially. According to the *Alloa Journal*, he had an orchestra, which played at dances – perhaps we might now call it a band. There was a Dance Club in Menstrie Co-operative Hall and sometimes, under more liberal Kirk ministers, in the Church Hall. The highlight of the year, socially, was the DCL Social, a dinner dance.

It's always the little things, isn't it? The connections. The fact that my grandfather, Matthew McKenzie, played the piano and the organ and loved to entertain people, like I do. Like I grew up thumping the piano. And the fact he had deformed feet and I look at my feet and I think, deformed or not? I look at them, I think about it, I think they're all right. But then there was the Jim Fisher thing – I walked with a toe turned in and I thought that made me Jim Fisher's son. When of course I wasn't.

How was Gregor's grandfather as a family man? The only surviving shard of family memory suggests he was not easy, 'a bit bolshie'. But perhaps all working men in Scotland, even the givers of music and entertainment, were stern and unbending by contemporary standards. There must have been an element of the joyless John Leckie in all labouring men of that era, for relentless work sours the soul. What seems without doubt is that Kit, the little girl who had never had her own mother, just various 'aunties' and a stepmother, was fast developing into a strong-willed child. 'Headstrong', she was labelled. If you were at all spirited, it was hard to meet the expectations of a strict, conventional, God-fearing family. Especially one dedicated to the Church of Scotland, which for decades had devoted much of its energy lecturing against the evil of pre-marital fornication, for fornication meant fatherless children.

For Matthew's daughters, rural Menstrie should have been a relatively healthy place, due to the plentiful spring water tumbling down from the hills, and the fact that Number 6 Glenochil Terrace was roomier and airier, had running water and was, by contemporary standards, advantageous. Kit, however, could not escape her early childhood. By the time she was a teenager her health had begun to fail. She had funny turns, spells of weakness, breathlessness, dizziness, when she was forced to sit down or she might pass out. At 18, she was diagnosed with mitral valve stenosis, the blight doctors later called rheumatic heart disease. They had no cure to offer.

Rheumatic fever was rife amongst those living in poor housing in working-class Scotland in the first half of the twentieth century. There was simply no way to escape it, no penicillin or universal healthcare. The fever followed a streptococcus throat infection; the body produced antibodies to attack the infection, but often, tragically, they also attacked the mitral valve of the heart. Inflammation of the valve would later turn into permanent damage – congestion of blood and fluid in the lungs, chest pains, chest infections, fainting – usually manifesting itself between ten and twenty years after the original streptococcus infection. Because it was a disease of childhood, therefore, symptoms tended to emerge after adulthood.

Kit may have caught the throat bug in the slums of Coatbridge. Today, improved housing standards and a simple course of antibiotics have eradicated the risk; then, it was a time bomb. Of course, in those days no one knew what caused rheumatic fever. She did not look frail as she moved into her twenties; indeed she was of medium build, with a round face. But from the age of 18, she knew inside she was vulnerable. She presumed, rightly, she might have the same heart weakness as killed her mother at her birth; indeed, perhaps she considered it a widespread inheritance, because her sister Isabella was frail as well.

During the 1930s Kit's big sisters married and left home. Isabella, the eldest, accepted the hand of John Henderson, a factory supervisor, and went to live in nearby Alva. The only healthy one of the three, Ruby, married Alexander Horne and moved into one of the smart, newly built local authority houses in Menstrie, at 22 Abercrombie Place. Such housing schemes, springing up all over in the pebble-dashed clusters that came to typify Scotland, were a welcome social revolution, created by the Addison Acts of Parliament, which gave councils both subsidy and responsibility to house people properly. The houses may look ordinary now, in the twenty-first century; in the

1930s they were five-star palaces compared with what had gone before.

Back at 6 Glenochil Terrace, in what was to set a pattern for the rest of her short life, Kit refused to let her affliction beat her. She missed her two sisters, who had mothered her since birth, but her dear daddy was still there and she took work where she could find it. There is a picture of her from around that time in a white overall and cap, which suggests she was on the production line in one of the local factories. Her young, broad, open face, half-ready with a smile, is unmistakably similar to Gregor's. Kit battled through her fainting fits and made the best of things; she could have been under no illusion that life was anything but tough.

And so it proved, when a family tragedy shortly before her 21st birthday turned her world upside down. On the evening of Wednesday, 9 March 1938, her father, Matthew McKenzie, working the night shift, was carrying out repairs on the ground floor of the fermenting room of the Glenochil yeast factory. At around 11.30pm he put up a ladder against a tank and began to climb, but as he did so his foot slipped and he plunged onto the concrete floor.

It was only a five-foot fall but Matthew landed on his head and suffered severe injuries. He was taken to Clackmannan County Accidents Hospital where, less than two hours after-wards, at 1.25am on 10 March, he was pronounced dead. The cause of death was head injuries, subdural haemorrhage and injury to his spinal column. Matthew was 49 years old. Perhaps, momentarily unstable on that ladder, his deformed feet and wartime bad leg were, after all, his nemesis.

We may wonder now at how little fuss surrounded Matthew's death. Life was certainly cheaper then. Those were the days long before the Health & Safety Executive. Work was extremely dangerous, a fact that went without comment. Census reports show only 2.6 per cent of Scotland's population were men aged 70 or over, and this was because their jobs either killed them swiftly and violently, or wore their bodies out in less than 30 years. At the mines, deaths were more or less everyday occurrences. John Leckie's father, for instance, had perished in a mining explosion above ground; five men were killed underground at the Rosehall Colliery in Coatbridge in 1934. Those miners who weren't killed abruptly died slowly of acute lung disease. Building projects were as deadly: up in the Highlands, near Kinlochleven, building a hydropower dam, the 'poet navvy' Patrick McGill described labourers being regularly blown up with dynamite or struck with sledgehammers, and then being buried more or less where they fell. Those who survived the day would then seek oblivion with drink at night; the booze either killed them quickly with hypothermia en route back across the hills from the pub, or slowly with chronic alcoholism. In bottling plants, corks would put out men's eyes; chemical fumes killed people in most industries; and in the iron and steel industry, or in ship-building, men were either swallowed by fire or crushed by falling metal.

No wonder it was still rare to reach retirement age.

Professor T. C. Smout quotes the poet Edwin Muir's description of life in a bone factory early in the century: 'The men and women who worked in the yard, unloading the bones and casting them into the furnace, never got rid of the smell, no matter how they scrubbed … they breathed it in the faces of their lovers … they breathed it out with their last breath, infecting the Host which the priest set between their lips.'

*We roll into Summerlee, which is practically visitor-free on a cold winter Monday, and almost immediately the museum staff recognise him. There is a bit of a buzz; they feel Gregor Fisher belongs to them. A real celebrity, he's been in all their living rooms with them. He's made their dull afternoon come alive.*

*'Can I get your autograph, Mr Fisher?'*

*'Can I get a picture with you?'*

*'I'm that star-struck, I can't work my phone.'*

*Meanwhile, they've found me an expert to speak to, Allan MacKenzie, a local studies officer with the council. He tells me what he knows about Long Row. It sure wasn't Buckingham Palace Mews. On the way out of the museum we see pictures of six-year-old boys in bare feet pouring molten pig iron into the sand moulds.*

*Then we're loaded onto an onsite tram, and trundled a kilometre or so round to the miners' cottages. I'm dependent on a wheelchair, so Gregor is helping me pile on and off the disabled ramp; we're like the paralysed man and his crazy Somalian carer in the wicked French movie,* Untouchable.

*'Just don't start frothing at the mouth,' he warns, 'or I'll just walk away and leave you.'*

*We get inside the sombre one-roomed, one-windowed cottage, replica 1910; part of a Row. Two double box beds recessed against the wall. A tin bath. A potty. Not enough room to swing a cat. There's a young volunteer there, warming herself on the cast-iron range, playing with her smartphone.*

*'There would have been two adults in one bed, perhaps seven children in the other,' she says jauntily. 'Apparently they slept propped up, to ease their lungs.*

*'When kids come in now, the first thing they ask is, "Where's the telly?"'*

Outside, under smirry rain, next to the entrance to the mine they have reconstructed for visitors, Gregor suddenly starts to sing, in that rich, loud stage voice of his:

*Daddy don't go down the mine.*
*A miner was leavin' his home for his work*
*He heard his little child scream*
*He went to the side of his little girl's bed*
*Oh, Daddy, I've had such a dream*
*Oh, Daddy, my daddy, oh, don't go away*
*For dreams have so often come true*
*Oh, Daddy, my daddy, oh, don't go away*
*I never could live without you*
*I dreamed that the mine was all covered with flame*
*The men all fought for their lives*
*Just then the scene changed, and the mouth of the*
*mine*
*Was covered with sweethearts and wives.*

In the canteen they give us free cake, because it's Gregor. A man approaches us and asks him to go and meet his pals, both in wheelchairs. Gregor toddles off, generous with his chat. Later, they join us in the disabled car park as they are loaded into a van, waving excitedly.

'You've made their day,' I tell him. 'In fact, you made the day for everyone in there.'

'I once forgot to turn up to open a village fete,' he says. 'My name was mud. I could never show my face there again.'

Sitting in the car, slums on our minds, we discuss the conditions workers endured.

*On the shoulders of giants, and all that.*

*I say it makes me angry and I can understand why Scotland is such a left-wing country.*

*'Doesn't it do that to you?'*

*He pauses. Shrugs.*

*'I was always too busy surviving to take up issues,' he says.*

The *Alloa Advertiser* and the *Alloa Journal* both carried reports of Gregor's grandfather's death, the latter hailing his status within the community. He was indeed a rather special and respected man. The record from Menstrie Parish Church was positively eulogistic, devoting a large entry to him, saying how, *'with very great sorrow, the Session resolved to record the loss sustained by the Congregation and the whole community.'* For 18 years, it said, he had been organist in the church. *'When first he came, he endeared himself to the Office-bearers and to the whole Congregation by his eagerness to help them in all their work for the Church or for the village and at once he became the close friend of the members of the Choir and especially of the children who were his care. Through the years Mr McKenzie retained the esteem and friendship of those who were associated with him and each year he added to the number of his friends. No one ever asked for his help in vain, for he was ungrudging and untiring in his service for Church and village and friends. As Organist Choir-master, Teacher of the Junior Choir and Sunday School Teacher, Mr McKenzie has had a great influence on our village life. The news of his sudden death casts a shadow on every house and the congregation assembled at his funeral on Saturday 12th March mourning the loss of a friend. As representatives of the congregation and of the whole community, the Kirk Session offers deepest sympathy to Mrs McKenzie and to the daughters who have been visited by so great a sorrow.'*

So Matthew, in his coffin, may indeed have taken with him to the grave the pungent, clinging whiff of the yeast factory, a symbol of a life dedicated to hard work, but he also took the affection of many people. His funeral service was held at Menstrie Parish Church and he was buried in Logie Cemetery, a mile away, at the foot of the hills. Colleagues from the British

Legion attended. So too did his fellow Freemasons from Lodge St Servanus 771, Alva. It is entirely possible that William Kerr, fellow Mason and work colleague, was amongst the funeral congregation and saw Matthew's widow and four daughters grieving for their father.

What was certain was that Matthew's death dismantled his remaining family. Mary McKenzie, his second wife, had to give up the tied accommodation at Glenochil Terrace, and she and her daughter Elizabeth departed for Fife. Kit, homeless and with her weak heart, moved in with big sister Ruby at her Menstrie council house.

Orphaned before her 21st birthday, Kit took the loss of her father with courage and stoicism, but she had lost her anchor point, her security. So too, perhaps, she missed the element of music and entertainment that he had brought. His death reinforced her sense that when you have little in life, all you can do is hold your head up high and get on with it. Loneliness and insecurity stalked her, physically and mentally. But she had a strong personality and a sense of fun.

During her twenties, through the passage of the Second World War, Kit took work as her health permitted. Loss was always there, a companion on her shoulder. In 1944 her older sister Isabella passed away too, aged just 32, of cerebral apoplexy. Isabella left a four-year-old daughter, also named Catherine in memory of the mother who had died in Long Row. This latest tragedy can only have reinforced the fatalistic message to Kit: death was never far away, and you must do your best to snatch any happiness where you could find it.

Around that time, while living with sister Ruby and her husband Alexander, Kit started going out with a man called

Peter Cameron. He, like her, was 27 when the romance started; he was a worker on the nearby Glenochil Farm.

Perhaps Peter was slow to commit; perhaps he wasn't sure. Perhaps he was using her. Certainly the courtship went on for over 18 months, longer than usual, before Kit succumbed and became pregnant. Maybe, despite all those years of stern church teaching, she became scared she would lose her chance of a husband unless she slept with him. And perhaps, much simpler even than that, it was just that nobody had educated her about the facts of life. Sex education did not exist in any organised form in those days, for anyone, and woeful ignorance was widespread, especially amongst girls who had grown up without a mother.

Interestingly, the stigma in Scotland upon a girl who lost her virginity before marriage was less harsh than in England, because, under Scots law, subsequent marriage legitimised a bastard child or one conceived out of wedlock. Not that virginity was quite the premium product some churchy people pretended it was. Menstrie was amongst several villages in the area with a high number of illegitimate births. Life could still be cheap, and casual. Only 40 years earlier, the Medical Officer of Health had reported crisply that in Clackmannanshire he was struck by the large number of deaths of children under one year old *and with this fact, that many of them were illegitimate. It would be of interest to know if these infantile lives had been insured or not.* Besides, on farms especially, where Kit's husband-to-be Peter laboured, it was fairly common practice for a girl to get pregnant before the marriage took place; a clever stockman liked to know a beast was not barren before he purchased it.

So Kit, 28 by then, was convinced they would marry and was happy to be expecting a baby. She was happy until she was four months gone, and just starting to show, when out of the blue her lover took a £5 emigration ticket to Australia and was never seen or heard of again. We cannot, from the vantage of nearly 70 years, and blessed with a completely different moral code, begin to understand how she felt – but certainly shock, bitterness, a sense of disillusionment and betrayal. Perhaps too, a sense of resignation. Everything she had loved, she had lost. All we can acknowledge, yet again, is that life had been unremittingly cruel to Kit. If this was the way things were, she was powerless to change them.

All she could do was keep hoping and roll with the punches.

On 12 March 1946 Kit gave birth to a little girl, Ann, and despite her circumstances, it was a joyous moment. This baby's life was neither cheap nor casual; she was precious. At last Kit, motherless since birth, had found someone who belonged to her and her alone. We should be under no illusions about the cultural pressures she was under to give away the baby. Those were the years of institutionalised cruelty to young unmarried women and their offspring, who were encouraged, if they wanted to maintain family respectability, to give up their babies for adoption. Many of these children became child migrants, exported like so much breeding stock across the globe – Australia, the US and Canada particularly.

To understand just how defiant Kit was, we need to understand the attitudes of the 1940s and 50s. Women who kept illegitimate babies were the exception, according to the historian Jane Robinson. Well into the twentieth century many people believed such children could not go to heaven. Illegitimacy was a potent sexual taboo. Fallen women were seen as morally weak; their children flawed characters who would inherit moral flabbiness, uncontrollable impulses, selfishness and a lack of self-respect. Little wonder, however much a woman loved her baby, *'the giving up of a child could be driven by all sorts of practical and emotional responses: shame; pride; a lack of money, confidence or support.'*

Kit lacked money and support but she was also stubborn and very much her own woman. She kept Ann – here was a little person to love. The father's name on the birth certificate was left blank. Sister Ruby, the last remaining bit of family, apparently continued to offer her a roof over her head, and the birth certificate states that Kit, by then working as a clerkess, was resident at Ruby and Alexander Horne's council house in Abercrombie Place, Menstrie. But it was a strained relationship and it was not to last; morality was at play.

Ruby had carried on her father's close links to the Kirk – her husband was the session clerk at Menstrie Parish Church and the family worshipped regularly. Her troublesome little sister and her illegitimate child, regardless of the mitigating circumstances of her conception, were an embarrassment.

Ann was christened in the church nevertheless.

*It's April 2015, and I read out to Gregor a snippet of a news report from* The Times. *According to a YouGov poll, one child in five is now present at the wedding of its parents. Illegitimacy isn't just dead as a concept; the word itself is meaningless, purposeless, obsolete. It's like the concept of no sex before marriage, or shot-gun weddings. Quite simply, all defy explanation to younger generations. The great weight of human hurt, shame, deception and abandonment caused by the stigma of illegitimacy will burden few of us again.*

'How do I begin to explain the stigma there was in the 1940s and 50s? How did you tell your children?' *I ask him.*

*He's in a twinkly mood.*

'The kids would say, out of the blue – "Dad, what is a bastard?"'

'"Well …"'

'"Are we bastards?"'

'"Well, I don't think you are, technically."'

'"Why?"'

'"Because a bastard is a child that has been born to two people, a man and a woman, and when they were born, the man and woman weren't married."'

'"Oh … But you and Mum weren't married."'

'"Yeah, yeah, yeah, but you're slightly more special than a bastard. You are the bastard offspring of a bastard, which means you're a git."'

'"What does that mean?"'

'"Well, I'm a bastard, OK, and I had you and you're a bastard, so that means you're a git."'

'"Oh, right." Light dawns on their faces. "So we're gits, we're all gits."'

'And they went away happy about that ... they were quite enchanted at the idea they were gits.

'But there was never any secrecy – we had that kind of household where from day one if there was something the children wanted to talk about, we talked about it, whether about sex or where babies come from, or illegitimacy or someone swearing at school, it was just the way it was.

'It was no big deal.'

The unmarried Kit and her little Ann lived at Abercrombie Terrace for the next two years, coming to terms with her status as a fallen woman, within and without the family. Ruby and Alex were disapproving enough; she also had to learn to live with being ostracised by the wider community.

In 1948, Matthew's widow, Kit's stepmother, died too. Mary was buried with her husband in the grave in Logie Kirk. That same year, Kit and her toddler were offered the chance of a home of their own, at 20 Glenochil Terrace, on the site of the distillery; the houses under the hills. She was returning to the place of her childhood, although not in the smarter of the two blocks, where she had lived with her father. This time she had a ground-floor single room in the second block, also parallel to the railway line. Though it was cramped, jerry-built accommodation by comparison, she was just delighted to have her own place. Did it occur to her that, at 31, she was the same age as her mother had been when she died after giving birth to her? Kit would not have been human, or a mother, if it did not cross her mind. Certainly she had very little in the way of possessions or money and her health was not good. But at last, in Ann, she had something that was all hers: someone to love unconditionally and hold in her arms, a tiny family of her own making.

Perhaps Kit rented the room on the basis of sentiment, the desire to give her little girl Ann a taste of the same childhood as her own. Perhaps there was nowhere else. Perhaps the house was tied accommodation, available to Kit through her clerkess job at the yeast factory.

Then again, perhaps somebody felt sorry for the determined, feisty invalid and pulled some strings on her behalf. Because it was around this time we know for sure that Kit McKenzie's path had crossed, properly, finally, fatefully, with a contemporary of her father's called William Kerr.

# CHAPTER 9

# The Deil's Awa' Wi' the Exciseman

'... there comes a moment when he knows
himself vulnerable; and then, as in a vertigo,
blunder upon blunder lures him'
Antoine de Saint-Exupéry, *Night Flight*

William and his mother headed down the dirt road towards the estuary, under a big, flat sky. His mother was pushing his younger brother John in a pram. It was a mile from the village to his grandfather's fishery at the edge of the saltmarshes, where the old man was waiting; he'd promised to let the boys watch him bring in the nets once the summer tide went out.

Such a strange sea it was to the child: vast and slow and shallow, and endlessly fascinating. The Solway Firth marked Scotland's south-west boundary. More than a mile across the sand and the tidal channel, which could be forded at low tide, England lay. Those were William's first memories. Such a treat it was, when the tide was receding, watching the line of men chest deep in sea, rocking on their heels to stay upright as a great sleek salmon thrashed into the netting between them. And then the joy of seeing them drag the unwieldly haaf-nets back in, especially on the days when they had smiles on their faces at the cache of heavy fish in the bag across their shoulders.

Here at the little fishery was paradise for the boys, stamping for flounder, the flat fish hidden in the sand when the tide went out. Or hunting for cockles and scallops and playing elaborate games – but not cops and robbers, or cowboys and Indians.

Oh no, the game was always smugglers and excisemen.

Even by 1900 and the dawn of a new century, the Solway Firth still felt like contraband country. Within living memory this great estuary had been Scotland's gateway for smuggled goods. It was in the blood of the people. Along this smuggler-infested coast generations had prospered from the illegal import of goods via the Isle of Man or France. Catherine Carswell, a biographer of Robert Burns, recounted wild tales of drinking on the farms, with every cup and pail needed to hold the French brandy; and of sodden servants boiling breakfast porridge in it. Fleets of small boats, wherries loaded with tobacco, brandy, tea, silk handkerchiefs, would sail up the firth, playing cat and mouse with the excisemen; and the biggest legend of all was Robert Burns himself, for hadn't the famous poet-turned-exciseman ventured onto the nearby sands and captured a smuggler's schooner?

Every local child knew the much-embroidered story; indeed, could claim to know the spot on the estuary, just to the west, where in 1792 the smuggling brig *Rosamund*, of Plymouth, had run aground. Burns, a government tax man, a gauger, had heroically waded out single-handed in breast-high water, with his pistol, and been first to board the ship. And while he waited for reinforcements from the dragoons, hadn't the poet composed an ambiguous, rollicking song about the Devil seducing an exciseman? It was not exactly true, of course; Burns had merely led one of three boarding parties in a second wave of Excise assault upon the stranded ship, but from then on every family sing-song would re-enact the thrilling, romanticised scene.

> We'll mak our maut, and we'll brew our drink,
> We'll laugh, sing, and rejoice, man,
> And mony braw thanks to the meikle black deil,
> That danc'd awa wi' th' Exciseman.
> Chorus: The deil's awa, the deil's awa,
> The deil's awa wi' the Exciseman,
> He's danc'd awa, he's danc'd awa,
> He's danc'd awa wi' the Exciseman.

William Kerr was born in 1895 to a rural existence much closer to the 1700s than the 1900s. His father was a joiner in the village of Dornock, Dumfriesshire, described by *The National Gazetteer* as 'a small unimportant place'. A mile inland from the estuary, it was home to around 900 people: fishermen mostly, and mill workers, plus the lucky few who in the 1910s got jobs in Grieve's cutting-edge Cycle Works, where push bikes, the modern craze, were made and repaired. Later came an abattoir.

William's mother, Ann, was the daughter and granddaughter of tacksmen, or tenants, of the local salmon fishery. A tacksman had legal and social standing; he was the more prosperous middleman who sub-let to others. Ann was the eldest of five daughters – her parents must have despaired of ever having a son – who grew up at the fishery. They had a manservant living there too, who helped with the fishing.

The fishing was unique to the Solway Firth. The village haaf-netters waded 100 yards out across the flats, their nets suspended on long poles between them. At other places along the sandy flats, they did it another way, hammering in posts with nets strung between them – stake fishing. Here, William recognised the familiar sight of the old man, Tom Graham, who led Mary Black, the fishery donkey, panniers on her back, across the sand to collect the salmon and the flounder.

Unlike the salmon, the flounder didn't swim out to sea – they relied on their camouflage, burying themselves in creeks and pools. The villagers would spread out upon the sand, feeling for them with their bare feet. It was a rare skill, learnt as children: once they felt the fish they would pounce on it, or strike it with a three-pronged fish spear, a 'leister'. Scary legends still abounded of the giant flounder caught in 1798: 'On Friday last there was got … in the parish of Ruthwell a most extraordinary white flounder; equal has not been heard of by the oldest person living in the place; it measured four feet and a half in length, was eighteen inches across the tail and weighed 67 lb.'

'You know your paternal grandfather was a fisherman?' I ask Gregor.

*Although his surname came, decades later, from his adoptive parents: pig breeders.*

'Too many coincidences,' he says.

'He used to catch salmon in hand nets, haaf-nets. And when your father was a boy, he learnt to catch the flounder lying in the sand.'

*His eyes light up. Flounder!*

'I used to go stamping for flounder, flukes, when I was a boy working on the farm at Langholm. We went out onto the Solway Firth, barefooted ... it adds a certain frisson, because a fluke is very shy and the whole object is to feel where they are ... You get your foot in the sand and – ooh – there's one, you feel the movement, and it goes shooting off, so you have to be quick and stand on it – but not too hard, otherwise you get mashed fish.'

*He's up on his feet, leaping round the living-room floor, miming the catching of fish with his feet. I sit laughing, but amazed too. That he, like his father, was a boyhood flounder catcher.*

*He's overjoyed by the memory.*

'If it was a little one, you left it, because there wouldn't be much eating on it. You wanted one big enough to fill a frying pan.

'We weren't far from Dornock. There were some standing nets there, stake nets, and the place was empty, just me, Billy and the kids out on the sand.

'One day we found a salmon shooting up and down in a wee pool behind the nets; they had missed it when they were checking.'

*He recounts how his cousin Carol's husband Billy Bell dispatched the salmon and they smuggled it up the leg of Gregor's trousers, just in case any fishermen were watching from the shore. Gregor hirples and staggers stiff-legged around my coffee table, miming how he walked back to the car, his hand down inside his waist-band, grasping the tail of a magnificent 15lb fish – the son of an exciseman poaching salmon on an ancient smugglers' coastline. They ate well that night.*

*'But the flounder ... Talk about another coincidence ...'*

*It is just one more thread linking past and present. Stamping for flounder is a very rare pastime. But here is father, then son, six decades apart: unknown, unknowing. Two boys out there on the same wet sand, relishing the ancient thrill of seeking fish with their bare toes.*

As a child, William Kerr was torn between his heritage, and yet, increasingly, by the sense of a new world beckoning. Every day, as he passed Bryson's grocer's shop on his way to school, he saw the steam trains on the Glasgow and South Western railway. They stopped at Dornock station to pick up fish, southbound for Billingsgate Market in London's East End. How good it would be, he thought, to get on one of those trains and see what lay beyond the flat expanse of sea and sky.

But a move was afoot in the other direction. By the time William was six, and his sister Jane just a few months old, the family had moved to Ayrshire. First they stayed in the village of Dundonald before moving to a more permanent home at 9 New Street, in the heart of Irvine. Where William went, he found the exploits of Robert Burns went too, for it was in the villages around – Mauchline, Tarbolton, Mossblown – and in Irvine itself that the poet's reputation lingered large as life. This was Burns's heartland, in an era when he was revered across the world. In 1905, according to biographer Ian McIntyre, the poet's birthplace attracted 100,000 visitors, four times more than Shakespeare's. For the young William in Ayrshire in the early years of the twentieth century, it was like growing up in Stratford today. The bard was heroic, his influence inescapable; his poetry was everywhere and if every working man was a Mason – and every man was – then almost every household had a print of Burns in his Masonic apron hanging on the wall.

The reason for the Kerrs' move was to enable their sons to get on in the world. As Robert Burns's father had done 150 years beforehand, the Kerrs moved their family a considerable distance, scraped money together for lessons and sacrificed everything they could to get the boys an education. They knew the only way to escape a life of brutal manual labour – *fighting for existence in that miserable manner'*, as Burns had put it – was through good schooling and self-betterment. William was sharp at reading, writing and arithmetic, and Irvine, a Royal Burgh and once Scotland's third port, boasted the famous Irvine Royal Academy, an ancient school established by royal charter. The school had reopened in a new building in 1901, the year the Kerrs moved there, and William went to study.

But after three years their family life was hit by tragedy. William's mother, at the age of 34, went into decline with tuberculosis. 'Galloping consumption', they called it. No antibiotics existed to cure it. She returned home to the fishery to be nursed by her sisters, hoping the sea air might rally her but she died there in 1904. William was nine, John seven and Jane not yet four. They were motherless; and her eldest son was bereft.

William did what she would have wanted: he studied hard and helped care for his sister. But four years later, when he was 13, his father remarried. His new stepmother, Margaret Glen Kerr, was small and heavy-browed, and the two did not get on. A fragment of family lore suggests she was hard on his little sister, whom he sought to defend. William was unhappy. In 1910 his stepmother produced a half-brother, David, and William, by then 15, laid plans to leave home.

He remembered the promise of that southbound railway. For certain he was inspired by childhood games of excisemen hunting smugglers. By spring 1911, this bright, ambitious 16-year-old, intent on escape and self-betterment, had bought a ticket and boarded a train to London to start a new life. He joined government service as a lowly boy clerk at Somerset House on the Strand, home of the Inland Revenue, Births, Marriages and Deaths, and the Stamp Office. William took lodgings at the home of Robert Russell, an office cleaner at the Board of Education, and his wife, Eleanor Russell, at 35 Bessborough Street, Westminster. He was one of eight boarders, young men aged between 15 and 23, most of them, like him, clerks in the civil service.

So the country lad had made his choice. He who could so easily have joined the elite ranks of the haaf-net fishermen was after a different kind of elite career in the white-collar world. In London he took on the gloss of metropolitan manners, joined a local football team and started to make his way socially. Sixteen-year-olds were perhaps more mature in 1911 than a century later.

Meanwhile, back in Irvine, his younger brother John had set his mind on becoming a schoolteacher.

'Now here's another coincidence,' says Gregor. 'Listen to this one.

'Back in the early 1990s, Vicki and I were living in the old manse in Dunlop, in Ayrshire, and our kids were at the local school.

'There was a fundraiser for the school, an auction of promises. You know the kind of thing. Someone organised a day with a fireman, or a visit to the STV studios, for parents to bid for. There was also some old school stuff for sale, including the headmaster's original chair.

'Vicki said she fancied this chair. I said, go for it. She bid strongly for it, paid about £50. And we had it at home, we still have it – a nice traditional captain's chair with arms and a rickety leg.'

Fast forward more than ten years. Gregor had finally tracked down his birth father's legitimate family and gone to meet his half-brother in Grantown-on-Spey. Who remarked on the fact that Gregor had once lived in Dunlop – and then asked if he was aware that his Uncle John had been for many years the headmaster at Dunlop school.

In other words, the chair that Vicki bought, unbeknownst to anyone, once belonged to Gregor's uncle. John Kerr, William's scholarly younger brother, had sat on it for years.

'Wow!' I say. The cogs are turning.

'But that explains something else: your grandfather, the joiner from Dornock, died in the schoolhouse in Dunlop in 1956, at the grand old age of 90. He must have gone to live there with John in his dotage. And surely, surely your father must have come to visit him there.'

'The old schoolhouse was just down the road from my house.'

Another uncanny link, past and present. A famous actor chose to buy a big, smart house in a random village. Here in the same village had once been his grandfather, uncle, father – then, 40 years later, him, the unacknowledged child.

Unknown, unknowing.

Decades apart, their footsteps overlapping; backsides resting on the same wooden chair.

'Bit bloody spooky, if you ask me,' says Gregor.

After two years as a lowly clerk at Somerset House, William Kerr had established a reputation for hard work and probity. In 1913 he was appointed assistant clerk to the Post Office. He was still too young to apply for a post as a Customs & Excise officer. Those jobs were for high-flyers; sought-after posts that brought good pay and pensions. Intelligence, integrity, maturity and a serious aptitude for mathematics were required.

But war was to disrupt everything. Dreams of an exciting, prosperous career gauging whisky and catching smugglers must be put on hold. William, by then living in Wandsworth, signed up as Private 952/527881, in the 73rd Sanitary Section of the Royal Army Medical Corps. He would later become an acting corporal and wear a stripe. Deep in the National Archives, the war diaries of the 73rd Sanitary, dutifully completed each day in the field by the officer's clerk, record his daily duties and routines. It is fair to say William's role in the Great War could never be described as the most glamorous, but there is no doubt it was deeply heroic – just not the kind of heroism that won a man the Victoria Cross. He was, effectively, a shoveller of excrement and a lavatory slopper-outer. For his first year of war he was a digger, cleaner and inspector of latrines, and subsequently the operator of a sulphur fumigator.

'He cleaned lavvies?' exclaims Gregor. 'As in, "What did you do in the war, Father?" "I cleaned the lavvies, son"?'

'Someone had to do it,' I say. 'And it meant he survived. If it hadn't been for lavvies, you might not be here.'

'Well, that's typical, isn't it? Typical! And here was I thinking the reason we couldn't find out this, that and the next thing about Papa's war record was, well, he was obviously doing something terribly important and very, very secret ... but he was actually digging shit pits. And you think, well, I suppose somebody's got to do it, haven't they? And you know, you don't get prizes or medals for work like that, so, I suppose, good on him!'

He laughs before adding: 'But there is a certain whiff about it, isn't there?'

He pauses.

'Did I tell you about the time a certain unpleasant whiff came off me?'

I shake my head.

'I was about eight years of age and I had a friend called Billy Fox, and we were, in our infinite wisdom, raking around at the bottom of a valley near Neilston, where there was a sewage works. As boys do, we thought, oh, we'll just climb this fence and see what's happening in here, and they had these big settling tanks with wooden slats over them. And Billy walked over. And I thought, I can do that. I walked over and when I got to the middle, I fell off and down I went into this concrete tank, and I could see his wee face above me and I was going up and down, because there was a current.'

'How deep was it? Were your feet on the bottom?'

'Oh, God, no! Deep. No feet on bottom.'

'Oh, Gregor!'

'And I went up and I went down, and I went up, and I went down. And I remember going down and coming back up, and Billy wasn't there. I tried to hang on to the sides, which were concrete, and I couldn't get a grip so I just kept going up and down and up and down in the dirty water. And I can remember, even as an eight-year-old, thinking, oh, this is the end of the story now! And feeling kind of terrified and calm at the same time.

'And I must have conked out because I don't remember much about the next bit, but apparently when I looked up and Billy wasn't there he had run to a big industrial laundry nearby and sounded the alarm. And a man called Mr Granger and one of his workers called Hugh Sweeney – I remember him to this day – they came. They brought a ladder, and Mr Granger held the ladder while Hugh Sweeney climbed down it and hauled me out. And I can only assume, because it was quite a feat, their adrenaline was running high.

'Then it was ambulance and hospital, stomach pump and all that kind of business, and two or three days in hospital. I remember the stomach pump being a hellish thing. I thought stomach pumps were maybe something like a foot pump for blowing up a car tyre, but oh no, a stomach pump was a tube. Right down your throat and a funnel with some water, and they pull it up again and you're bleeeeurgh! So there's nothing pumpy about it. And no matter how much I protested … ooh, God!

'Now, the newspapers must have got wind of this and as Cis and I came out the hospital there was a reporter and photographer on the steps of the Royal Alexandria Infirmary and they wanted to take a picture. I think it had made the news in some form before that and this was the follow-up story – Miracle Boy

*Returns Home,* or whatever. And as the guy put the camera up, Mother said, "No publicity, please!"'

He roars with laughter at the innocence of the memory from a pre-celebrity, pre-paparazzi age.

'No publicity, please! My wee mother!

'I was just standing there; I didn't know what this was about. Anyway, he must have been quite oily, the reporter, because he said that they had a car and that they would be more than happy to drive us back home if that would be helpful … and the idea of saving a bus fare from Paisley to Neilston appealed to Mother, so we were taken home, by which time they obviously had charmed her. I was sitting in the back, saying nothing.

'And so when we got home, I was told that I had to go and put my school uniform on because they were going to take a picture. Sitting there, me and my ba' [ball] face. It went in the paper.'

On 17 November 1915 the 73rd Sanitary embarked at Southampton, where the soldiers' first job was, appropriately, to inspect the ship's latrines. From Le Havre, they travelled to join the Allied front in northern France – Thiennes and Steenbecque, Busnes, Lillers, Béthune and Les Quesnoy – where their job was basic cleaning, disinfecting, constructing canvas latrines, digging urine pits and inspecting the billets for thousands of infantrymen. They were an early field version of an infection control unit.

Pte William Kerr is mentioned frequently by name. He spent the first few months looking after the latrines and billets of, amongst many, the Cyclists Corps and the Signallers, before filling in the urine pits as the men moved on. As 1915 drew to a close he was involved in building a sterilising plant at Béthune and working in the sulphur chamber. Most notably, he began training in the use of a new invention called a Clayton disinfector.

Even 73rd Sanitary had Christmas Day 1915 off. By early 1916, Pte Kerr's regular job had changed from cleaning field toilets to sterilising 800 articles of clothing a day.

A man could only take so much excrement.

His fiercesome machine, the Clayton disinfector, was the size of a Smart car and was, in its day, cutting-edge – the best thing yet invented to combat plague and disease. Once fired up it burnt sulphur to create sulphur-polyoxide gas, which it blew through fumigation tubes into a sealed room. From anything placed in the sulphur room for eight to twelve hours, the gas would eradicate bubonic plague spores, cholera and typhoid. The machines were used in hospitals and laundries to kill infestation.

Maintaining hygiene behind the lines and delousing clothing was safer than being an infantryman. While it lacked glamour, the work of the Sanitary Sections was in fact vital for victory in the Great War, because infection and disease, especially typhoid, were far more deadly than shells and bullets. In the Boer War, 12 or 13 years earlier, some estimates were that nearly 70 per cent of men died from filth, and the minority died by steel. The statistics had been too awful for even the traditionalists to ignore. The British Army had had to learn enough from this experience to ramp up medical and sanitary strength. As Professor Francis Cox has pointed out, historians still argue over whether the First World War was indeed where the balance was tipped; if it was the first great conflict in which disease caused fewer deaths than steel. Either way, young William was one of its unsung heroes.

Certainly more men from the Royal Army Medical Corps than from the infantry divisions came home physically unscathed when war ended. Psychologically, it may be another story, for we can only guess the sights they saw and the filth they battled daily. For William Kerr and his machine, amid the pervasive stink of sulphur and excrement, the sour reek of dirty uniforms, stale blood, ripe wounds, dirty sheets and bandages and gangrene, it must often have felt like Hades. But it was another way of winning the battle.

As war progressed, records show that the 73rd Sanitary's role evolved. The men were sent to investigate cases of cerebrospinal meningitis and scarlet fever. They inspected slaughterhouses and visited trenches to test the quality of water in newly discovered wells. But always, the basic task was managing the bodily waste of 100,000 desperate men. In November 1916 the 73rd were at Montauban, inspecting the billets around Trônes Wood.

*'Only a few scattered shallow dugouts are here. The wood itself is shelled daily and the shell holes used as latrines. In order to cope with its use for these purposes public roadside latrines were erected by the section,'* their officer serenely wrote.

Unlike his men, he didn't have to use a shovel.

In late March 1917, Gregor's father, William Kerr, and his grandfather, Matthew McKenzie, were in the same location on the Western Front, at the tail end of the Battle of the Somme. Matthew had just arrived and was succumbing to trench fever from the lice. Nearby, in the war-razed French villages of Suzanne and Corbie, Pte Kerr was fitting out a room for his Clayton disinfector.

Back home in Coatbridge, Kit, the daughter of one man, the future secret mistress of the other, was waiting to be born.

William Kerr loved poetry. As we have already learned, to his dying day he kept certain harrowing war poems in his wallet and his private papers, as if to articulate things he could not express himself from the sights witnessed in that terrible period. There was the well-known 'In Flanders Fields' by John McCrae:

> We are the Dead. Short days ago
> We lived, felt dawn, saw sunset glow,
> Loved and were loved, and now we lie
> In Flanders fields.

There too 'The Hell-gate of Soissons' by Herbert Kaufman, a harrowing narrative poem that describes the martyrdom of 12 brave English soldiers trying to take the bridge over the Aisne.

⋆ ⋆ ⋆

In 1917 William returned home to Ayrshire and the family gathered in the garden for a special photograph to celebrate his return: him, in his RAMC uniform, with his new corporal's stripe; and his brother, sister, father, grandfather, stepmother and half-brother. William looks young, bold and confident; a more worldly, assured figure than the others.

It was time to pick up his ambitions. At the end of the war, the government's Customs & Excise were desperate to hire officers and secure revenue for rebuilding. Above all else, the war-weary country needed money. In 1919 the decision was made to waive the usual entry qualifications and hire large numbers of ex-servicemen as Unattached Officers without requiring them to go through lengthy formal procedures. The men had to prove themselves bright and mathematically adept, it was true, but it was mostly considered that they were academically and ethically qualified by virtue of the war. Even without his previous service at Somerset House, William Kerr would probably have earned a post as an exciseman; as it was, he was a certainty. Records show he began his career in 1920, and from 1921 was based in Belfast.

The Belfast Customs & Excise station area included much of Western Scotland. William was posted to Port Charlotte, on Islay, one of the Western Isles and home to many famous distilleries. Although a long way from anywhere, he was self-sufficient and resourceful. And it is worth considering what a prestigious and ancient job he had landed, with a social status that set him apart. In the eighteenth century Dr Samuel Johnson described excisemen as 'wretches hired by those to whom the excise is paid', brilliantly pinning down their ambiguous position. With greater powers than the police, tasked with the safety of the state's taxation, an exciseman had to be mobile, live a separate life, be morally above reproach, remain aloof from the taint of local connections yet know absolutely everything that was going on. At least that was the theory.

According to Catherine Carswell, writing in 1930, the exciseman's post depended on a combination of harshness and obedience, an attention to detail and a perfection of book keeping. Certainly Gregor's father would spend years of his life, firstly by oil lamp, then gas, then electricity, handwriting reports and totting up figures. All with fountain pen in his neat, punctilious hand.

It seems that the excisemen were onto the idea of flexitime centuries ahead of their day. This was a world in which William Kerr was able to carve out freedoms as long as he completed his many and diverse tasks. An exciseman worked hard. He must regularly visit every public house to check the spirit books. He must also check for smuggled goods or 'grogging' – putting water in an empty cask to extract spirit in wood – or diluting the beer. In breweries he must test the gravity of the brew. As Robert Burns once wrote, good-humoured and jaunty, *'I am a poor, damn'd rascally Gauger [sic], condemned to gallop 200 miles every week to inspect dirty Ponds [sic] and yeasty barrels.'*

But the job extended far beyond alcohol. Since 1 January 1909, when old age pensions began to be paid, excisemen had to administer them. Like lawyers, they were authorised to obtain probate on small estates, getting applicants to swear on the Bible. They had to write reports on everything and give evidence in court. In short, they must have their fingers on every pulse and eyes in the back of their heads.

Posted on Islay in the Inner Hebrides, home to some of the world's most famous malts, the young William Kerr had one of the excise's most enjoyable jobs of all: distillery control. He had attained the same status as Robert Burns as a gauger: the age-old art of checking the alcohol content of spirits and overseeing bonded warehouses and their precious hoard. It was a terrific career. In 1927 the salary was £3/10s per week rising to over £8 per week, with an annual pay rise, six weeks holiday, pension and sick leave – and status, *serious* status. Officers were often asked to stand for election on local councils, as William would later do, and they were considered on a social par with solicitors and doctors.

There is a photo of William as a young officer, sitting on the grass with the family dog, back home in Irvine. He is handsome, smartly dressed, upwardly mobile, with a bow-tie, a white collar and a waistcoat, a very grown-up pipe clasped self-consciously in his teeth. He was enjoying his job, catching smugglers and cheats for real. Within two years, he had also met the woman he wanted to marry.

Twenty-eight-year-old clerkess Margaret McCulloch McDowall Barr was two years his senior. Her father, now dead, had been a fisherman – we must presume a reasonably success-ful one – and Margaret lived with her widowed mother in a substantial stone-built terraced house on Harbour Street, Irvine, with a magnificent sea view. It is possible that she and William knew each other from childhood days, perhaps even church, for his old home in New Street was a stone's throw from her house.

The pair were married in 1921 by the minister of the local Church of Scotland and their first home was with her mother in Harbour Street.

*It's another of those coincidences.*

*Gregor Fisher used to live in Harbour Street, Irvine, too. Sixty years later.*

*In the early 1980s, while working with Borderline theatre company, he shared a cottage overlooking the sea with Morag Fullerton, the artistic director, and musician Tam Harvey at the north-east end of the street. At the other end, a quarter of a mile along, were Borderline's offices and rehearsal room. Every morning Gregor would head out of his front door, turn left and walk along the waterfront; and some days the sea would sparkle in the sun and the seagulls cried; other days the prevailing southwesterly would bring driving rain off the Irish Sea and he would put down his head and hurry.*

*Many years later, after his friend Sheila Duffy had helped him find his father's marriage certificate, he and Maureen drove down to Irvine to see where William Kerr had lived. When they turned into Harbour Street, Gregor said: 'Good God, this is where Borderline used to be! I know this street.'*

*Then, slightly incredulous: 'Good heavens, I passed these houses every day!'*

*They found the house and there on the door, in very large letters, was the name Kerr. It must have been pure chance about the name, because William and his family had moved away, 80 years previously. But the fact was that, once again, he had been walking in his father's footprints.*

*He found it decidedly strange.*

While William was posted away, Margaret stayed with her mother in Irvine and the couple's first child, Sarah – Sadie – was born in 1923, at the Harbour Street address. Fifteen months later, when baby John arrived, William Kerr had moved his family into a much bigger detached townhouse further along the street. Everything he did, it seems, was mature and modestly upwardly mobile.

In 1928 he transferred to the jurisdiction of the Edinburgh station. There was a vacancy overseeing three distilleries west of Stirling – at Menstrie, Cambus and Carsebridge, near Alloa. These were three of the six founding names that had become the giant conglomerate Distillers Company Limited, later Diageo. It was too far to commute from Irvine and William was given temporary accommodation during the week in the excisemen's tied houses at Menstrie – the houses under the hills.

And so our wheel turns its first full circle. Here it was, at Glenochil Terrace, that the exciseman's path first crossed with that of the McKenzie family. Did Matthew McKenzie, at 39, view the eager, proper 34-year-old officer with a certain wry detachment? For all that he was churchy, Matthew knew that working in a distillery was a timeless game of goodies and baddies, poachers and gamekeepers. Then, as now, the industry contained many fly men, who knew every trick in the book to lay their hands on some of the precious spirit – then claim it was missing due to the quasi-mystical 'angel's share', evaporation. Everyone who worked in a whisky plant was regarded as a potential thief by the excisemen, just as every exciseman was sized up for his sharpness by the employees – that was the way it was.

John Adamson, who wrote the history of Menstrie, describes the inventive methods used by DCL employers to smuggle whisky off site. They used bodybelts, strapped hot water bottles to their chest or stomach, or placed flasks inside wellie boots. One crafty carter, who delivered to the distillery, would give his horse a nosebag while he waited to get unloaded. Beneath the chaff was concealed a container of whisky and no one thought to search there as the horse stood at the exit gates, munching away contentedly.

Sometimes it was easier just to pilfer whisky on site. The spirit continued to seep out of the wood after the casks were emptied and the distillery workers siphoned it into pails, which they hid in the corner, topped with straw. Come tea break, they would brush the straw aside and dip their mugs. Those were days long before CCTV.

The historian T. C. Smout reminds us of a world in which every trade, every industry, had its own drinking rituals. For the majority of working people, alcohol was their sole release and recreation. Illicit distilling, common everywhere rurally, had been a special tradition in the farms and villages beneath the Ochil Hills but that was being stamped out at the same time as, between 1918 and 1920, the government raised the duty on spirit from 30s per proof gallon to 72s/6d. The price of whisky rocketed just as The Licensing Act 1921 cut back on pub opening hours. In other words, reduced availability, extortionate prices and less time to drink. William Kerr had much to enforce and was greatly resented as a result.

The distilleries stored their whisky in vast bonded warehouses, covering many acres. These were effectively state holding pens under customs control. One of William's critical jobs was stocktaking there. The warehouses were fitted with two locks – one the official excise lock, which he held, the other in the possession of the company managers. One partner in the system couldn't get in without the other; it symbolised perfectly the lack of trust on both sides and explained the sideways glances that the smart young excise officer got from the workforce as he explored his new domain. How fly was he? Would he turn a blind eye?

Gauging of spirit in an oak cask was indeed an elite and mysterious art. The officer drew samples from the casks by means of a valinch, a narrow tube, and the whisky was then put in a jar. Once the sample had been tested with a hydrometer, the gauger would ask for it to be put back. 'Putting it back', however, could have more than one meaning for both wily distillery workers and sometimes even the gaugers. Former excisemen dined out on tales of fellow officers who made lunchtime soup laced with remnants of wines or spirits they knew how to acquire.

The 'angels' share' was the portion of alcohol lost to evaporation during aging in oak barrels. In higher humidities, like rainy Scotland, more alcohol was lost and the strength of the product reduced. Which is why bonded warehouses and the area around them – the roofs, trees, chimneys, cars, washing lines and houses – grow a dirty dark fungus, the angels' share fungus, *Baudoinia compniacensis*.

As William Kerr settled into his new enforcement role, he became acquainted with Matthew McKenzie. They met on the factory floor or on the short path between their respective flats and the factory. William saw Matthew's children playing outside on the stone steps or on the drying green. They were much the same age as his own little ones, still living in Irvine, waiting to join him. Perhaps he learnt their names: Isabella, Ruby, headstrong little Kit.

Matthew and William were both Masons, which made them sworn brothers. In fact almost every man from that period – teacher, solicitor, police, tradesman, businessman, builder, labourer – was a brother. It is hard now, from the liberal, feminised twenty-first century, to grasp just how pervasive freemasonry was. All Protestant working men belonged, all women were excluded – it was a fellowship as natural as breathing.

For excisemen, the Masonic movement was essential. It promoted trust, access and communication; it was the way to be in the know. As Horace Sheppard, William's contemporary in the Excise, intoned a trifle pompously: '*So many of the traders and businessmen of the area were Masons too, but I did not let that interfere with my official controls required as an excise officer.*' William Kerr, his boyhood shaped in Dumfriesshire and Ayrshire, had grown up with Robert Burns the Masonic hero in his bloodstream. And as a boy he had seen how, when a Mason died, a splendid deputation was sent to the funeral by the local lodge. In bowler hats and black suits, wearing their Masonic aprons, the men marched two abreast behind their Master with the white stick, their attendance duly noted in the local press.

It was simply the way of things then.

William Kerr arranged for his family to join him as soon as he could (an officer was given an allowance for a move). In December 1929 he and Margaret had their third and final child, Dorothy, who was born at a rented house in the village of Cambus, close to the bonded warehouses. William was very busy then: within a few months of Dorothy's arrival came the introduction of pensions for widows over 50, which meant a big expansion of his workload, but he was well compensated by a one-off lump sum of £40 – about £1,175 today.

By 1933 electric light had arrived and William was settled, prosperous and an experienced gauger. He had a car for work, a good wife and three bright children, whom he wanted to see do well, just as his father had done for him. Unmistakably, the job offered conscientious, hard-working men like him the chance to rise in social class. Soon the Kerr family moved into a stylish new semi-detached at 2 Park Terrace, Tullibody. That was another perk – excisemen were recompensed on mortgage payments. If the rented house in Harbour Street had had a beautiful view over water and sea marsh, then Park Terrace had at least a large open park facing it and space for the prestigious motor car. It was a good life, well paid and secure, with high public standing.

In 1938 the distillery community learned of Matthew McKenzie's terrible accident at the Menstrie yeast factory. It was a big funeral and William may have gone as a matter of neighbourly and Masonic duty.

At home, William and Margaret's children were high achievers. Sadie was training to be an accountant, but John, who had done well at Alloa Academy, had taken what his father thought was a strange notion to become a journalist. William spoke to his contacts within the industry and diverted his boy to a proper job with Inde Coope Brewery – John duly went off to Leeds and Burton-on-Trent to train and qualify as a brewer.

In 1945, as William reached the statesmanlike age of 50, he was invited to stand as an Independent candidate for Tullibody on Clackmannan County Council. He was duly elected. William Kerr, in middle age, had made it; liked and well known, he was at the pinnacle of local respectability. As a politician, he found a pressing problem of the time was the shortage of housing. Council houses, controversially, were being given to incomers rather than locals, and there were unavoidable rent and rates increases.

Sometime in these immediate post-war years, Kit McKenzie enters the story again. In 1948, by now with an illegitimate baby and failing health, she was about to be made homeless. Sister Ruby and her husband Alexander had given up the tenancy of their council house in Menstrie and could not, or did not wish to, shelter the fallen woman any longer. Did Kit seek William's help because he was a familiar, avuncular face, now a councillor, and acquainted with her late father? After all, they both worked at the distillery and perhaps she knew him from works dances.

Could it have been, because he was a kindly man, that on her behalf he managed to pull some strings with the bosses at DCL, who owned the flats at Glenochil Terrace? Did he persuade them that one of their clerkesses was a worthy tenant, especially as she was the orphaned daughter of the unfortunate Matthew McKenzie? We cannot know precisely how things came to pass but later that year Kit and Ann moved into a primitive single-room flat in the older of the buildings, the houses under the hills.

By the time William Kerr stood for re-election to Clackmannan County Council in May 1952, his main concern as a councillor, he announced in his campaign literature, was the residents' welfare. Note the precise, cautious wording of a civil servant with a lifetime of writing official reports: *'Housing problems have always had my careful and impartial considera-tion. I have tried to carry out my public duties conscientiously –*

*without fear or favour.'* The vast increase in the size of the community had brought problems of overuse of shopping facilities, water supply, sewage and sanitation, he regretted. He promised to do all he could to tackle such matters.

There was no doubt about the size of the problem. Scottish housing was always abysmal, to use T. C. Smout's uncompromising adjective, and especially in comparison with England. At that date, south of the border only 2.6 per cent of the population were still being forced to live in one or two rooms. The equivalent figure for Scotland was a devastating 25 per cent, nearly 10 times more.

At home, in William's well-appointed, comfortable house opposite the park, his loyal and kindly Margaret, a dedicated wife for more than 30 years, kept his food warm for him when he was delayed at election hustings. His constituents saw him as a modest but influential man, who tried his best for them.

Everyone trusted William. Why, he'd just become a grandfather, did you hear?

Who knows what the voters might have thought, as they picked up their polling cards that May morning, had they known William Kerr's secret mistress was eight months pregnant with the first of their two children, and living in a single-room with an outside toilet, no electricity and no running water, down a little-used railway track at the back of the old distillery. In those old houses under the hills, now shabby and nearing demolition.

Because by now the Devil really had gone awa' wi' the exciseman.

We're on another expedition together, Gregor Fisher and me.

After a bit we reach Stirling and turn east, in a straight line along the bottom of the Ochil Hills. The road runs flat along the valley floor and, at our left shoulder, the hills rear up dramatically, a long, forbidding line. Craggy. Landscape the way a child would draw it. To see the top of the hills, you have to lean towards the windscreen and peer upwards.

We pass through one former industrial village in the shadow of the hills. Then approach the next.

'This is Menstrie,' I say. 'This is where you come from.'

'Yeah, um, yeah, never quite fancied the name ...' He squirms like a schoolboy.

'How d'you mean?'

'Well, you know ... Menstrie ... you know, Menstrie ...' That rich, droll voice.

'Oh,' I say, starting to laugh. 'Women's things, periods.'

'Yeah, all that.'

We turn right and suddenly the layout that I've memorised from old maps and aerial photos is upon us. Here's the old hump-back bridge. I pull over in front of it, eager to show off the results of my detective work.

'The house where you lived with your mother was just down there on the left, where those trees are. It's gone now. This was a railway line; it ran behind your house. Behind your house was the field, then the steep hills.'

He stares out of the window, is silent for a bit.

'So my mother would have pushed me along here, over this bridge in my pram?'

'Well, yes, I guess so.'

*When he speaks again, his voice is abrupt. He's still looking out of the window.*

'What I can't understand is why I was abandoned. How did that happen?'

*And all at once I'm anxious to try and ease his hurt; and at the same time eager to defend the memory of a woman who exists for me only as a name on a death certificate. To defend her for the sake of every mother who screws up. Which means all of us.*

'But your mother didn't abandon you. She died, Gregor. She couldn't help it. She died. You know that. She must have died desperate about leaving you.'

'Yeah, I'm not talking about my mother. I'm talking about my father.'

*I pause, searching for words.*

'He had no choice, did he? Not in those days.'

# CHAPTER 10

# Evening Comes, I Miss You More

But pleasures are like poppies spread,
You seize the flow'r, its bloom is shed;
Or like the snow falls in the river,
A moment white – then melts forever.
'Tam O'Shanter', Robert Burns

Just like his mother's birth, 37 years earlier, Gregor Fisher's arrival was not particularly auspicious. He was illegitimate, for a start, which was a difficult label to be lumbered with the minute you drew your first breath, when you hadn't done anything but be born, but that was the way of things in sanctimonious 1953. His mother, Kit, was a very sick woman with a long-term heart complaint, who already had two other fatherless children.

When Gregor was taken home from the old Airthrey Castle Maternity Hospital, near Stirling, it was to what, these days, we'd call unfit for human habitation. Kit's place in the houses under the hills was just one room, one window, no running water, no sink and no toilet, but there was also a warm fire, hot food, devotion, unconditional love and clean clothes. Make no mistake, however, this little family, the unmarried mother with three young children, were outcasts and living in poverty.

That's how it was. We can't embroider those facts. We can't say it was *Angela's Ashes*, because things weren't that bad. It was simply a tough start, and it was where the comic actor Gregor Fisher, the man who made Scotland laugh, came from. One day, his legendary Rab C. Nesbitt character would enter every living room, say the unsayable; tell a country the blackest, funniest truths about itself. And it all began there, with a scandalous, hidden affair between a vulnerable, lonely woman and a venerable married public figure, a man old enough to be her father.

Say it like that, in tabloidese, and it may be shocking. In fact, however many times you walk around the facts, look at them from different angles, couch them in softer language, it's never an easy story.

So was Gregor a lovechild, born of a genuine but doomed romance, or was he just, well ...

*'Welcome to a bastard wean,' says Gregor harshly, shrugging, putting on the 'I-don't-care' hard man face.*

No one on the outside ever understands what brings two people together in a lasting relationship. We can make the usual guesses, of course: lust, love, loneliness, need, power, ego, friendship ... they all play their part. Whatever dreams William Kerr and Kit McKenzie shared will never be known. We have little more than the bald facts of a pairing that in its day was scandalous.

William Kerr, Gregor's father, was a man whose reputation went before him. He was a politician and a government officer in a supposedly unimpeachable, quasi-judicial role. Plus, he was an old man, by the standards of the day. Nearing 60 years old, he was prosperous, well connected and lived a comfortable middle-class life with an impeccably respectable wife and three high-achieving, well-educated children.

A cautious Victorian, you might say, with a lot to lose.

Gregor's mother was a Nobody to her lover's Somebody. Kit was 22 years younger than William Kerr: that is, much the same age as his daughter. Considerably lowlier and poorer in status than him, she was a clerkess in a factory where he officiated and when they began their affair she already carried, cruelly, the stigma of being a fallen woman, mother to one illegitimate child. Some folk in the community ostracised her; others, who knew she suffered chronic ill health and had had a tough life, felt sorry for her. She and her daughter Ann, when they first moved into a rented place of their own at Glenochil Terrace, were poor, socially isolated, had few possessions and no luxuries. Photographs taken from works dances show a woman with a wide, intelligent face, attractive but care-worn, with an ever-hopeful look. You can tell that she has had a hard life but you can also see her spirit in the tilt of her chin and proud shoulders.

She put on a brave front, said her eldest daughter, because it was all she had.

William Kerr, from contemporary photographs, was dignified, verging on portly, and had a twinkle in his eye. Can we discern a faint version of the expression on Gregor's face, one that suggests a laugh is never very far away? We can make the case that Kit had known him most of her life; he had always been pleasant to her. Now that her little Ann had started school and Kit was able to pick up her work as a clerkess in the yeast factory, she saw more of him. It is possible she did some secretarial duties for him. Maybe in the beginning William made Kit smile; or maybe it is even more basic than that – that he noticed her, spoke to her, simply made her feel that she wasn't invisible. When a woman is ostracised in a community and feels alone in the world, with precious little going for her, and even less to look forward to, then attention from a man can stir heady emotions. Kit was in her early thirties, with little prospect of ever finding a husband, and a woman's heart flutters readily when she is lonely. A flirt, a wink, eyes meeting across an office … these things sparkle in a dull life and take on a disproportionate meaning. In the head of a solitary girl a crush will blossom fast; daydreams of romance will grow wings.

William was, by all accounts, a well-intentioned man. He knew her father; knew her sad past. Maybe he felt sorry for her and tried to help her. Then again, maybe he was an opportunist.

For Gregor and Maureen, the children he conceived with Kit, here lies the centre of their pain: they don't know what the truth is, they can only wish.

*The archive of the global drinks giant Diageo, happily for us, is in Menstrie, at the old Glenochil Distillery. We're inside its cool white splendour, in late autumn 2014. Gregor and Jo, the archivist, are discussing the mysteries of yeast production.*

'Hey, listen to this!' I interrupt (*I'm reading an account of Menstrie's history*). 'It says Glenochil Terrace was built in Victorian times to house visiting customs and excisemen.'

*We stare at each other.*

'That's our link – William Kerr was an exciseman.'

*Now I'm testing the narrative.* 'He knew the houses. He almost certainly stayed there, way back in the 1920s.'

'And that's where my mother lived when she had his children ... us.'

'The pictures prove the houses were still there in the 1950s.'

*It's another smoking gun. We're transfixed with the drama.*

'What a boy!' *Gregor is twinkling laddishly.* 'His second family. Maybe he tucked her away there, maybe he pulled influence with his friends at DCL to get her a house.'

*Jo is looking from one of us to the other, wide-eyed, caught up in it.*

'And customs officers have to be above reproach,' *she says.*

'Think about it,' *says Gregor.* 'Why not? He's been married a long time. He's been through the horrors of war. He says, "I'm going to take happiness where I can find it." He's a practical man, he's going to go for it.'

'But maybe he really loved her,' *I say.* 'Remember the poem.'

*Gregor rolls his eyes at me.*

'Ach, female romanticism.'

'You're being very cynical.'

'Maybe you're both right,' *says Jo.*

*I know which version of the story Gregor, secretly, desperately, wants to believe. But I still haven't found Number 20 Glenochil Terrace, where he lived as a baby. His birth certificate says so. The house just doesn't seem to exist.*

Whatever the circumstances that led William and Kit to come together, we will never know. Lovers are always inventive. In the distilleries and the yeast factory William had the familiarity and sense of entitlement that come from being in authority for 25 years. It was his fiefdom and had been for a generation. People called him Mr Kerr, said yes, sir, no, sir; treated him as a big boss. This was a deferential age. We know William could organise his working day to suit himself; we know Kit was strong-willed and feisty. However the romance started, the couple's first child, Maureen, was born on 12 June 1952. Only Kit's name was put on the birth certificate, and she brazenly kept the baby instead of giving it away. She alone was happy to have another child to love and cherish; others were horrified. Events were cloaked in subterfuge, but people doubtless judged Kit harshly, wondered why the baby wasn't adopted and speculated on the father. We can be fairly sure it was then that Kit's sister Ruby distanced herself. Her disgraceful sister really had gone too far this time. As the social historian Jane Robinson puts it, unmarried mothers were trouble – they disrupted family relationships and embedded a fat, dirty, unbidden secret into everyone's lives. The fact that the rumoured father was married, and therefore an adulterer, made the situation doubly scandalous and embarrassing.

It is interesting to note even Thomas Barnardo, who started a home for destitute street children in Victorian London, had his limits when it came to illegitimate children. Robinson points out that Doctor Barnardo would help the single mother, but if she were to 'fall' again his doors were closed; one mistake was your limit. He would not condone sin and he did not accept that illegitimate children were morally untainted. As if to confirm this, little Maureen was christened in the vestry at Menstrie

Kirk – in private, in other words, presumably because the minister considered it too shameful to christen a bastard baby in front of the congregation. The Church's compassion did stretch to allowing Ann to attend Sunday school, though.

In public, things carried on as normal. Nobody said anything openly about Kit's scandalous behaviour, especially not at work. In the 1950s these things were buried deep. But there are few secrets in small communities; few office romances ever go undiscovered. And the timing was uncomfortable. William Kerr had newly become a grandfather, when his eldest daughter, Sarah, gave birth to his grandson Martin. Just seven months later his illegitimate daughter Maureen was born. Did he celebrate one christening, and feel sad over the child who could not be christened openly? As if to raise the stakes, five months after Maureen's arrival Sarah gave him a second grandchild, this time a daughter. What glorious illicit gossip: Bill Kerr at the age of 57 having an illegitimate daughter, book-ended by legitimate grandchildren. One child to shun, the others to boast about.

Robert Burns did things like that 200 years ago, and maybe William had long envied the licentious spirit of the poet; but surely to goodness no one in his position could get away with it now? The potency of the secret, dangerous as sweaty Semtex, must surely have seized William Kerr when he woke in the middle of the night and considered the possibility of discovery. After nearly 40 years as a meticulous, controlled bureaucrat, he had thrown all caution to the winds in a quite spectacular way. Love can indeed be a form of insanity.

Plainly the feelings between the two lovers were strong and their hidden relationship endured, despite the risks. Whatever the wisdom of their behaviour, Kit became pregnant again. Why on earth, given the circumstances, did they allow themselves to create another child? And why did she choose to keep this one as well? Several interpretations are possible. Naïvety, we can surely discount. Fecklessness seems highly unlikely. Clearly Kit desperately wanted a family, and was strong and determined enough to refuse to part with her babies when society, reason and lack of money all said she should. When you are very poor, love is one of the very few things that is free. Besides, William, by continuing to see her, was giving her strong signals that he cared.

Kit's reputation, though, was truly beyond repair. As the gossips might see it, perhaps she might be forgiven the first baby – that Peter Cameron had been a bad lot, hadn't he, to leave her like that? But to do so again? And, word had it, to do so with a married man the same age as her father. And to think of that dear father of hers, Matthew McKenzie, God rest his soul, playing the organ in church all those years and she's done this. And now another one, a *third* baby out of wedlock? And she's keeping it too. Shameless! Dearie me …

Oh yes, the cheap script is always easier to write. Illegitimacy was always, but always, the mother's fault. Did anyone, in those judgemental days, blame William Kerr? Did anyone think: dirty old man in a position of power taking advantage of a poor sick lassie like that? And if they had, was that interpretation any more correct? There is nothing to rule out a high-risk, consensual romance between a lonely, nothing-to-lose woman and an old man in a long worthy marriage set alight by passion like a teenager. It happens; reason deserts lovers. When it comes to behaviour, to quote the writer Gavin Francis, few of us manage to be who we aspire to be.

There are many differing ways to look through the prism at this doomed private drama. Ann, Gregor's older half-sister, tells a painfully authentic version, seen through the eyes of the child carer of a sick mother. Kit was so disabled by her bad heart valves that her eldest daughter had to look after her throughout their time together. Latterly, Ann used to run home from school as fast as she could along the open path beside the sparsely used railway track where the train drivers knew her and waved at her. Often she had to run home in lunchbreak as well, to give Gregor his bottle and to check that her mum hadn't fainted. She had been taught by the doctor and Mrs McAdam how to revive Kit. When her mother did have one of her frequent funny turns and passed out in a chair or on the bed, Ann knew the drill. Gently, she was first to tap her mother's cheeks to bring her round; she then had to lift up her head and put a glass of water to her lips. Mum would recover after that if she just sat and rested for a bit.

'It was just my heart taking a wee funny turn,' she would tell Ann, with a brave smile. 'Don't worry about me.'

Despite her weakness, Kit still had to work – there was no disability benefit then. She got five shillings a week in family allowance. She sustained two jobs, as a clerkess at DCL and as a cleaner of big private houses. One of the houses she cleaned was a grand place up the hill in the nearby village of Blairlogie – Ann remembers playing quietly in the big rooms while her mother cleaned. The house seemed like a palace to the little girl. Sometimes Kit supplemented her income with bar work in the village. If William Kerr helped pay for his children, it was never obvious. Life was a struggle.

To Ann's knowledge, William never came to their home in Glenochil Terrace. She never met him. To this day she does not know what he looked like.

'I can only ever remember Mum and the three of us,' she says.

When Maureen was born, nothing was said to Ann about the absence of a father. Maybe, and she would not be the first mistress to do so, Kit fantasised that one day William would leave his wife and they would be together; daydreams, happily, were also free. It seems clear she yearned for a family to recreate the love and togetherness that life had repeatedly denied her. Possibly she was rebellious, rejecting the Church teachings imprinted upon her; a woman who snatched at passing pleasures, and never mind the consequences; and then again, maybe she was so mentally strong that she didn't give a damn about convention. Sensing her time was short, she would make the best of it. We would not now dream of questioning the motives of a modern single woman, but to seek and keep illegitimate children in the 1950s was, at the very least, a moral curiosity.

When Gregor entered, stage right, 18 months after Maureen, he was the star of the show even then: a chubby, healthy baby, good enough to eat, with blond curls and bright blue eyes. His mother had thrown public censure to the wind and he was her reward, the best gift of all, a new life arriving on 22 December 1953. Christmas babies are special, and this one was celebrated and fussed over by his mother and young sisters, even if shunned by everyone else. For the little family, home in the houses under the hills was the gas-lit single room on the ground floor, with the solitary window facing south towards the yeast factory. It wasn't quite Long Row in Coatbridge, but it was still very primitive. Ann and Maureen remember a double bed in an alcove, where Kit and Ann slept, with the two younger ones in cots alongside. They had a wardrobe, a gas cooker and a fireplace, a table and chair, a dressing table and an easy chair. Water was fetched from a standpipe outside; and outside too was a shared toilet and washhouse, where they washed in the sink and their mother boiled water and scrubbed their clothes by hand.

The Diageo archive is just a couple of hundred yards from the former site of the houses under the hills, where Gregor spent his first Christmas. There's an overpoweringly pungent smell of yeast in the winter air – almost vile, almost pleasant, always unforgettable.

'Phooar!' he says.

And then: 'I remember that smell ... quite like it, actually.'

The rooks are cawing loudly, circling in and out of the bare trees.

He's got something pressing to ask Jo the archivist.

'Menstrie, what does the name mean?'

Deadpan.

'The plain on the strath,' says Jo.

He beams. 'Oh, I'm happy about that,' he says. 'I really am.'

No more women's things.

By the time Maureen and Gregor arrived, Ann had effectively become the carer for the whole family. Kit's dizzy spells were getting more and more frequent. Regularly, after Ann had patted her mother's face and brought her round from a funny turn, the little girl would put Gregor and Maureen in the pram and take them out for a walk to give her mum peace and quiet to recover. The brave little gang would go along the tracks around the yeast factory and the bonded warehouses, passing the farm and the piggery. Ann remembers the day when a pig, a pig as big as she was, got loose and started chasing her, and she was running, running, heart racing in terror as she pushed the pram with the babies in it. She also vividly recalls another incident when they were playing outside, after another of her mother's episodes, and a bee went up Gregor's nose. She had to cope. Thinking quickly, she held his nose and squeezed his nostrils to make him sneeze. The bee backed out rapidly without stinging him.

In reality, there was precious little time to create memories and Ann herself was fragile. With the kind of bad fortune that never left the family, when she was eight she was rushed into hospital to have a kidney removed in an emergency operation. She remembers how it began – being in bed at home, in excruciating pain. Her mother gave her a cup of cocoa while the doctor went to phone for an ambulance. 'I was much more anxious of spilling the cocoa and giving Mum more washing to do than I was about going in an ambulance,' she says. She ended up spending seven months in hospital, being fed tripe and raw eggs whipped in milk, and when she came home she was so frail she went to stay with Aunt Ruby for a little while.

By now, with the children aged nine, three and one, Kit's own health was becoming an insurmountable issue; as her heart valves deteriorated she became weaker. From 1954 onwards Ann, Maureen and Gregor were in and out of children's homes, placed there temporarily while their mother was very ill. When she recovered enough they came home.

From Ann, a wise and warm survivor of her past, there comes a moving picture of an embattled family unit, desperately precarious because of Kit's health, but nevertheless strong – fighting setback after setback. They were, in Ann's words, 'terribly ostracised' by parts of the community, but there was one good friend in Mrs McAdam in the village and the old gentleman in the flat next door to them. Ann would ride over on her bike and do Mrs McAdam's shopping for her, and the older woman was a great support to Kit. Decades later, as we have seen, when both lovers were long dead, Mrs McAdam was still loyal enough to be reluctant to speak William Kerr's name.

How brave can a woman be? Despite her fast-failing heart and the social isolation she faced, Gregor's mother demonstrated astonishing resilience – a feisty person, mentally strong, whose attitude, Ann recalled, was, 'We'll get on with it. We'll get back on our feet and keep fighting. Our mother was wonderful.' Kit cared tenaciously for her babies, making it clear they were precious, wanted. And if people judged her, she squared her shoulders and remembered how much she loved her family and her mystery man.

Don't forget, this was a proud woman whose cakes always had to be put in a nice posh box.

Kit was, in her eldest daughter's memory, a terrific cook, too; she made a great clootie dumpling (a rich fruit pudding). But above all else she left implanted in Ann's head the surety that she had total love and adoration for her children. It is one of the great sadnesses of this story that Maureen and Gregor were too young to understand that.

'We were her priority. I never remember feeling hungry, cold or unloved – and we all want to be loved, don't we?' says Ann.

The children were always as smartly turned out as possible, as was Kit. They certainly did not live in squalor. There are pictures of Kit at works dances, careworn but in a long satiny dress, almost certainly homemade. Her head was up and proud, she had a good figure too; she was plainly determined to enjoy life as much as possible. Ann has memories of family laughter, and fun, dancing around the room to music on the acid battery-powered radio.

Her mother occasionally went out. One evening, after Ann, the babysitter for the two little ones, had fallen asleep, she woke to a great crash. Kit had thrown something through the window to wake her daughter up, and whatever it was had landed on the floor.

'Happiness was there. Mum didn't have an easy life but love was there and love is self-sustaining.'

And there was another poignant little memory. As an underdog, Kit McKenzie seems to have had compassion for creatures even further down the pecking order than she was. Ann recalled the time when mice ate the family's cheese.

'I remember Mum said: "Well, they deserve to live. They have got the cheese."'

*We're still in the archive and I'm pursuing the houses under the hills. I'm determined to solve the mystery of Gregor's first home: the phantom building. I'm sure it's the key to things. I've found the haunting picture of Numbers 2–12 Glenochil Terrace, where Gregor's grandfather lived. But nothing next door, no Number 20. I'm convinced it was once here; I just need that final bit of proof. While I'm doing detective work with maps and aerial photos, Gregor is doing what he does best: charming everyone to bits.*

*They are swapping stories of family illegitimacy; cautiously, at first.*

*'My grandfather worked at the factory here too,' says Jo. 'He and my grandmother lived in Menstrie.'*

*'Maybe we're related,' cries Gregor.*

*'Oh, probably.'*

*'These small villages …'*

*'There is a certain Menstrie look,' she says.*

*They pose together, facing me, and ask me to spot the resemblance.*

*I think he's feeling better about things.*

*I've found a picture from 1928 that clearly shows three build-ings by the railway line. The houses under the hills. The mystery of 20 Glenochil Terrace is solved. There was a second tenement of flats and a washhouse. Now there's proof: Numbers 14–20, bull-dozed long before Numbers 2–12.*

*I've also got the magnificently atmospheric photograph of the bigger tenement.*

*'I remember standing in that allotment,' says Gregor, looking at the picture, a record for posterity taken before final demolition in the early 1960s, by a man from the Royal Commission on the Ancient and Historical Monuments of Scotland (RCAHMS).*

Then he says: 'I also remember stone steps.'

Jo finds a magnifying glass and we zoom in on an aerial picture taken from the north in the 1950s.

There they are – outside stone stairs round the back of the building.

His memory is correct.

Later, we drive up the bumpy back track, past the molasses tanks for the yeast making and the vast acreage of bonded warehouses. The angel's share fungus from the whisky, Baudoinia compniacensis, streaks the walls and roofs of all the buildings. Everything is dirty green and black, like the contents of a mouldy fridge.

'That's where the house was,' I say. 'Go look.'

The rooks are still noisy. He wanders off along what was once the railway line, lighting a fag. When he comes back, he shrugs.

'There's nothing there now, not a stone. The only memory is the smell … and the hills. I remember them. Thinking back, I've always loved mountains, they've always been there. Am I making this up? For a child, these hills are like Alps.'

'No, you're not making it up,' I say.

What of William Kerr, who was plainly never a presence in his children's lives? What did he offer her, this old man with twinkly eyes? We can speculate – charm, humour, attention. Perhaps a sense, albeit fleeting, of security. Fun. Laughter. A few stolen nights out, when she felt young again and wanted as a woman; a few moments of escape and happiness; dreams. A warm body to hold in intimate embrace, something she had been starved of. All of these are very human cravings.

Did William's relationship with the frail, headstrong creature endure because behind all the subterfuge and the stigma, there was love? Why else would he risk so much? Ann is pragmatic. With hindsight, she believes it was a love affair, and thinks that the knowledge that William cared about her mother was what sustained her. It gave her the strength to deal with the rejection of others, just as she had learnt to deal with the first rejection by Peter Cameron.

The tragedy is, of course, that William Kerr's secret family was not one that he was ever able to visit, love and cherish. There was too much at stake for him. We do not know if he ever saw them or held them; or ever visited her deprived accommodation, this county councillor who broadcast his concern about the state of overcrowded local housing and lack of inside toilets. It was indeed a man's world, and a hypocritical one at that.

William drove home from work at Glenochil, half a mile up over the bridge across the River Devon to his nice house at 2 Park Terrace, Tullibody, and a welcoming supper on the table from his loyal Margaret, a woman two years his senior, by this time a pensioner. In an era when women aged quickly, she was twice as old as his mistress and looked very much the elderly, kindly grandmother she was.

Such were the uncomfortable facts of his betrayal.

It's mid-afternoon, November 2014, and the school run is in full swing in Tullibody. Down the road from the school, on Park Terrace, I drop Gregor off outside his father's old semi-detached house opposite the park. Back in the 1930s, when they moved in, it would have been a smart, spacious home, this, for the middle class. Several bedrooms upstairs, a large, stylish roof, extravagant enough to prove there was an architect involved, and money to pay for style over substance.

Gregor has finished chatting to the woman on the street outside and returns to the car.

'She says new people live there now. She's not been here long herself.'

He's silent for a bit before adding, 'Did he have a dog? Did he walk around the park?'

I don't say anything.

'I wonder if he ever lay at night wondering about Kit's children? His children? About us?'

There is evidence, however fragmentary, that he did; indeed that he cared very much. If we seek proof that William Kerr really loved Kit, it is in the fact that he went back even after his wife had discovered about the affair and the existence of Maureen. He refused to stop seeing her. Not only that, but he remained so much in touch with her that he fathered another child with her fairly soon afterwards. These are not the actions of a man who seeks only casual sex, or an inveterate womaniser; they speak of a man who is emotionally involved. Kit McKenzie can be seen as William's Jean Armour: Robert Burns used Jean, seduced her, two- or three-timed her, sired her several children out of wedlock, but ignored the shame and kept returning to her.

> Ay waukin, Oh,
> Waukin still and weary:
> Sleep I can get nane,
> For thinking on my dearie.

The difference is that Burns eventually married Jean and legitimised his children with her.

But something else points to William's affection for Kit: the fact that he was prepared to put so much at risk for her. Nothing he had done in life up to this point gives the impression he was a gambler. On the contrary, he had been an obedient soldier in a particularly filthy job and then a lifelong civil servant, schooled in precision and measurement, a stickler for upholding laws, rules and regulations. Yes, for sure, an exciseman's role had ambiguity at its core, as Burns had shown, but William's had been a lasting, careful career. He had so much at stake: he had a reputation in the community for steadiness and integrity; his three children had done well at Alloa Academy and were all upwardly mobile; his job, his political future, his home, his family, his pension … all these could be placed in jeopardy. For a man of such a sensible temperament to behave in such a rash way and then to persist in his rashness suggests the madness of love.

There is another reason why Kit may have touched his heart: their lives had a strange symmetry. She was left motherless as a baby; and he too was only a small boy when his own mother died. Plus, his mother died not long after giving birth to his sister Jane, and he had cared for and protected the little girl. He knew what Kit had gone through and he felt paternal towards her.

It was also, of course, a whole lot more simple than that. As Gregor suggested, his father was a man who had been scarred by his experiences in war, then made dusty by decades of probity and book keeping, and was now staring at his own mortality. He wanted to snatch some forbidden joy before he died. The 1950s, as the comedian George Burns once put it, was the decade when 'the air was clean and the sex was dirty'. But men and women still wanted each other.

However it happened, William was found out. Either he had volunteered the information to his wife Margaret – which seems unlikely – or someone had gossiped. In the early 1950s their youngest daughter Dorothy, in her twenties and still living at home, was upstairs one evening when she heard her parents shouting below. It was not a house where people rowed and she crept to the top of the stairs to listen.

Decades later, recounting the story to Gregor and Maureen, Dorothy became deeply emotional. What she had heard impacted on the rest of her life. From the raised voices travelling up the stairs, Dorothy gathered that a woman in Menstrie had given birth to her father's child, a little girl. Her mother knew and she was falling apart. Dorothy gripped the stair rail, listening to her sedate, respectable, going-on-elderly Mummy and Daddy, their shared life dissolving into deceit and anguish.

For Margaret Kerr it must have been indescribably painful. For Dorothy, the baby of the family, it was shattering – the revelation that her beloved father was unfaithful to her mother; that he was not the perfect man she thought he was, that he was a sexual being. And there was an illegitimate child. The knowledge was profoundly shocking and she buried it deep inside her. As was the way of it in the 1950s, these things must simply be closed off.

The turmoil and distress within 2 Park Terrace was profound, but nothing was visible to the outside world. Nobody knows how long the atmosphere in the house remained difficult. At some point, presumably, there was some *rapprochement* and the couple made an attempt to get back to normality, as countless partners have done after such a betrayal. William Kerr had to gamble that his wife would keep quiet for the sake of a comfortable life, sure in the knowledge that divorce in itself, balanced on the 1950s morality scales, was as much of a scandal as a mistress and bastard child. His poor wife probably felt she had little option but to accept and bury the horrid secret. Those were the days when few people walked away from their marriage vows. And we have no reason to believe she was anything other than devoted to him.

Of course, as we know, William returned to the arms of his mistress – indeed perhaps he never left them – and in the spring of 1953 Kit became pregnant again with Gregor. She was expecting at the same time as his eldest daughter Sarah and, as we have seen, gave birth five months before her. These parallels are cruel in the telling. While Mr and Mrs Kerr, grandparents again, cooed over Sarah's new baby in middle-class suburbia, the infant boy, unacknowledged, kicked his heels in the damp little room under the hills.

William's boat was becoming increasingly unlikely to be rocked. In 1954, the Kerrs' son John announced his engagement to Jane, the daughter of a wealthy family with a large estate in the Borders. They had met at the National Trust for Scotland, where John, anxious to avoid a brewing career, was pursuing a writing livelihood. The wedding was a fairly grand affair in Knightsbridge in London. Dorothy was a bridesmaid. The ceremony took place in February 1955 and pictures show William as a dignified, avuncular, balding man of 59, wearing coat tails. He definitely had a face that looked as if it liked to laugh, and you would not mistake him for anyone other than Gregor Fisher's father. His wife Margaret looked like a sweet, proper, be-gloved old lady. She was 62 and wore homely round glasses, a sensible, well-cut woollen coat and thick tights on swollen ankles. Dwelling on her wistful face rather breaks one's heart. For a man leading an outrageous double life, William Kerr looked remarkably content. As the biographer Catherine Carswell said of Robert Burns, 'At the best he is confronted by two conflicting evils, between which he must choose; at worst by two conflicting truths from neither of which he can escape. Such was the warp and woof of Robert's life.' But William, like Burns, seemed perfectly able to live with himself.

The following year brought catastrophe. Early in the spring, after a tough winter in that single room, Kit's health was failing badly. The rheumatic endocarditis, dating from childhood, plus two babies to look after, was taking its toll. Moves were made to get her into hospital in Edinburgh for a pioneering heart operation, as yet tried on very few people, which might help her condition. As she deteriorated towards the end of February Maureen and Gregor were dispatched once again to a children's home in Clackmannan, and Ann went to stay with Aunt Ruby nearby. Kit was taken into Stirling Royal Infirmary and plans were made to get her transferred to Edinburgh as swiftly as possible. The last time Ann visited her, before the planned surgery, Kit told her eldest daughter that if anything happened to her, Gregor and Maureen were to stay together. Kit knew exactly how mortal she was.

On Monday, 12 March, Ann went to school as usual and that evening celebrated her tenth birthday – though 'celebrated' is altogether the wrong word – at the house of Aunt Ruby and Uncle Alex. That night, the lonely birthday girl prayed for her mother. At 10.30 the next morning, Tuesday, 13 March, on the day Kit was due to go to Edinburgh Royal Infirmary for immediate surgery, she died of a cerebral embolism, brought on by 20 years with mitral stenosis. If history is written by the winners, 38-year-old Kit was never given a pen. She left a world in which, however brave and feisty she had been, tragedy and disease had blighted her from the minute she was born.

Every birthday since then, Ann has remembered the anniversary of her mother's death the following day. Family events imprint inescapable patterns in our lives. In the same way, Kit, dying of the same time bomb of a disease that had killed her mother, knew history was repeating itself: she too might leave three little children motherless. She had fought so hard to stay alive to look after them, but could do no more.

The pity is that Kit did not reach the operating theatre, for in 1956 Edinburgh was one of the leading centres in tackling the fall-out from rheumatic fever. Cardiologists in the 1950s were just becoming familiar with the ravages of mitral stenosis on the heart valves. In the words of one surgeon, by operating to open up the 'shrunken, guttering orifice of the mitral valve' he could enable many young women to go on to bring up their families. Sadly, Kit just missed being one of them, and she took those poor, shrunken, guttering valves to the coffin.

Astonishing as it may now seem, in 1956 neither father nor mother of an illegitimate child was entitled to act as the child's tutor or curator after either parent's death. ('Guardian' is not a term used in Scots law.) This was a relic from the days when an illegitimate child was regarded as *filius nullius* – in the eyes of the law he or she was literally nobody's child. Illegitimacy placed them outside the families of both parents. Kit's three children, aged ten, three and one when she died, were outcasts with no status or legal standing whatsoever and only the authorities could be forced to step in and take responsibility for them. Gregor and his siblings, strictly speaking, had no legal relationship with their parents, indeed with anybody. Now their mother was dead, and their father, or fathers, officially unproven, what was to become of them?

Word reached William Kerr, and we can only wonder how difficult it was to deal with such news. It must have had a profound impact, bringing grief, guilt and fear in equal measure. He too had lost his mother when he was nine years old so he knew the despair and the lasting sadness. He had also experienced the awfulness of an unkind stepmother, who had upset him and been hard on his baby sister. What was he to do to protect these children? And equally, what could he do to protect his own reputation? With his immediate family forging respectable professional lives, he had far too much at stake to acknowledge two illegitimate children. To ask his long-suffering wife to take them on was unthinkable. Had she known there was a second child? Did he tell her that Kit had died? Even if he did, he could certainly not then reveal to her the depths of his sadness.

As a well-known public figure he was as trapped by society as his mistress had been. At the same time, Gregor's father was not legally bound by anything. He was honourable enough to know, however, that doing nothing was not an option so he duly telephoned his lawyer, confided in him the shocking secret and made an appointment to meet. He reached for a pad of blue Basildon Bond, took out his fountain pen and consigned his two children to continue in the care of the county council, paying 3s a week for each. If his hand shook a little, it was understandable.

We may wonder, a little wistfully, whether he cared enough to engineer a visit to Maureen and Gregor while they were in the home, to see them for one last time before adoption. Concealing his relationship with them to the staff, of course. It would have been easy to arrange as a councillor. Somehow it is nicer to wish that he did make that effort, rather than just washing his hands of the whole terrible business with the curt blue note. But we will never know.

Seven months later William went back to see his solicitor, Victor E. Cuthbert, in Alloa. Having acknowledged paternity of the children by volunteering to pay for their keep, he had now formally to shed it. Sitting in the lawyer's office, he picked up his trusty pen once more and signed the legal document giving his consent for James and Ellen Fisher to adopt Gregor McKenzie.

I, William Blake Kerr, Officer of Customs and Excise, 2 Park Terrace, Tullibody, being the father of said child, hereby state that I understand the nature and effect of the Adoption Order for which application is made and that I understand that the effect of the order will permanently deprive me of my parental rights.

He then signed an identical document with regard to Maureen. We may wonder whether Victor Cuthbert looked appraisingly across the desk at his client, and if he passed silent judgement on his behaviour. Did William himself find this a difficult and embarrassing business to conclude? Thank heavens Cuthbert was an old friend; thank heavens for professional secrecy. Hopefully, all this would die down soon.

Even those who do not believe in fate accept, if they look back, that life is riddled with uncanny coincidences. William had another painful one heading towards him like a steam train. On 22 December 1956, exactly three years to the day that his illegitimate son Gregor was born, his grandson came into the world. John and Jane had had a new baby, Nick. One wonders what went through William's head that day, or whether he had by then been able to compartmentalise the past and shut it out.

His son John was on the cusp of becoming an author and journalist. Indeed he would become a respected political commentator on the BBC, and write for the *Glasgow Herald* and the *Guardian*. William took great pride in his son and his family. Their prosperity reassured him that he had carried through the project his own father had started: through brains, good education, aspiration and extremely hard work he had successfully launched his children into a higher social class.

William's final deed regarding the scandal was to visit his solicitor again to sign the final document consenting to permanent adoption. That was the occasion when he neglected to fill in the word 'father'. His role in his natural children's lives was effectively over. When, five years later, he returned to Victor Cuthbert's office to sign his will, only his three legitimate children were mentioned. To do otherwise was not possible. That is not to say he forgot his illicit family or that he felt no pain. Just as his wife Margaret and his daughter Dorothy never forgot the distress of his betrayal, what fragments of evidence exist suggest William mourned the brave and feisty Kit for the rest of his life. Those sentimental lyrics of the poem found in his wallet, 'Just A-wearyin' for You', are proof of a kind:

Evening comes I miss you more
When the dark glooms round the door,
Seems just like you ought to be
There to open it for me.
Latch goes tinkling, thrills me through
Sets me wearying for you.
Just a-wearying for you.

William retired after at least 40 years in the government's service, which entitled him to a pension of half his handsome final salary. He and Margaret enjoyed a quiet and comfortable retirement together, obviously reconciled into old age. William remained a prominent citizen in the area. Their grandson Nick fondly remembers trips in the car to Tullibody to visit them, a benign, elderly couple. His granny was kindly, his grandfather modest. The old man used to take the children to play in the park opposite.

The scrap of paper with the romantic lyrics lay in William's wallet for the rest of his life: treasured, well thumbed. Death came abruptly. He was sitting in the chair in a barber's shop in Tullibody one morning when he collapsed and died of coronary thrombosis. At seventy years old he took his secrets, his regrets and his emotions with him to the end, leaving only a mystery love poem about someone other than his wife.

His funeral took place at the new crematorium in the nearby town of Falkirk.

After Kit's death her three children were unceremoniously wrenched apart. Maureen and Gregor were dispatched to another home and then, a matter of only a few months later, adopted by James and Ellen Fisher from Coatbridge. Ann, meanwhile, was under the impression they had been taken to Banff, far away in rural north-east Scotland, and for almost a decade she learned nothing more of their fate. She continued to live with Aunt Ruby and Uncle Alex in a house where neither her mother nor her sister and brother were ever mentioned again. *Omertà*. Not a word about the past, no explanation. Not long afterwards, the houses under the hills were bulldozed. It was as if Ann had never existed, as if her family had never happened, and the little girl struggled, lonely and unhappy, through what remained of her childhood.

Later, as we have seen, when tragedy befell the adoptive mother Ellen Fisher, Maureen and Gregor were separated against their dying mother's wishes and brought up by different women. Within months all three of Kit's children, therefore, were lost to each other. Maureen, as much as her big sister Ann, struggled with her feelings of abandonment and the lack of love and nurture every child needs.

And Gregor – well, Gregor was the lucky bastard, wasn't he? The luckiest of the three; the one who if he landed in the midden would come up smelling of roses; or if he fell in the stream would come up with a salmon in his shirt pocket (or perhaps down his trouser leg). We all know where Gregor ended up – with the love of Cis; and then Vicki's love; and on the strength of all that the ability to build a stable family background of his own and a remarkable career.

# CHAPTER 11

# Rab C. Nesbitt

'Never complain about your troubles; they are
responsible for more than half of your income'
Robert R. Updegraff

There was perhaps one moment when Gregor Fisher finally realised how big the whole Rab C. Nesbitt thing had become. It was the evening of 9 June 1992 and he was hovering in the wings of the Hammersmith Odeon, wearing a string vest and a dirty bandage around his head, while a few feet away sat 3,000 people in high expectation, aching for him to appear. Nesbitt, his comic character, had achieved cult status. The live show was an extraordinary sell-out across Britain, the TV series having bust the BBC Two ratings figures. Right then, in that moment, he knew what a rock star felt like.

'And I'm thinking, "I'm 38 years old, I'm terrified, and isn't this altogether a rather silly occupation for an adult human being?"

And then, fleetingly, 'I wish I'd strangled that bugger Nesbitt at birth.'

The plot for the stage show centred round the World Cup in Italy. Nesbitt had gone to Italy for the football and forgotten to come home, as you do. When the curtains opened, he wasn't there. Nesbitt's two sons were running wild around the auditorium, his wife, Mary Doll, and her friend, Ella, were piling into the sherry. There were ten minutes of comic chaos, the four of them battering and insulting each other, screaming 'Bastard!' and 'Keech!' Seven pages of Ian Pattison's brilliant script – without Rab. But it was his absence on stage that was creating the comic tension. Everyone was expecting him.

And I'm standing there in the wings waiting ... and waiting ... and the tension is rising. Ten minutes is a long time and the audience are laughing, but you could feel them waiting too, you know. Without wishing to sound like a complete luvvie, oh God, it was intense, you could feel the tension and the anticipation, and you're standing at the back and you think: 'God, I wish they'd hurry up, get this bit by.' You'd have to be a complete zombie not to sense what it's going to be like when you actually walk on.

Then Mary was alone on stage, sitting on the settee, her lip trembling. She said something like: 'Oh, Rab, where are you?' which was Gregor's cue. He didn't appear at first, just a voice off—

'Mary Doll, that's me back, then.'

And the second they heard his voice, before they even saw him, the audience gave an almighty roar, an explosion of emotion, enthusiasm and greeting. It was like the noise from the bear pit at a football match when the winning goal is scored; or when the opening chords signal the greatest hit at a rock concert. Actors talk about the warm wave but this was like fireworks going off, and for Gregor it was both exhilarating and terrifying at the same time.

And that really was when it came home to him how huge Nesbitt was. First, the brief cameo for a TV sketch, then the development of the lovable drunken buffoon, the street poet, the pitch-black, bleak-pitch humour; finally, the mega-famous pub philosopher who spoke universal truths. Nesbitt had grown into something larger than anyone ever dreamt of. Owned and beloved by the public, he was a caricature, a monster, a shackle, a friend, an alter ego, an Everyman, a crazed King Lear shouting down the storm … all of these things. Every man, every woman, knew a Nesbitt, loved him and hated him, and everything in between. For a while it seemed half of Glasgow drank with him; the other half was married to him.

And he – *he*, Gregor Fisher, he *was* Nesbitt. He had that power; he made them all laugh. Because as Nesbitt himself once said: 'There's nothing that restores yer faith more in human nature than meeting some poor bastard that's just as mad as yourself.'

That night was the premiere gig in a crazily successful tour. There were ticket touts, people clamouring for an already sold-out show. It was London, too, meaning Nesbitt was not just a provincial Scottish cult. The cast had played other venues on the tour, filling bigger and stranger places, like an ice rink outside Belfast, but the Hammersmith Odeon was different. There was something about being in the capital, about the reception Nesbitt got, that made it so special. In those torrid few months the stage show had played at least 35 nights in England and dozens more in Scotland. From Aberdeen to Plymouth it had sold out and the organisers simply kept adding more dates on, until the point when Gregor said, 'Enough, no more, I have to go home and see my family.' But that night of 9 June 1992, if ever there had been any doubt about whether the Nesbitt phenomenon was real or not, that night he knew.

With the genius of both Pattison's writing and Colin Gilbert's direction, it was a successful stage show. People laughed a lot. The plot had the usual universal truths in it. Nesbitt's excuse for being four months' late back from Milan was that he met a wee mate and got talking. It was the Glasgow boozer's classic excuse – an anywhere boozer's excuse.

He brought Mary back a bit of stale pizza, in his pocket.

'Have yi not missed me?' he asked, all hurt.

Because of course now he was back she was furious with him, ranting sarcastically about missing his sweaty Y-fronts and the barnacles of his snot stuck to the table legs.

'I see, playing hard to get, eh?' said Nesbitt.

When a show went right, as this one did, it was an extra-ordinary feeling for the actors. When it clicked, and they got over their fear of forgetting something and letting everyone, including the audience, down, it became an absolute joy. Gregor felt as if the audience were one big animal that he had made connection with: they loved him and he loved them. Inside Nesbitt, incorrigible, hopeless, irresistible Nesbitt, he could feel a huge amount of love, affection and understanding for the character. But the most interesting thing about Rab C. Nesbitt is Gregor's ambivalence towards his character: a real love–hate relationship. He grew to be inordinately proud of what they achieved with Nesbitt, and the pleasure it afforded so many people, but if he had had his way, the old waster might never have survived the initial editing process. In fact, he did his level best to sabotage Rab at birth.

*'Shows you how much I know,' he says wryly, from the perspective of 30 years.*

It all began with a sketch on *Naked Video*. The modus operandi for that particular show was to start off with a pile of scripts and whittle them down and down. A lot of stuff did not make the cut – that was the nature of sketches. One was a surreal vox pop theme, written by Ian Pattison, in which West of Scotland characters were approached in the street and asked on camera to give their views.

And it was pretty random as to which actor was given which sketch – this one happened to land on my lap. This particular script was pretty incoherent and didn't make much sense to me – a Glaswegian guy, a bit of a nutter, rambling to camera. I wasn't best pleased I got it. I really didn't want to do this sketch one bit.

The crew used to take a stack of vox pops with them when film-ing so they could maximise the time; an actor not involved in the next big sketch could be deployed to do a vox pop while the others were changing and being made up for the main event. On the day of Nesbitt's intended creative birth they were filming a sketch with Tony Roper entering a furniture warehouse, somewhere west of Maryhill. Opposite was a patch of waste ground so they decided to use it to try out a strange new char-acter – the angry drunk, who referred to himself as 'scum'. The head bandage and rancid string vest had been specified by Pattison, and instead of the show's standard street drinker's outfit of the time – a 1970s cast-off suit with wide lapels – Gregor, for some reason, ended up in a pinstripe suit. It was different, but Colin Gilbert, the producer and director, signed it off.

Gregor filmed the sketch once and it didn't work. He admits he kept forgetting the rambling lines, which he couldn't seem to get into his head. They tried to salvage it by getting Johnny Watson to play a reporter doing 'noddies' so that they could stitch it all together in the edit. Then, on Colin Gilbert's insist-ence – and he wrote the cheques – they had one more go. Yet again it wasn't very good and Gregor went home fairly sure he had driven a stake through the heart of the character and it would not be resurrected. Several days passed, another episode of *Naked Video* was just about finished, and the vox pop presented again, last thing, when the light was fading, because Gilbert still thought it had a distinctly interesting feel to it and Gregor, despite himself, felt it was worth trying again.

There was a cameraman at the time for the BBC called Norman Shepherd and Norman was a Yorkshireman, very down-to-earth, a very good cameraman. We were shooting film, none of that video nonsense, so we tried it several times. Everyone was saying, 'Christ, aw naw, it doesn't work.' We were doing it in Glasgow, on the pavement opposite what's now the Marriott Hotel, just me to camera. The sketch opened with some question – I didn't know what the question was, I only knew what the answer was – so I just had to let rip with the nonsense.

And he slips into Rab C. Nesbitt's voice, that profane, indignant stream of consciousness as familiar as the smell of toast or the sight of rain falling on a Glasgow pavement. The sketch can still be found on YouTube: a young, angry Nesbitt, interrupted by the camera while walking along a city pavement after dark, the lights of the hotel behind him, a rolled-up newspaper in his hand: 'You talking to me, you talking to me? Don't you talk to me! Listen, I'll tell you, the trouble with this Tory government is what they're doing to people like me, see, see people like them, see people like me, OTT altogether … Yeah, and I mean you can talk about your Thirties, your Thirties – see, I lived through your Thirties. I had TV, I had ringworm, I saw *The Jazz Singer* four times, I know what you're talking about. You can talk about your holocaust, fair enough, but that was a skive compared to this, that was a doddle compared to this. I mean, have you tried to get a sick line after five days, eh? No? Well, don't you talk to me, don't you ask me questions!'

Gesturing with his newspaper towards the hotel: 'You can see the buggers, sitting there on the telly and that, in their dinner jackets, in their dinner jackets, sitting there having their dinners with their la-di-da this and their la-di-da that, and see when it comes down to it, they're no better than I am, they're no better than I am. In fact they're worse than I am, and I'm scum and then maybe you can work it out because I can't but then again, who am I? Who am I? No, no! See, when you scrape it all away, all that crap and you get right down to it, right down to the bottom of it, the bottom line, they're all a lot of jumped-up fascist bastards and I'll tell you something else, I should know, for I was an inspector on the buses and maybe you can tell me the answer because I'm Donald Duck if I know the answer. Wha' … wha' was your question again?'

But Gregor didn't screw up the lines this time and Norman took the camera off his shoulder, took out a roll-up, spat out some tobacco and said in his emphatic Yorkshire accent: 'That was it, that was it. That was it.'

He then turned to Colin Gilbert and remarked: 'It makes it all worthwhile when you get something as good as that.'

But that *was* it, as far as Gregor Fisher was concerned – '*The one thing I didn't like about it was the feeling of "Let's diss the rest of the West of Scotland, because this was a UK-wide show; let's show everyone what a bunch of drunks and ne'er-do-wells live here."*' He admits too that he always had an eye to the future and was ambitious to make the transition from being purely a Scottish actor to something broader. And so he thought no more about it.

Norman the cameraman was right, though; as were Colin Gilbert and Ian Pattison. There was a bit of a buzz about the character; people thought it was funny. For the next couple of series the vox pop man in the bandage and the string vest became a regular on *Naked Video*, spouting off his stir-crazy monologues. The powers-that-be in the shadowy world of TV commissioning were impressed and a Christmas special titled *Rab C. Nesbitt's Christmas Greet* was ordered, based entirely around the character and his attitude to the festive season.

Initially, the idea made Gregor uneasy – '*Uh well, I don't know ...*' – but by this time it was easier to go with the flow. They filmed for Christmas 1988, with a medley of well-known faces from Scottish entertainment, such as Peter Capaldi, Rikki Fulton and Alex Norton, and he found he really enjoyed doing it. It was great fun, and he reasoned it might get an audience in Scotland. Gregor knew that Pattison was a very gifted writer and observer of humanity, and that the developing character of Rab C. Nesbitt was acutely funny, but he still shrugged it off as local, and that was the end of that. Nothing could have prepared him for the shock when Alan Yentob, then the Controller of BBC Two, suggested a series based entirely on Rab.

I was flabbergasted, just flabbergasted. I couldn't believe it. Then we did the series and it's a funny thing when you're doing TV; you're cut off from reality. You're just a band of brothers, you're there with a restricted time to do this, that and the other, and you're working with your friends and you're trying to get something done and make it funny. In a way it's a very private thing; there's no audience, no immediate feedback, so you don't actually know until you play it back to an audience how it will be received. Even then, it's maybe only 200 people in a BBC studio somewhere, laughing, and you think, 'Well, we got away with that.'

As to how they're going to respond in Wigan or Crawley, and wherever the BBC broadcast, you just never really know. So you trot off and become what you really are – a husband or a parent or washer of dishes and occasional changer of a nappy – and it's not until you meet the outside world, as it were, that you realise people actually liked it and the show's a hit.

Gregor's world at the time was quite a small one. He and Vicki lived in Ayrshire, bringing up a young family. He only got feedback when he went to the supermarket, and even then the messages were mixed.

I would go into a shop in the West End of Glasgow.

Some woman would say in that very West End accent: 'Oh, you are the boy that plays that chap on TV, that Raspberry Nesbitt thingy, and it's very funny but why, oh why, do you have to swear so much?'

And I'd think, 'Oh well, I suspect you've missed the point, missus.'

And then you'd get someone else saying: 'Aw, it's pure dead brilliant by the way, we're loving it,' and you think, 'OK, people are watching it, but it's not en masse.'

It wasn't until the second series of *Rab C. Nesbitt* began in May 1992, as the character and his family developed and the ratings soared, that the penny dropped. The show was getting ground-breaking figures across the UK, about 6.5 million on BBC Two. Gregor remembers going to Ayr Flower Show with his children, infants at the time, and inevitably a nappy needed to be changed.

*'And I was sitting on the grass changing the nappy and suddenly I realised a crowd had gathered all around us to watch, five-deep, and I thought, "This is odd, this is very odd." So the realisation of how big the whole thing was sort of crept up on me, a very gradual thing.'*

So, where did he come from, Rab C. Nesbitt? Who made him? Why did he become so famous? According to the *Herald* newspaper in Glasgow, *Time International* magazine once featured Nesbitt on its 'People' page, a place normally inhabited by the world's rich and beautiful. In a piece headed 'Rabscallion', it quoted Ian Pattison's script: *'All of us is rats, but none of us is ONLY a rat!'* That was from the scene where Rab finds his children, Gash and Burnie, have made a hat from a silver milk bottle top and put it on one of the rats that have infested the Nesbitt home.

> 'That's no' how I brought you up. To rip the piss out of dumb animals.'
> 'It's only a rat, Da!'
> 'All of us is rats, but none of us is ONLY a rat!'

It was dark, anarchic nonsense with, as always, some sliver of truth. That was about the same time, the summer of 1992, when it was confirmed Rab had topped the BBC Two UK ratings again.

What goes before matters, and Billy Connolly had whetted people's appetites for funny Glaswegians. You could even make the case that Nesbitt continued the Scottish working-man's, or in this case *non*-working-man's, culture, which 200 years earlier Robert Burns had made into an art form. The trick was to capture the bawdy unsayable stuff and then say it, performing to a crowded bar and entertaining everyone. Glasgow had a great tradition for telling it like it was – that up-front humour, born of the shipyards, transposed to the music hall.

> Gregor Fisher recalls one classic story with a shiver of sympathy. 'There's Roy Castle at the Glasgow Empire, last house on a Friday night, Roy's not going well. Roy's tap dancing, he's playing the trumpet, he's got the saw out, he's doing everything, and there comes a wee voice from the gallery, "Is there no end to this man's f****** talent?"'

In any group of hard, tough West Coasters, there was always a comedian, the man with the one-liners and lightning put-downs who kept everyone entertained. In Tony Roper's autobiography, Billy Connolly recounted his first day as a van boy at Bilslands bakery, listening to another van boy – Roper – holding court with mercilessly funny patter. *'Better keep quiet,'* thought a young Connolly, all the while longing to be half as amusing as Roper (who of course went on to fame, acting with Gregor, from Dundee Rep to *Rab C. Nesbitt*).

Nesbitt was based on that kind of funny man but he was subtler than that. In terms of performers, he was an original. As Andrew Young, writing in the *Herald* newspaper, put it, before him the underclass had only featured in bleeding-heart, hand wringing *World in Action*s. But seeing misery through the eyes of a comic character, both cheerful and profound, opened a different perspective altogether. He was the waster who spoke wisdom. You might say that if it hadn't been for Nesbitt, we'd never have had *The Royle Family*, *Shameless* or *Still Game*, or reality shows like *Benefits Street*. Or even the character of the mad drunken Scottish Groundskeeper Willie in *The Simpsons*. He paved the way for them all. The waster's waster. Nesbitt was the granddaddy of all of them, the ultimate anti-hero. Gregor Fisher's skill was to make him human as he stumbled through life.

As Rab himself put it: '*When you get right down tae it, there's only birth, copulation and death. Everything else is pure bloody guesswork.*'

Many critics, and many more viewers, said *Rab C. Nesbitt* was one of the cleverest and funniest shows ever made, and it was voted amongst the top 50 best TV comedies of all time in a BBC Two poll in 2004. The first sketch appeared in 1985; the first series started in 1988 and to date there have been 67 episodes. The show was either first, second or third in the BBC Two ratings for about six years in the 1990s, and it is still going, appropriately garlanded. It won a bronze medal at the New York Film and TV Festival in 1986, best sitcom at the Royal Television Society award in 1991, was nominated for a BAFTA in 1994, scooped prizes from Montreux and the Banff Film Festival in 1992, and won two Scottish BAFTAs in 1991 and 2009.

The inestimable Nancy Banks-Smith, writing in the *Guardian* in September 1994, is worth quoting at length about an episode of the show that is fairly close to the bone in light of what Gregor Fisher's life contained. But maybe that was why he was so good at it. Banks-Smith wrote:

All comics are enraged individuals – or mad, as we say in the trade – and they don't come much madder than *Rab C. Nesbitt* (BBC Two). His 'Bastards that ye are!' would awaken the dead. But not quite. 'Is there a problem, nurse?' 'It's Mr Nesbitt. He's going mad, screaming and shouting and swearing. I don't know what's wrong with him.' 'His mother is dead.'

Ian Pattison has the nerve of a burglar to use that as a subject for comedy. That and perfect confidence in his accomplice, Gregor Fisher. We've all seen comedies about relatives who would merrily murder each other but I don't believe I've ever seen a monologue delivered over a stiffening mother before.

Suddenly, as if he had seen her lips move, he started and shouted for the nervous nurse. 'Look! D'you see that woman lying there ...? That's my mother. One of the finest human beings that ever walked this earth. She Has Not Got Her Teeth In! Her gob is a calcium-free zone! And this is a woman that was so self-conscious she used to put a dish towel over her knees when she was watching telly because she thought Trevor McDonald could see up her

bloody skirt! Now look at her lying there like a
plucked chicken for all the gawping eyes of the
swining world tae see.'

Importantly, Nesbitt had moral standards. Gregor remembers
one sketch in the pilot show where a character played by Iain
Cuthbertson was lying drunk. His money and his carryout were
lying beside him and the script required Nesbitt, himself in a
state of stumbling inebriation, to make off with both the
carryout and the cash. Gregor refused and there was a bit of
debate.

I filmed it so that Nesbitt picked up the carryout but
put the money back in Cuthbertson's inside jacket
pocket and patted it ... it was right. Nesbitt had a
kind of moral centre, a sense of decency about him.
That particular instance was my suggestion, but the
show was like that – I would say something, and
Gilbert would say something.

Rab's world was honest about itself, too. When it began the show
was based upon the anarchic family life of a work-shy alcoholic
during Margaret Thatcher's reign. In the early scripts unem-
ployment, domestic violence, child abuse, alcoholism and
substance abuse were things to make jokes about. In more
recent shows, there are food banks and the bedroom tax, a
middle-aged Rab has given up drink to stay alive and Mary Doll
has become an entrepreneur, but the outrageous dark humour
is still there. The fact remains that Nesbitt took ownership of the
term 'scum' from that first, stuttering monologue on a pavement

on Glasgow's Argyle Street, and from then on nothing could be said about him that he had not said himself. Nothing has ever been out of bounds.

> Nesbitt: (to London beggar): Aawright there, pal? (Points) No legs, eh? (Giving thumbs-up) Good career move!'

Often there was dialogue so rude the audience couldn't believe they were hearing it.

> Rab: I mean, I had tae start drinkin again, didn't I?
> Doctor: Oh really, how so?
> Rab: Aw, it was her. She said foreplay wusny worth a toss since ma hon stopped shakin!

Sometimes the show would take the cast to places where they felt very uncomfortable.

> It was like ... 'Can we do this, can we really do this, is this the one that's going to fail, can we laugh at this?' It did feel that close to the edge sometimes. But it worked.

In one episode Nesbitt has cancer. Of course, Gregor's mother Cis had died of cancer and he found acting the scenes hard, but rationalised it afterwards. It was right; cancer was what happened to people. Nesbitt was a drinker and a smoker, so why shouldn't it happen to him? Afterwards Gregor received a lot of letters from people saying how pleased they were, because they themselves had cancer, but they had laughed and laughed and thanked God someone was talking about it.

Then there was the sketch where he had chosen to have a sleep, after a good drink, in a freshly dug grave, and woke up angrily when the coffin was lowered on top only to start berating the stunned funeral party.

> Hey, whit's the score? You wannae watch what you're doing with that thing. You could kill someone with that.

What then were the personal influences that inspired Gregor Fisher to bring Nesbitt alive and furnish him with inner humanity? The street life of Glasgow, for one: the dreadlocked down-and-out who once roamed Central Station, raking through the bins and talking to the moon. And the black guy he saw on New York's 42nd Street, who did the same thing. Acts of humanity he had witnessed, occasions when someone ran to help someone else. He cites too the famous TV advert for the *Guardian* newspaper from the 1980s, featuring the skinhead running towards an old lady with shopping bags – running, running, running, as if about to mug her, but instead he was saving her life – 'The *Guardian*, a different perspective'. It struck a chord with Gregor; he knew instinctively that *Nesbitt* worked because it was about a real human being. And human beings were pretty decent folk even if at first glance they appeared not to be.

Into Nesbitt too he put the people he had grown up with, worked with and observed – skivers in the factory jobs, men overheard in bars; the funny men, the angry men, the cynics, ever-hopeful chancers, the men who were simply joyful in their skin. In there too was the inarticulacy of simple Uncle Wull and the negativity of John Leckie. Especially John Leckie.

Because he was a huge influence on my life; a huge influence. Although we never communicated or talked, the fact is that when I was growing up he was omnipresent, growling away, 'Don't do that, don't do that,' and by *Nesbitt*'s time I understood a bit better why he was like that and wished I could have had the relationship with him all over again.

When a script arrives you've got to read what's on the page, but also you've got to read what's in between the lines – and ask yourself why. So we played it that undercurrent way.

With *Nesbitt* we weren't making a documentary about low life in Glasgow, we were making a sitcom. It's a comedy – it's about turning on your telly for a good laugh and if it also makes you think, then great. That's the best kind of comedy. But there is nothing new about *Nesbitt* – never has been. The Greeks were doing this thousands of years ago – a guy paid by the local community to come out and take the piss out of the authorities. Rab is just where the steam comes out, I suppose. The show was never about looking down on people, it was always understanding. Things were heightened but I didn't want it ever to be that we were taking the piss out of Nesbitt. I wanted to get the audience involved in his world, to be on his side, to understand – maybe not all of it, but some of it.

The fondness and the sense of engagement mattered. There had been some criticism that Nesbitt was a one-dimensional drunken bum, especially from the worthies on Glasgow City Council, but if he had been the TV series would never have gone UK-wide and he would not have been invited to debate at the Oxford Union. It worked on all levels. It was that rare thing in acting: a moment of alchemy. Pattison, Fisher and Gilbert created a character, the eternal optimist; the man who had nothing, who was vaudeville as much as Shakespeare. He could stand on set and announce: 'I am a citizen of the world. "Mr Happy," they call me. Everywhere I go, folk shout out, "Err goes that big, fat, happy bastard."' And everyone simply loved him, even if it was reckoned the English understood just one word in six. Maybe it survived because it was good enough to transcend meaning.

But let's not overcomplicate it. As Gregor Fisher says, it *was* sitcom.

And if the ironies of the character had resonance with Gregor, if he thought about the layers of his own hushed-up family past, of lost mothers and those who were less than happy bastards, or had nothing to their name but humanity, then that was something he kept private. But he was certainly a natural in the role.

Not quite everyone was familiar with Nesbitt. Gregor had a London accountant, who ran an amateur football club in Reading and was trying to raise funds for it. He nobbled his famous client and asked him to come down and do a Rab C. Nesbitt interlude at the football club's 1988 dinner, at the Ramada Hotel in Reading.

'Oh yes, they all know it and love Rab,' he assured Gregor.

Sporting the requisite unshaven look, Gregor went up to his room to change into his uniform of dirty vest, grubby bandage, wig and stained pinstripe suit. Fully in costume, he went downstairs and through the kitchens, from where he was to make his entrance to the stage, and found the meal wasn't yet finished.

'I thought, "I'll just nick out of this fire exit and have a fag," so I did and it happened – I heard the door go click, you know, the automatic door.

'And I thought: "Oh shit, I'm locked out."

'So I had to go right round the front door of the hotel, whereupon the very officious chap said: "You can't come in here."

'"No, no, I'm terribly sorry, you see, I'm the cabaret," I said.

'"No, you can't come in here."

'Then somebody else turned up and they threw me out of the hotel, and I had to go through a great long explanation before I could get back in again – and I just made it in time to do the gig.

'Well, you wouldn't let Rab C. Nesbitt into your hotel, would you? Let's be honest. Fine to watch him on television but you wouldn't like to sit next to him on a bus. That's the difference, isn't it?'

The simple fact, though, was that Nesbitt, like Gregor Fisher himself, was a lovable man when you got close to him. The joy bubbled up when it could. Ironically, the character of Nesbitt made Gregor the member of yet another family, the fifth in his life. There was Mary (Elaine C. Smith), his long-suffering and hardworking wife, who coped better with the real world than Rab. Their children were Gash and Burney, bad boys, toerags, ne'er do wells and themselves fathers of illegitimate babies. His best friend was Jamesie Cotter (Tony Roper), whose wife Ella Cotter was played by Barbara Rafferty. The 'C' in the middle of Rab's name didn't actually stand for anything, merely that Rab's grandfather was Rab A. Nesbitt, his father was Rab B. Nesbitt and he was Rab C. Nesbitt. He lived in Govan, a poor area of Glasgow, and claimed he was the only surviving family member, being the only one able to understand a benefits form. Is it just coincidence that Gregor Fisher, of all people, was able to make this ridiculous, chaotic backstory funny?

Because of Rab C. Nesbitt, Gregor Fisher remains one of the most recognised people in Scotland. But there was always something of a double edge amid the laughter. When a character becomes that big, the actor becomes its prisoner.

Stirlingshire, 2014. We're sitting in the sunshine, discussing newspapers. Gregor has that look on his face, that mixture of mordant humour and bitterness.
    'You know what will happen when I die, don't you?'
    I glance up at him.
    'You know what the headline will be in the *Daily Record*?'
    Silence.
    'Rab's deid.'
    Pause.
    'That'll be it, story of my life: "Rab's deid".'

But he's not Rab C. Nesbitt. He's Gregor Fisher – a million miles from Rab. And it's not the story of his life. An actor, as the American novelist Gail Godwin once wrote, is a ghost looking for a body to inhabit, and maybe the truth is that for years Gregor simply didn't know who he was, or where he came from. Deprived of two mothers by tragedy, unwanted by his father, passed on unofficially to others, his story is one of survival against the odds. He'd never found his secrets. From his first three families he received desertion, evasions, fictions, clues and a polite cover-up, which for a while he thought was true. So that's what this book has been all about: not acting, but finding out who he really was.

# CHAPTER 12

# A National Treasure

'Being illegitimate is the story of the everyday
strength of the human spirit'
Historian Jane Robinson

Bong!
*Pause.*
Bong!
*Pause.*
Bong!
Upstairs in his old farmhouse in the south-west of France, the noise stirs Gregor Fisher half-awake. Outside, the barn owls are calling and he can hear the frogs in the nearby stream. It's about five o'clock in the morning.

*'Bloody clock,'* he thinks. And pulls up the duvet, hoping it will shut up and he can get back to sleep.

Bong!

With a curse, he rolls out of bed, trying not to wake Vicki, and then, stark naked, pads downstairs to the living room where the old mantelpiece clock sits, silent now, smug. The clock that keeps no time and is not wound up, but every so often comes to life and starts chiming.

'You effing thing!' he tells it, but very affectionately. Picking it up gently, he tilts it to stop it chiming anymore. Then goes back upstairs to bed, reflecting on the strange and unknowable things in life.

It's W. B. Kerr's clock, you see. William Kerr, the father he never knew. When his half-brother John died, the Kerr family wanted to pass on to Gregor some of the old man's possessions. One was a dark wood mantelpiece clock presented to the young officer when he left the Belfast Customs & Excise station in 1928 and transferred to Clackmannanshire. His name and the dates were engraved on the back.

> And that clock, that effing clock … I have to say, I'm sure people will think I make these things up, but at any time of the day or night that clock could spring into action. You try and ignore it and then, bong, it's off again and you think, 'Oh, God, come on! Give me a break, W. B. K.'

Gregor was also given his father's oil lamp. It might be the reading lamp William had had since Irvine Royal Academy days when he studied late into the night. Or it might be the government-issue lamp he got when, as an exciseman, he was sent travelling. Gregor doesn't know for sure; what matters is that he knows the lamp went everywhere with William, to all the postings in remote places where there was no office and he had to sit in his digs, writing up the day's reports long before electricity came.

Another possession passed on to him is a black brolly with a bamboo handle. He is very protective of it. His wife Vicki thinks it's quite sweet how no one is allowed to use it, even when it's raining. Gregor's sister-in-law Jane also presented him with a piece of Mauchlineware that once belonged to William. Small, high-quality Victorian souvenirs, they were beautifully carved and varnished wooden objects with scenes painted or transferred onto them. They were made of pale sycamore to begin with and they were produced by the Smith family in Mauchline, Ayrshire, who sold them in the thousands to affluent tourists of the day, many of them American and most of them Robert Burns aficionados. Then, as now, pieces of Mauchlineware were valuable. William's was a little wooden book cover containing a notebook for recording birthdays. On the front cover, black against the golden, fine-grained sycamore, was a romantic scene of Burns's birthplace.

On the inside front, top left, the small boy had written very carefully in ink, with a certain self-important flourish: W. B. Kerr, 9, New Street, Irvine, Scotland, N. B. – North Britain; a record of another political age, apart from anything else. As William grew older and his handwriting matured, he copied out his name and address three more times underneath, perfecting it. The hint of extravagance on the initials 'W' and 'B' would last throughout his life, recognisable even to the signature on the adoption papers. At some point later on, his son John has added in pencil, 'J. Kerr, 2, Park Terrace, Tullibody, Alloa', and drawn an arrow linking it to his father's name with the words, 'His Son'.

Elsewhere within, the young William had entered one or two family birthdays and at the back meticulously copied lists of names in neat rows – his family's names, his grandparents', possibly those of schoolfriends and neighbours. Clearly he showed early promise as a methodical keeper of neat records.

Gregor Fisher still treasures Wavell's anthology of poetry, belonging to his father, which John passed on to him at the first clan gathering, some years earlier. Field Marshal Archibald Percival Wavell fought in both world wars and became Viceroy of India. A love of poetry led him to publish his favourites in a book called *Other Men's Flowers*, including, of course, the rollicking 'She Was Poor But She Was Honest', which Gregor had had so much fun with. Wavell's selection is very traditional and of its time, including Burns's classics, such as 'My Love Is Like a Red Red Rose'. Perhaps the father's love of poetry has been passed down, for Gregor keeps a more modern anthology by his bedside, often reading a poem before he goes to sleep – *'Sure as fate, often as not it's something that's quite apposite to what's going on at that minute in your house or your life. I don't read one every night but I like to have it there.'*

There is one final, significant William Kerr memento given by Dorothy. It is a little silver medal, from Irvine Royal Academy, which William received for perfect attendance. Gregor keeps it on his keyring. A hallmarked Maltese cross, it is cut from within a square, with thistles, roses, a shamrock and a Fleur de Lys on it. Inscribed on the back are the words, 'Irvine Borough School Board. Presented to William Kerr for five years perfect attendance'. On the front are the initials 'W. K.'. Also on the keyring hangs something Vicki gave Gregor: a silver charm of two conjoined masks, one laughing, the other crying (the classic Greek comedy and tragedy symbol). The diligence medal, the acting charm. The twin achievements of two men, therefore, father and son, dangle side by side.

\*  \*  \*

The mistake made, says Gregor Fisher, is that people think there's something fascinating about adoption, the basic status of being an illegitimate or abandoned child. *'Maybe there is if you're looking in from outside. But it isn't fascinating if you're the one on the inside, if it's you who's been adopted. Then you just have to get on with it.'*

He cannot remember any particular surge of emotion when finally he put most of the pieces of his life together. If anything, he felt a bit flat. Even to this day his abiding feeling about the whole matter is one of *'What a total mess this had been. What a f\*\*\*-up.'* And at the same time he was, and still is, intensely grateful that he was young enough to escape some of the pain his mother's death inflicted on his sisters. He knew how lucky he was, eventually, to be scooped up in the arms of Cis Fisher. Nevertheless, everyone in his story gets hurt in some way, he says.

*'Everyone gets it in the neck here.'*

Even in the uncovering, there is fresh pain; nobody comes out intact from a process in which lifelong secrets and lies are revealed, assumptions and pleasant memories challenged. Family history, as the writer Alison Light has said, is never neutral in what it wants to say about the past. Peeling back the layers of identity is a tough business. We have to realise that our grandparents, our parents, had lives as we ourselves have – fallible, well intentioned, incomplete – and we must understand that. Gregor has had to learn that even when he found out the hard facts, he would never have satisfactory answers. Because nobody ever knows what goes on between two people. He bounces the question back to anyone who asks too much.

And what's your manner of coming? Do you know what went on between your mum and your dad? Was it this, was it that, was it …? You don't know, do you? You can never fill all the bits in between the lines.

It's the same when, as an actor, he gets a script, and he reads it and thinks, *'bit boring, actually'*. But he knows it's not the words, it's not just the lines, it's what's between the lines, it's how the actors say the lines – that's what counts. It's the spaces in between that make the thing come to life. And that's what's missing from his own history. What he has are the names, dates, births and deaths – the rest is guesswork. He is convinced there was a passion, a love affair, between William Kerr and his mother Kit, but in the same breath he says he thinks that because it's what he *wants* to think. All he can base his conviction on is that sentimental poem in his father's wallet.

In that poem, was that really his father thinking about his mother? *'Just a-wearyin' for you./The door latch tinkling in the dark'*. Was it a grand passion, or an affair with a secretary that went too far? From the letters John Kerr wrote to Gregor, oblique though they were, it seems he believed their father was emotionally involved with his mistress. But Gregor will never know, and whatever way he spins it, indeed cannot help but spin it, the verdict is open and cannot be proved. Other people will have to make up their own minds.

What he has learnt is that nothing is ever in isolation; everything is connected. At times, he's not proud of the part he played – he recognises that he was desperate to be loved and cared for by Cis to the exclusion of the rest of her family, which had a lasting effect on them. He recognises that his past has had an influence on the way he deals with his family and his own children and others in his daily life. No man is an island. His early life has affected him, just as it has affected those who have been in his life. Unconsciously or otherwise, that's just the way it is. Get on with it.

Hopefully, he's brought enough joy and laughter to the world to be forgiven, he says.

Along with the comedy, life has made him wiser. There are always reasons, always consequences. He now looks behind first impressions in order to be more understanding. There are posthumous apologies to seek. At a cursory glance, John Leckie, Cis's husband, was a grumpy old man, but there was a reason for it. He was that way because he had lost both his parents at a young age and never in his wildest dreams did he expect, when nearing retirement, to be lumbered with another child. And if he did lean across and tap the boy's plate and say sourly, 'Eat that, it's the same price as the rest,' it was because when he was living in a little flat in Battlefield Avenue during the 1914–18 war parenting his three younger brothers, there was nothing to eat but bread and dripping. And it wasn't a Monty Pythonesque 'I-lived-in-a-cardboard-box' joke, it was for real; there *was* only bread and dripping, and here was Gregor, not finishing a bowl of good soup. Little wonder John Leckie shouted sternly, 'Finish your food! You don't know how lucky you are.'

Gregor caused him a lot of grief.

Everybody, everybody, everybody but every single person we've talked about in this book has a story to tell. They've been rattled about, they've had highs, they've had lows, they've had good times, they've had bad times and that's what makes people who they are. And if you can find some sort of line through all that, it will help you understand why that person's screaming and shouting at you. People are the way they are because of what's gone into their computer system beforehand. I'm not always good at it, sometimes I'm still too quick to judge people, but what has happened to me has made me look beyond what I see at first glance and try to get a handle on people. Walking a mile in another man's shoes is a very good exercise actually, a good exercise.

There are times, of course, when he doesn't quite manage it. Overcoming the negativity of illegitimacy has been huge. It can put a chip on his shoulder; it can make him, to use that old Scots expression, 'a bit of a jaggy nettle'. Sometimes people irritate him intensely by the assumptions they make. He remembers once, while at drama college in Glasgow, dropping in to the upmarket department store Forsyth's just before he got on a train to Langholm to see his cousins.

'I was a student, I didn't have much money, but I was determined to take them a bit of smoked salmon. A bit. And they were a snotty bunch of people in that shop. God, they were snotty. Anyway, in I went.

"'I'd like a piece of smoked salmon."

"'Mmm-hmm." A posh Glasgow voice. "Do you realise it's £14.20 a pound?"

"'Yes, I do realise that," I said. Red mist rising. "In fact, I'll have the whole side of salmon," I said.

'Thinking, you're not going to pass judgement on me, you jumped-up little Bearsden shop assistant!

'It cost me an absolute bloody fortune and I was cleaned out for that week and the next bloody week too. But I wasn't going to be beaten by her assumptions. People should think before they open their trap.

'I think that reaction has got something to do with my childhood.'

**When pressed on the question of identity Gregor is unflinchingly honest.**

I don't know if I know who I am or not. I know roughly where I've come from and how I've been brought up. I know who I've come across and how I've dealt with things, and I know I'm sometimes terrified that there's going to be no money to pay for something. I know I always like to drive smart cars and have the occasional pair of hand-made shoes – I think that's something to do with adoption. It's kind of, 'Hey, look at me. Look at me, I'm the one that used to wear the plastic shoes, I'm the one that came out of the care system in Clackmannan. I'm the one that's driving the nice car and lives in a nice house.'

You know I bought a Rolls-Royce. Why on earth did I buy a Rolls-Royce? Just to show off, probably. I think that's absolutely true. It doesn't show me in a good light, but it's true. Why did I think I should have hand-made shoes? Well, I told myself it was because I have fat feet and shoes don't normally fit me. No, it wasn't, it was because I wanted hand-made shoes. I was showing off, as my mother would say. And I think there's a direct connection with all that and my early life and the plastic shoes, which I hated. Now, interestingly enough, it doesn't really matter to me but maybe that's a thing that happens with age. I drive a very old car now.

Gregor regards it as a strange kind of blessing that both his parents are dead. He has heard terrible tales of adopted people who sought out their birth parents and were rejected, effectively for the second time. Indeed he encouraged one adopted girl he met to seek out her origins, although at the same time warned her to be a little cautious of the reception she might get. Sure enough, next time he met her she told him it had been a disaster. Her mother was living a smart middle-class life in the Home Counties with a husband who didn't know anything about it. Nobody knew about her past, nor did she want them to. She didn't want to know; her daughter was to remain a stranger. The girl had made a big effort to track her down, her mother agreed to meet her in a quiet place and said in a very polite, firm way, no. Gregor has known other encounters like that. And then, to lighten things, he recounts the story from the maternity ward with Vicki.

'There's a pregnant woman, has quite a bit of a gas in the birthing room, big stramash, eventually gets the baby out.

'"Would you like to hold your baby?"

'"Noooo," she says, "I don't want to hold the bloody thing. Oh, take it away and get me outside, I want a f****** fag!"

'But her reaction is as legitimate as the next woman's – nobody's the same.

'I've been lucky that I don't have to sit and have that conversation with my birth parents. Because I can put their relationship where I want it to be, where it's comfortable for me. I can spin it, shelve it, frame it, idealise it, condemn it ... Whatever I want.'

Those integral to Gregor's story, though, what happened to them? Many of the people directly affected in one way or another by Kit and William's secret affair are now dead. After William himself passed away in 1965, his widow Margaret lived for another 12 years, moving to be near Dorothy in Cumbernauld. She was 85 when she died. Gregor's half-brother and two half-sisters by William Kerr are all gone too: John in 2012 and Dorothy, childless, the following year. Sadie had died before Gregor made contact with the Kerrs.

John's widow Jane lives in the Borders. She and John had three children – Nick, Barbara and Willie, who remain in touch with Gregor in the easy, relaxed, affectionate way of cousins. The shame and the secrets have been swept away; the Kerr family have behaved with great dignity and warmth towards him. He can never thank them enough for that.

John Leckie died in 1978 and Cis in 1983. They had worked as hard as human beings can, attended church, survived two wars, rationing and recession. Living within their means, they never entertained any luxuries, loathed waste until the very end and the sum total of their thrifty lives was £14,000 and a house. Their two daughters, Gregor's unofficial adoptive sisters, Una and Margaret, are now retired. Una still lives in the old family home in Neilston, blessed with a grandson. Margaret lives on Tiree in the Inner Hebrides.

Jim Fisher is gone, and so too are all his brothers and sisters.

Aunt Ruby is dead. Ann, Gregor's half-sister through Kit, survived the trauma of the loss of her mother and siblings but endured a difficult adolescence with Aunt Ruby. She married young and had children, and now enjoys her grandchildren. She and Andrew McDonald, her husband, have recently retired to Scotland after many years in Plymouth. Ann is saddened by the decades clouded by secrets, but happy that everything once withheld from her is now in the open. Love, she believes, sustains people.

Maureen, Gregor's only full sister, has for a long time worked with disadvantaged people, the homeless and those with substance problems. She has a happy marriage and grandchildren, whom she dotes upon. Despite this she still seeks answers for the way she was treated.

Johnny Monaghan, Gregor's childhood friend and also adopted, is regarded by him as a brother. Although Johnny now lives in Poland, where he runs a successful business, the two men remain very close and speak often on the phone.

And what of Gregor himself? He and Vicki have also had a long, loving and successful relationship. They have three children, Alexander, Jamie and Cissie, now in their mid- to late twenties, who were all at their parents' wedding in 1990. His family unit is precious to him; he guards their privacy closely. Growing up, the kids had little interest in their famous father's mysterious beginnings – or his career, for that matter.

'I never sat them down and made a big deal of it … they just grew up kind of knowing things had been a bit different for me.

'They were proud of being gits.

'I'd try and start a conversation, maybe to explain a bit more.

'"Listen, Dad, we're watching a really good Tex Avery cartoon here, can we talk about it later?"

'I used to do personal appearances, and for that I had to get the full gear on, the string vest, the suit, the works, so I'd come and say goodnight looking like Rab C. Nesbitt.

'"Night, kids!"

'"Night, Dad!"

'Kiss.

'Oblivious.

'Kiss. Kiss.

'Dad just had his work clothes on.

'Invariably there'd be something on at Christmas that I was in. They'd say: "Dad, can we watch the other channel?"

'"Yes, of course."

'Click

'And do you know what, it doesn't matter to me because I love them and I know they love me, and I've never been so sure or so happy about anything in my life. We all want to be loved, don't we?'

Often, as a treat for tea, he'd rustle them up a cheese dream. He made a proper cheese sandwich with nice thick bread, dipped it in beaten egg and fried it. The end result was a wodge of crispy eggy melted cheese and carbs, which they ate with tomato ketchup. Family life was characterised by Gregor's love of cooking and by moving house. Both he and Vicki are very peripatetic, combining the thrill of moving with the fun of doing up grand old houses: at several places around Scotland, then Lincolnshire and most recently France. The only time they were rooted was when the children were at school. Gregor rationalises his itinerant nature from his childhood; from an early age he was used to being shuffled from one children's home to another, from house to house, family to family. He calls himself a 'suitcase boy'. He doesn't remember feeling unsettled by that; he just got used to it. Even when he is back in Scotland working, camping in Johnny Monaghan's flat, he feels happy and comfortable.

Being a parent was a big game-changer. The near-loss of Vicki when Alexander was born, then the arrival of the next two babies, affected Gregor deeply. As a parent he suspects he was a bit too liberal – it was a hard one to get right. Easy enough to be firm about not touching the fire or making sure they crossed the road safely, but less so when it came to letting them follow their own instincts and pathways. As when Alexander and Jamie expressed an interest in learning to play the piano and he was happy to oblige – only for them, after three or four weeks, to say no, it's too hard.

And I should have said, 'Well, you signed up for it, kids, see it through to the end' – but anything for a quiet life. It's that thing about wanting to be loved, too; you cannot bear not to be loved. I think maybe that's got something to do with my background – I couldn't bear not to be liked so the kids got away with absolute bloody murder actually. They were very happy but maybe a bit spoilt as well. When I was young it was different and that was just the way of it – I was brought up with older people and it was the make-do-and-mend generation so I would have hand-me-downs from my cousin. I wanted something that was just for me. So with my children it was totally the opposite – I was doing a film about Popieluszko in Paris and I remember buying a whole outfit for Alexander in some flash children's shop in the Boulevard Wherever, the whole sort of designer outfit: because I could. But it was absolute silliness on my part because if they wanted something – not needed something – they got it. And I do not know to this day how they've turned out to be such sane, normal people.

True to the laws of parenting, they've all kind of gone the other way. Jamie walked in the other day. God, you should have seen him! I mean, he's a good-looking boy but if he'd just buy himself a T-shirt that didn't have any holes in it, it would be very good. But he just couldn't give a stuff.

Even worse, Gregor's children have grown up with a love of leftovers. He rolls his eyes in extravagant horror.

'Leftovers are anathema to me. I mean, the idea of eating the same meal twice is just ridiculous.'

Had he not been an actor, he would have liked to be an architect. Fiddling about with old houses is a passion, the grander the better, as if to confound expectations of how little bastards end up. He does a lot of the deconstruction himself, handy with a sledgehammer and wheelbarrow, hash-bash before getting the experts in to do the nice bits. In France they have turned part of their old farm into a gîte, which they rent out. But there's no swimming pool – ever since that close encounter with the sewage tank 50-odd years ago he has had a fear of water.

He never learnt to swim, although holidays have seen them in exotic seaside locations all over the world. Bora Bora, for example, and there's Vicki off snorkelling in the clear turquoise sea and then there's Gregor, the water lapping around his waist, going not an inch further from the shore, thank you *very* much. Round at friends' houses, where there are swimming pools, he may venture into the shallow end, feet firmly on the bottom, and stand and have a drink. Enjoy the sun. Make people laugh with his intrinsically comic expressions and body language. Feet on the floor – lovely. Perhaps even very occasionally a vain attempt at floating, but *only* at the shallow end.

They have a garden in France too, and it's a double act, him and Vicki. She looks after the flowers and, as he puts it, the girly bits, while he does the potager, the vegetable garden. They spend long, happy hours out there, losing track of time. He cooks splendidly with the fruits of his labours, and they take great pleasure having friends round when he might rustle up some-thing quick – seared magret de canard, duck breast, perhaps, with some mashed potatoes with a tiny bit of mustard through it and some nice green vegetables from his garden.

And he is so glad to be alive, this complex, bright, humane, kindly but very guarded man, who has survived much more than most of us. Humour bubbles out of him, often dark, but always funny. The built-in physical comedy of his face and his body defies translation onto the page. He believes that most people, even those who go off the rails at some point, are pretty decent human beings. The bulk of the people in his story are just ordinary human beings with warts and flaws, the same as anybody else. That comforts him, because he says he's got faults galore. The story of how and why he came into the world is a tale of ordinary people in a society that judged them more harshly than today's.

Finding his roots hasn't made him any more, or any less, settled; it is just the way things are and he knows whatever his past circumstances, he has to get on with it. He is aware he has had so much more in his life to compensate for the bad bits; that there are some people in his situation who know nothing about their parents. Most of all, he acknowledges that if he had found nothing in his childhood to fill the aching gap caused by a lack of family, things could have been very different.

'If it hadn't been for Cis, and lots of other people, I would have ended up in permanent therapy, or worse.'

His luck, his great good fortune in life, was that there was always somebody to help fill the gap, to meet his need; someone he could share what he had with. The initial person who did that for him was Cis. But there was a whole team of other people, mainly women, who rescued the little boy with kindness: Aunt Agnes, Margaret Monaghan, Miss Fay and his cousin Carol. They nurtured, cared, wiped his snotty nose ... even sent him Valentine's cards when they knew no one else would. People who made an effort to help him along his path. Some people who are adopted or abandoned don't have that and he realises how fortunate, blessed, lucky – *use all three words, use any word you want to describe that* – he has been when he compares his life with theirs.

*It's April 2015 and Gregor has just announced his comeback on stage – after 25 years – with the National Theatre of Scotland. His mobile pings.*

*Laughing, he reads out a text – it's from the theatre press officer.*

'"According to the leader column of The Scotsman, *you are a national treasure."*'

'That's nice, Gregor. *[trying not to laugh]* You are a national treasure.'

'I don't actually know what the hell that means. Does it mean I'm an old bastard now?'

'The Queen Mother was a national treasure. Desert Orchid was a national treasure.'

'Oh, God!'

'Clare Balding is a national treasure.'

'Oh, I like her, actually.'

*I pull up the article on my iPad and start reading aloud:* 'Gregor Fisher is a national treasure who has given Scottish popular culture some of its best-loved characters. In the Naked Video TV sketch show he created the Baldy Man ... blah, blah ... and, of course, with the help of writer Ian Pattison, he gave the world Rab C. Nesbitt, an instantly recognisable figure ... blah, blah ... often accessorised with a blood-stained head bandage.

'At first glance, Rab was the worst kind of Glaswegian stereotype ... blah, blah ... but great writing allowed this superb actor to imbue him with an unexpected pathos. There is a bit of Rab C. Nesbitt in more of us than we would care to admit ... one of Mr Fisher's great talents is the physicality he brings to a role, and a larger-than-life range of emotions, from rage to despair.'

*The national treasure is looking very happy, as indeed he should. But he knows his story is not yet complete for there's one final big thing missing. And we've simply got to find it.*

# Epilogue

'I'm here now,' he thought. 'I can do no more.'

William Golding; *The Spire*

How much more do we know of Gregor Fisher's story? We know enough to know that we will never know it all. The truth about what happened has been concealed by the passage of 70 years, by death and lies and secrecy, by change and renewal, by bull-dozers and buy-outs. History exists for those who succeed, who carve out their achievements in property and public service. But occasionally, against the odds, we can peel back some of the layers of the past and find out what happened to the little people.

There are many elements that will always elude us: secrets and whispers, joy, colour and laughter. Such is the nature of intimate lives. As Gregor is fond of saying, how much does anyone know about how their mother and father met, what they felt, why they fell in love? You don't have to be adopted not to know the whens and whys and wherefores. For him, however, there was still one important piece of the jigsaw missing, and that was Kit McKenzie's final resting place. Gregor's birth mother: the ever-optimistic girl who had had the cards stacked against her from the word go, who had lost almost everything and everybody she loved. She had fought ill health, poverty and loneliness, defied the gossips, gave birth to three much-loved children but then died so young. So what had happened to her in the end? Where did she lie?

We had a death certificate. From this dry document we knew that Kit had died on 13 March 1956 in Stirling Royal Infirmary. And this time too, we could fill a bit of the space around the stark line in the ledger. Ann, Kit's eldest child, could remember that her mother was due to be transferred to Edinburgh for an emergency operation to try to make her better. But when the little girl came home from school that afternoon they told her it had been too late – Mum had died before they could get her there.

Not another word was spoken on the matter. Ann was sent back to school as normal the next day. Aunt Ruby hushed everything up to the extent that the child was not told when or where her mother's funeral was taking place. There was certainly no question of her attending; she was too young. And so the little girl had to grow up unable to grieve, and because she wasn't allowed to talk about her mother she found out nothing more. Then, after Ruby died, it was too late to ask.

She had a vague memory that one day at school, later that terrible week, a schoolmate had said something like, 'That's your mum away today,' which, years later, she presumed was on the day of the funeral. After Ann and Maureen found each other in 1964 the two sisters had tried to solve the riddle. They had walked round various local cemeteries and asked the local councils for any record of her burial, but nothing could be found of Kit. They couldn't even find their grandfather Matthew McKenzie's grave in Logie cemetery.

Gregor and Maureen also searched for their mother's final resting place, back in the 1980s. They wandered round the graves in Logie cemetery but again had no luck. Maureen put forward the theory that Kit was probably in a pauper's grave somewhere because she was penniless and there wouldn't have been any money to bury her. This would explain why she wasn't in the churchyard or didn't have a headstone. Gregor saw the logic, although he thought the natural place to bury her was in the family grave at Logie with her father – but precisely where? They still hadn't found Matthew.

You would have thought if there was a spare place they would have laid her in there, wouldn't they? But maybe the Rubys of this world would have said, 'You're not putting her in beside Dad after her behaviour.'

As we came to write Kit's story, and she began to emerge for Gregor as a real person, not just a name from the past, the need to find her became pressing. Surely, before we closed the pages of this book, we could track her down. Experts and amateurs, everyone tried to help. Surely she must be in the family grave, if only we could find it. Enthusiasts from the Logie Old Graveyard Group volunteered to scour the old cemetery yet again, scanning for Matthew and/or Catherine McKenzie, but both remained oddly elusive.

'I am sorry that I have drawn a blank,' emailed a kindly member of the group. 'Last night I "walked the lines" but no stone. I can only assume the Cemeteries department made some sort of error in recording, which has been carried on in the present records. It is an intriguing mystery but I am afraid it will remain one.'

Further searches of the burial archives in Stirling and Clackmannan failed to find her. We were baffled. In those days of oppressive morality, where would you lay to rest a penniless fallen woman with few friends, an adulterous relationship and a family who felt disgraced by association? Could her body have gone to Edinburgh University for medical science, given her heart condition was one of the challenges that surgeons were starting to tackle?

Gregor was in Scotland, rehearsing for the play *Yer Granny* with the National Theatre of Scotland. One Saturday in early May 2015 he had the impulse to go and look in Logie graveyard for himself. The cemetery is a particularly pretty one, in the dip between the rock bearing Stirling's Wallace monument and the base of Dumyat Hill.

He got out of his car, lifted his face to the hills, walked through the gates; looked about. Then a feeling came over him, an impulse, *'Maybe it's down there, I just think it's down there somehow,'* and he turned left and started scanning the gravestones farther down, close to an area of the cemetery under repair. Almost immediately, there it was, bold as you like, shouting at him, with a large art deco-styled headstone like the Empire State Building or an old Odeon cinema: his grandfather's grave, the family grave. He had found them.

Or so he thought. The headstone read:

In loving memory/of/Matthew McKenzie/who died
10th of March 1938/aged 49 years./And of/Mary
Jamieson/his beloved wife/who died 6th June 1948/
aged 53 years.

At the bottom was engraved: *'Erected by/his wife and family/and fellow workers at/Glenochil'*.
In front of the big stone, at its foot, leaning against it, was a little stone, older and much less grand. It said:

A/Token of respect to/Matthew McKenzie/
accidentally killed/Glenochil Distillery/10th March
1938/aged 49 years.

The name James L. McKenzie was inscribed along the bottom. He was one of Matthew's brothers and he must have erected it some years before the bigger stone. Gregor stood there, shaking his head at it all. No mention of Kit – but it was all very odd. He phoned me from the graveside:

It just gets weirder and weirder, this story. There's a new princess been born today and I find Grandpa's grave. When nobody else could. So there you go.

Re-enthused, we redoubled our efforts. At the very least, it seemed, we had an unproven positive: that Catherine was there in the grave, unmarked, above her father and stepmother, and the council records of the lair had been lost. Then Stirling Council came up trumps: they found the records for Matthew McKenzie and Mary, his second wife. Officially there were only two spaces in that lair, but the council said that in some cases it was deemed possible to fit a third person in (some families did that). However, they assured us Kit definitely was not in there with her father. So we tried the crematoria. But it turned out that none of the local ones – Falkirk, Perth, Dunfermline – existed at the time of her death in 1956. They had been built in the 1960s and 70s.

And then, the following weekend, Ann, Gregor's older sister, remembered another fragment. Wracking her brains, something had come back to her; something she had hidden deep away because it was so hurtful. She remembered being at school, that awful week, and a classmate saying to her, 'Your mother will be in the fire now.'

It was late May before the text arrived from a friend who had gone hunting for Kit in the records of the Mitchell Library, in Glasgow. The message was short but thrilling.

Found her. She was cremated in Glasgow.

And so, one rainy day, we drove to the Western Necropolis Crematorium, on the hill above the housing schemes of Maryhill. It is a strange yet peaceful place, quirky Victorian Gothic in red sandstone and marble, and boasts an ugly industrial chimney – just in case you wondered what purpose the building could serve. The crematorium has stood there since 1895, the first in Scotland. It took a while to catch on; cremation was initially so unpopular that after the first ten years only 191 bodies had actually been disposed of there.

It is pouring down as we park under the cherry trees fringing the visitors' car park: proper pelting Glasgow rain.

Gregor and Vicki get out of their car. He pulls one of those comical faces, opens his arms to the heavens.

'What about this then?'

He looks up at the sky.

'I mean, give us a break, Mother.'

Theatrical pause.

'I mean, come *on*! Could you not do something about the weather for this?'

By the time I have got into my wheelchair the rain has stopped and patches of blue sky have appeared. She must be listening.

We cannot find any brass plaque on the wall of the lobby to commemorate her. Gregor goes exploring, opening the door to the chapel.

'Gregor, you *can't*! There's a service on,' Vicki hisses.

'No, there's not,' he says.

He reappears.

'I'll tell you what, I'm not being smart here, but there's the hell of a heat.'

'Gregor, stop it!'

We enter the empty chapel, walk towards the descending catafalque. It is indeed very warm.

'I like to think my mother would find things funny,' he says. 'My real mother, Kit, I'm sure she was good for a laugh. I rather think she had a sense of humour.'

He starts rooting, very respectfully, around the catafalque, looking at the caskets. There's a plaque for a Jessie Nisbitt Clapperton on the wall. We smile. Maybe that's Rab's Aunt Jessie.

'I think we're romanticising it to think we might find her casket,' he says. 'I don't suppose anyone would have paid to keep her here. I don't suppose there were many people at her service.'

Just then a young man approaches us, one of the crematorium workers, offering help. Gregor explains that a relative of his was cremated here. Would there be any records, plaques, anything in the book? We give him the date.

'I can check what we have got up the stair. I can check that, no bother.'

After five minutes he comes back with a battered, dusty old ledger, repaired with tape, its cover worn down to sludge-brown card, the pages yellowed and curled. Cremations from 1955 to 1957, it says on the front.

And there, on the bottom of a right-hand page, Gregor found his birth mother. Handwritten, in fading ink. No: 29952, Miss Catherine McGregor McKenzie, housewife, of Glenochil Terrace, Menstrie. Age: 38, 'unmarried' written under her age. Death: March 13th; cremation: March 15th. Undertaker: Alloa Co-op Society Ltd. Ashes: Scattered. Remarks: None.

'And that's the original book?' asks Gregor.

'That's the original, yes.'

'Number 29952,' said Gregor. 'I'm glad we found her.'

'Her ashes would have been scattered here, in the Garden of Remembrance,' said the young man. But he has no further details, such as who paid for the funeral. Later, the Alloa Co-op Society confirm that records from that far back are gone; Gregor will never know whether the cremation was paid for by William Kerr or Aunt Ruby. Kit McKenzie, it now seems painfully obvious, was whisked away out of the area and her body disposed of with almost indecent haste. Dead on the Tuesday morning, death registered the same day; reduced to ashes by the Thursday. She was the only name on the page in the crematorium book from outside the Glasgow area. The message couldn't be clearer:

Kit might have been squeezed into the family grave with her father but she wasn't. Ruby didn't wait long enough to pursue it; she wanted to erase her sister's memory as quickly as possible. So Kit's body was hurried away to what, in those days, especially in country areas, was a most unusual end. The word must have spread like wildfire, and behind closed doors the Menstrie locals had gossiped about her sudden death and cremation. Hence, in an act of unforgivable cruelty, their children had gone to school and told Ann that her mum was to enter the flames.

Gregor is asking the crematorium man about his job.

'There's five of us work in here. One week you're upstairs, bringing people in, showing them where to sit, dealing with families, helping carry the coffin. And then the week after that, you work downstairs.'

'How do you find that?' Gregor asks. Deadpan.

I catch Vicki's eye, glance surreptitiously around for the cameras. For about the tenth time in Gregor's company I feel we're trapped in a comedy script.

'It's my job, I'm used to it. The first time, you're a bit ooh, but you get used to it. Then we disperse the ashes from a brass scattering urn; you press a button and the ash gets spread on the grass.'

'Must be pretty fertile out there then,' says Gregor.

'Oh aye, definately!' Laughing.

'That looks like a new roof. Was there a fire?'

'Aye, there was. In the 1990s, actually.'

'What was the cause of that?'

'Electrical fault.'

'Pleased to hear it ... if you see what I mean.'

They're both laughing.

We could only be in Glasgow, where ordinary life is always a heartbeat away from both tragedy and comedy. We thank him and leave the chapel.

The Garden of Remembrance is a small, walled area, with a grass rectangle in the middle and flowers around the edges. Here, Gregor Fisher's mother lies, found but still elusive.

'I would like to think Mrs McAdam was here for her service,' says Vicki.

'Well, exactly – who *was* there?' Gregor says. 'Or maybe Mrs McAdam was told to keep away. Maybe Ruby went. Maybe W. B. Kerr sneaked in the back.

'We don't know and we never will, that's the truth of the matter.'

Pause.

'But we know she's here.'

The moment is solemn but serene. In the distance, from the streets of the council estate, come the peals of an ice cream van. As we all pause, lost in our own thoughts, Gregor nods up at the cherry tree. We turn and look. There, very close, almost within touching distance above our heads, unfazed by our presence, a large magpie is rubbing its beak on the branches, shaking the blossom, watching us.

Gregor laughs; it's a happy laugh.

'Good old mother! You couldn't make it up.'

And you couldn't, but it was true.

As he drives away, another flash of black and white – and a second magpie flies across.

One for sorrow. Two for joy. I'm sure Gregor saw it.

# Bibliography

Adamson, John. *Menstrie – A People's History*, Clackmannan
District Libraries, 1996.

Andrew, Patricia R. *A Chasm in Time – Scottish War Art and
Artists in the Twentieth Century*, Birlinn Limited, 2014.

Carswell, Catherine. *The Life of Robert Burns*, Wm Collins,
1930.

Cox, Francis. 'The First World War – Disease, The Only
Victor', Gresham College, 2014.

Dillon-Malone, Aubrey. *Cynic's Dictionary*, McGraw-Hill,
1998.

Francis, Gavin. *Adventures in Human Being*, Profile Books,
2015.

Light, Alison. *Common People – The History of an English
Family*, Fig Tree, 2014.

MacGill, Patrick. *Children of the Dead End*, H. Jenkins Ltd,
1914.

McIntyre, Ian. *Robert Burns – A Life*, Constable, 1995.

The National Archives: British Army War Diaries 1914–22.
The National Records of Scotland, Edinburgh.
Pattison, Ian. *Rab C. Nesbitt: The Scripts*, BBC Books, 1991.
Report of the Royal Commission on the Housing of the
    Industrial Population of Scotland, 1917.
Robinson, Jane. *In the Family Way – Illegitimacy Between the
    Great War and the Swinging Sixties*, Viking, 2015.
Roper, Tony. *I'll No Tell You Again: My Autobiography*, Black
    and White Publishing, 2014.
Scottish Government Research Document: 'Health in
    Scotland, 2000'.
Scottish Law Commission: 'Consultative memorandum 53
    Family law: Illegitimacy', February 1982.
Sheppard, Horace. *Beyond the Call of Duty – The Memoirs of
    an Exciseman*, Old Museum Press Limited, 1998.
Sisman, Adam. *Boswell's Presumptuous Task: The Making of the
    Life of Dr. Johnson*, Penguin Books, 2000.
Smout, T. C. *A Century of the Scottish People: 1830–1950*,
    Fontana Press, 1986.
*Through the Lens 27: Glimpses of Old Dornock and Eastriggs*,
    Dumfries and Galloway Libraries, Information and
    Archives, 2005.
Wavell, A. P. *Other Men's Flowers: An Anthology of Poetry*,
    Pimlico, 1944.
www.monklands.co.uk – Monklands Memories
www.scotlandsplaces.gov.uk: Medical Officer of Health
    Reports, 1891 – Clackmannanshire
www.solwayheritage.co.uk

# Acknowledgements

To Victoria, Alexander, Jamie and Cissie, my family, without whom nothing but nothing would be possible.

Very special thanks must go to Annie Maw, who introduced me to Melanie Reid, the writer who put flesh on the bones of my past. Melanie says her primary thanks are to the Royal Commission on the Ancient and Historical Monuments of Scotland (RCAHMS), whose haunting picture of Glenochil Terrace inspired her detective work; and to Professor T. C. Smout, whose seminal writings gave her the confidence to recreate a world not long past, but one that we can now hardly recognise. She is grateful to Angie Mackenzie for enthusing her, Archie Whitehead for lessons in Robert Burns and Lindsay Passemard for support.

My story would never have been uncovered had it not been for the tireless efforts of my good friend Sheila Duffy, the professional genealogist; or without the help of Jo McKerchar, Diageo's senior archivist; members of Menstrie Parish Church of

Scotland; Jane Laidlaw, who scoured council burial records and came up trumps just at the crucial time; the staff at Summerlee Museum of Scottish Industrial Life in Coatbridge, and Eleanor Young from Logie Old Graveyard Group.

Sincere thanks go to Ian Pattison, for his brilliance as a writer and for allowing me to quote from *Rab C. Nesbitt* scripts; likewise to Colin Gilbert, the vital third element in our comic creations and also the best fact-checker known to man. The Comedy Unit has been generous with archive material; and I am grateful to the BBC for giving us permission to quote from sketches and the *Guardian* for letting us reproduce a review by Nancy Banks-Smith.

Many thanks are due to Kate Latham, our editor at HarperCollins, for her patience with us; to Jane Donovan and to Jenny Brown of Jenny Brown Associates for having faith in our ability to tell the story our way.

I am deeply grateful to my sisters, Maureen Doonan and Ann McDonald, for digging up their painful memories of our fractured childhood. My extended Kerr family has shown me immense warmth and generosity. I'd like to mention Una Brown and Margaret McIntyre for nurturing a small troublesome boy and making him part of their family, and who will always be my 'big sisters'.

Thanks too, to John Monaghan, my younger, smarter brother, whose support has taken my breath away.

And lastly, to Mel, Melanie, Ms Reid, without whose kindness and understanding and sometimes junior psychology, not to mention enormous talent, all of this would never have happened. Thanks to her nagging, I drink lots of water now and don't get so many headaches.